Creative Step-Parenting

Gayle Geffner

ISBN-10: 0-86690-593-6
ISBN-13: 978-0-86690-593-0

Cover Design: Jack Cipolla

Published by:
American Federation of Astrologers, Inc.
6535 S. Rural Road
Tempe, AZ 85283

www.astrologers.com

Printed in the United States of America

This book is for

my husband James Geffner

and

Dana, Seth, Tina, Marty and Gavi

Contents

Illustrations

Introduction

This book is written from love and practical experience. I have been a step-mother for more than twenty years and have known my step-children since they were five and nine years old. I have been an international astrologer for more than thirty years. I have combined these two areas of my life for this book.

While earning a degree in history, I also took numerous college classes relating to the psychological and sociological foundations of education. During this time I was trained to look for warning signs of troubled children—not just the large immediate signs of acting out due to a newly broken home, but the smaller actions that are easily missed and may develop over a longer period time after an event such as a divorce. These little signs may reappear or intensify or you may actually begin to notice them after a divorced spouse remarries. I also did additional psychological research at the time of writing this book.

Over the years I have had countless clients who have had problems adjusting to life as step parents. Many of these clients had actually known their step children for many years and found a very new and different atmosphere after the marriage. Many others were together for a shorter period of time before marriage but experienced many of the same adjustment situations.

My method of using a step-by-step delineation of a child's natal chart, certain planetary and nodal placements, and the step-parent's planets in relation to the child's placements has evolved over the years into a practical approach which creates clear and concise picture of how to bring two people together, even when the child is resistant. The areas of work are the areas where the step-parent and child can bond through such things as school work, sports, music, hobbies, social activities, family gatherings, and the like, or wherever they can come together with good aspects and planetary combinations. Although I write about tough placements as well, and places where you must work harder, my emphasis is on the positive. I also use the child's secondary progressions to search further for places to bond. The method of synastry used in this book actually guides the step-child, as well as the step parent in finding common ground for a successful family life.

If you are an astrologer with clients who seem to have difficult problems, and you are not a licensed and state certified professional counselor, it is advisable to refer the clients to a professional counselor along with the astrological help you give them.

Gayle Geffner

Chapter 1

The Astrological Basics of Step-Parenting

BEING A STEP-PARENT can be very tricky. Children do not want to take orders or advice from their own parents, let alone you. They may feel they already have a home and you are an intruder. They may have always liked you and seem to have changed their attitude toward you after your marriage to their parent. This is not to say all situations are extremely difficult; but they are different. At best, when you marry someone with children, there will be adjustments. Many of those adjustments may be easy; however, there also may be difficult ones.

When you become a step-parent, there are many astrological factors to consider. The dynamics of the situation do not only take into account your new role in an already established family. You must look at each child's chart, your spouse's chart, and even your spouse's ex-spouse's chart in synastry with your own to really get a clear picture of what is happening.

As a step-parent you are establishing a family nucleus within an existing and already established family nucleus. The existing, established family nucleus may have physically or tangibly broken up, but the dynamics are still there. It becomes very complicated. For example, the ex-spouse of your current spouse will always be in the picture since he or she has a child with your spouse. There are weddings, birthdays, grandchildren and more. In an ideal world everyone will get along, at least for the sake of the children.

Even if your spouse is a widower and his former spouse is no longer physically in the picture, the first spouse's influence in child rearing is still there. Therefore, the ex-spouse's chart can be very enlightening to your new family dynamic. It is often difficult at best, and disastrous at worst, when you do not consider all factors involved in the situation. The new family dynamic may also be wonderful. There are so many factors to consider, and that makes this book a necessity.

Astrology gives you insight into your family situation and may help you deal effectively with perceived problems. Astrology can show you different sides of an issue that you, in the midst of a situation, may not recognize. It will help all of the family adjust and live together in a healthy, happy relationship with each other. Since you, as the step-parent, are the new factor, it seems reasonable that you will probably have to make a little extra effort. Remember, your step-children are just children. They did not divorce either parent. This new situation is harder on them than anyone.

At the beginning of your relationship with your spouse, you are dating and your relationship is read from your spouse's fifth house as a romantic interest. The fifth house (defined further below) is that of romance, creativity, speculation and children. You and the children share the fifth house and you are "on a par" with the children. Perhaps you are sometimes in competition with each other, either in your mind or in the child's mind. Perhaps you are very friendly with the children. You are not positioned "over" them. The playing field is level. You are not a parent and you are not part of the family.

When you marry, you go from your spouse's fifth house to his or her seventh house of marriage and partnership and become the spouse of the child's parent. You then may be viewed as a figure of authority. At the least, you appear to have a position "over" the child since your relationship has changed from on a par to a parent of sorts. The child who once may have really liked or even loved you may take on a whole new attitude toward you. Things can be and often are very good. But because of this new position, things may not be so good at first. Things may go back and forth from good to difficult. It depends on each individual, each child and how the situation is handled. Child psychologists say it can take from five to seven years to really establish a family dynamic and form a family bond between step-children and the step-parent, even with those who really liked you in the first place. This is why looking at all of the astrological charts involved is so important. It helps each party understand the situation and leads to an earlier bonding experience.

My ideas come from a foundation in psychological and sociological factors in learning and how to spot troubled children, as well as practical, personal and a very happy experience as a step-parent.

One of the first things to learn to avoid is any indication of negativity toward your spouses's ex-spouse. Your spouse may complain about his or her "ex" to you, but you must both always be positive in front of the children. They love both parents and I feel it is very damaging to the children's relationship with you, your spouse and even the ex when anyone makes statements that the child perceives as disparaging, whether the remark is intended that way or not. It is just not fair. Remember, your spouse thought enough of the ex to marry him or her at one time so the ex must have some very good qualities; and, if your spouse right now feels very negative, it may be due to current circumstances. As in all things in life, this too will pass. More than likely, your spouse will eventually help create a friendly atmosphere with the ex. In fact, most people I know are very careful to keep any negative remarks away from the children during the divorce and they always try to spare the children's feelings. This is incredibly important for the future of your relationship with the children.

Also, it is important to remember that you are not "the" parent. I find it advantageous when dealing with step-children to express my opinion to my spouse, but say it is really up to you and the ex to do what you feel is best—this is just my opinion. Your spouse will probably consider your opinion and incorporate it or not. Of course, if the children live with you and are in imminent danger or doing something truly wrong, you have to step up to the plate. Your common sense should tell you when to act and when not to act. In the long run, are the little things so important that you want to create animosity? The children are not young very long. Let the parents be the parents. You are an adult in the house and of course your rules and opinions matter, but why hassle with the small stuff?

Children of divorce often have trouble finishing things they start. One of the best ways to relate is to help and encourage them to complete tasks without pestering them about it. Helping is a very good bonding method.

Probably the most important thing to remember is that children have the same feelings, ego and sensibilities as adults. They are just not as mature. Therefore, you must always treat a child with the respect with which you wish to be treated. Listen to the child's opinions. You can suggest alternatives or tell them that although their opinions are different, you value them. You must really listen and engage the child in conversation in order to develop a mutual respect. You would not want to be told to be quiet or have the feeling that what you said did not matter, and neither does the child. I find that children live up to expectations, so if you expect them to behave in a civilized, considerate manner and set an example, that is probably what you are going to get.

The houses, signs and planets as they pertain to a child growing into an adult, with a view toward step-parenting, are defined here. They are geared toward family dynamics and the motifs presented by the signs, planets and houses. Later in the book, I delineate the natal charts of an extended family and the synastry of family charts showing how each is affected by a spouse, a step-child, a step-parent, a sibling and even a spouse's ex-spouse and what you can do to create a healthy, happy family environment. The use of progressions and transiting planets are very important to development, and retrograde planets and Nodes are critical considerations.

Although this book was written for astrologers, if you are a student you can refer to the books listed in the bibliography in order to gain an understanding of the terms used in this book. There is some basic information included here, but if your knowledge of astrology is limited you may wish to use a beginning reference along with this book. If you are an astrologer or advanced student, the definitions are a starting point for you to look at the charts with a view toward step-parenting.

The Houses

The houses as they relate to adults are slightly different than for children or adolescents. As you look at the definitions of the houses, you will see how the definitions of a child's houses lead to the definition of the adolescent and then the definition of the adult as the child develops into the adult.

First House

Child's First House: The child, being ego-centric, expresses himself or herself first through this house. The child comes into self-realization here. Also, the sign on the cusp of this house suggests how the child will dig his or her heals in and take a personal stand. It is important to acknowledge the child's self-assertion and to help the child develop.

Adolescent's First House: This is the house of rapidly moving self-realization and the way in which the adolescent copes with growing up. Look at the astrological sign on this house to see how the adolescent handles positive and difficult situations, and how the adolescent feels he or she appears to the peer group. Peers are very important at this stage of life and your child's feelings here are also very important.

Adult's First House: This represents you personally, your nature, disposition and the face you show to the world. It represent your individuality. This individuality is what you bring to your step-parenting skills. It is how your step-children will perceive you. Thus, work through this house toward a positive perception from your step-children.

Second House

Child's Second House: The child is looking for personal belongings and personal comfort here. It is also the house that suggests how the child's personal value system will develop.

Adolescent's Second House: This is the house associated with the adolescent's developing personal values that will lead to adulthood. It is also the house of possessions and how the adolescent begins to make money. This house also will suggest just how important physical beauty is to your adolescent.

Adult's Second House: The second house represents your money, financial affairs, possessions, financial prospects and your personal value system. This house most importantly suggests what you really value and enjoy. These values are a clue as to what is valuable to you in regard to step-parenting.

Third House

Child's Third House: This house may primarily relate to the child's siblings and how the child consciously learns to deal with them. It suggests how he will mentally learn, school and field trips, short vacations and going away alone to camp. This house also represents the expression of the child's opinions, which is very important. The child's opinions are valid and should be considered along with opinions of the adults in a given situation.

Adolescent's Third House: This house represents brothers and sisters, short distance travel, how the mind is developing into the adult mind, as well as attitude toward school, and how your teenager expresses himself or herself. This house suggests how your teen may prepare for higher education, or how he or she sets a foundation for further learning. Since most teens do not really like to talk a lot to parents, the sign on the cusp and the planets in this house, if any, suggest ways to help open doors of communication.

Adult's Third House: This house indicates your conscious mind and mental activity, communication and writing, brothers and sisters, elementary education and short distance travel. How you communicate with your step-children will manifest itself in this house. Look at the ruler of your third house and your step-child's third house, as well as the planets in both, to see how well you communicate with each other.

Fourth House

Child's Fourth House: This is a crucial and important house for a child. It represents home, security and foundation. Traditionally, it represents the father, but in today's society it can represent either parent. If the father is out of the picture, mom must take over, and thus this house may be confusing in today's society. If the father or mother is gone, it is also a confusing time for the child. The child's foundation is shaken to the core in a divorce and this will create tremendous insecurity even in the most well adjusted child. Look at your step-child's fourth house to get a picture of his or her security or lack thereof and how the child relates to his or her parents.

Adolescent's Fourth House: This house suggests how well the adolescent will get along with his or her father (or mother, depending on the strength of authority figure). The adolescent's emotional foundation is represented here and the emotional outlet for a broken home can also be found here. Also, this is the house the adolescent breaks away from as he or she grows up and becomes an adult. Thus, the sign on the cusp and any planets will suggest how the adolescent will begin breaking away, and how you can deal with it.

Adult's Fourth House: This house indicates your home and your foundation. As with the adolescent's fourth house, your father's influence was felt in this house. Your emotional foundation is crucial to a healthy emotional foundation for your family, children and step-children. An adult must look at his or her own fourth house if there are issues of personal insecurity.

Fifth House

Child's Fifth House: The child expresses this house a lot through the arts and creativity. A good way to keep the step-parent/child relationship fun is through activities. You may have moved your relationship to the seventh house, but keeping the fifth house relationship alive with art, music and shared hobbies is a great way to make the child feel secure. This house suggests friends (not just the eleventh house), so activity here helps keep the situation friendly, even in trying times. Sports are also represented here and a good way to bond.

Adolescent's Fifth House: This is the house where your teenager grows up and falls in love. At this critical time, hints of how to talk to the teenager about life are found here. It is also the house of creativity and your teenager's childhood creative activities will further blossom and often change. The teenager will begin to take more risk and he nature of the risks taken is found here. It is still a good idea to try to find creative outlets and recreation that can be shared so lines of communication are kept open. Also, a new-found pride may appear. Power struggles between the child and parent or the child and others may also show up here. Teenage girls are especially prone to "drama" and just how much "everything is a disaster and life will end because of something" will be suggested by the sign on the cusp and the planets in this house.

Adult's Fifth House: This is the house of romance, creativity, speculation and children. Your spouse's fifth house will give you insight into your step-children. Also, your spouse's attitude toward children will show here. This house shows whether the adult is willing to gamble either literally or by way of risk-taking.

Sixth House

Child's Sixth House: This house is a double-edged sword for the child: work and fun. It is also a house of learning. The child may have a pet but must ensure the pet is taken care of or must do chores to earn the pet. The child also learns health issues and develops a sense of how to take care of self and live a healthy life. Development of the child's work ethic is shown in this house.

Adolescent's Sixth House: This house suggests how your teen works toward finishing tasks, even school work (also indicated by the third house). It shows how your teen begins to take on more responsibility, maybe through an after-school job or babysitting or offering to do extra chores to work for something desired. It is a good idea to work along with the teenager, not by doing the job for him or her, but by example suggesting ways to expedite work, thereby showing that hard work pays off. This is also a health house and teenage problems with health may appear through this house, especially by transiting planets. For example, a teen with Neptune in this house may live in a fantasy world during adolescence, but also may be more likely to try alcohol or drugs. On the other hand, neither of these things may manifest and the teen with Neptune here may discover a vivid imagination and take a shine to creative writing, art or music. This house is very important regarding how your teen develops, and you can get a lot of clues as how to approach the adolescent and help his or her positive development. Remember, children of a divorce often do not finish what they have started. Use the sign on the cusp of the house and planets in the house for suggestions of ways to help the teen finish what is being created.

Adult's Sixth House: This house indicates work, service, health and small animals. The methodology (how you work) you developed as a child and teenager will manifest here. This house also suggests how you relate to coworkers. It suggests health difficulties and strengths.

Seventh House

Child's Seventh House: This is a crucial house for the child. It is a house of partnerships, and on the child's level, the partner may be his or her closest buddy. The child is learning how to share with a partner. This is the house through which the child sees the parents' divorce, how he or she learns to relate to the break up of a partnership. Since it is the house through which the child also sees the new marriage, it suggests how the child learns to compete with a rival.

Adolescent's Seventh House: This house of partnerships may suggest a study partner or lab partner for the adolescent. It shows how the adolescent is growing into an adult and the type of partners he or she will look for. Also, it shows any contractual situation the child may have; for example, did the child contract to work on weekends and will he or she be paid when the work is complete?

Adult's Seventh House: This house indicates partnerships, contacts, marriages, dealing with the public in general and open enemies. In an adult chart, it is one indication of the financial condition of your employer (the eleventh house being the other). It is also the house that shows how you deal with the termination of a marriage or partnership.

Eighth House

Child's Eighth House: This house is karmic, and the child may relate instinctively, without question, to those he or she feels drawn to. This is the house of trust and of sharing innermost thoughts and things with others. The child will begin to equate his or her own life (in a microcosm) in light of the mysteries of life (the macrocosm). The child has a very basic curiosity of sexuality.

Adolescent's Eighth House: The adolescent kind of leaves the macrocosm idea behind for a time and relates what is happening to him or her as distinctly unique—no one understands or has suffered or felt such joy. The adolescent begins exploring issues of intimacy and sexuality. The teen years are the years your child is vying for personal power, and how this takes place often comes from this house. This is the house that indicates whether your adolescent may develop an interest in hidden matters, the occult or investigation. It is a time to look at astrology charts with your teenager and see how you can relate to each other.

Adult's Eighth House: This house points to legacies, death, taxes, insurance, government and other people's money, as well as the financial house of your spouse or partner. It suggests how you and your spouse will handle issues of money with your step-children and how you will teach them to invest or save. It is also the house of crime and may indicate criminal tendencies. It may point to psychology, occult studies, research and investigation, and issues of intimacy.

Ninth House

Child's Ninth House: This house suggests how the child's belief system develops, his or her social consciousness and need for humanity, and the quest for foreign objects or places. Maybe your child is interested in his or her ancestral country. Planets in this house suggest how you can teach your child about the world and other cultures.

Adolescent's Ninth House: This house suggests how to help your teenager reach his or her goals, whether they include higher education or other matters. Perhaps foreign travel and related occupations such as the airline or travel industry are very important to your teenager. Look to planets in this house or the sign on the cusp of this house as to how to relate to your teenager with regard to his or her personal world philosophies and understanding of other cultures and those who are different, as well as to help develop tolerance for all persons. This house also suggests how your teen will develop a personal belief system.

Adult's Ninth House: This house is your house of beliefs, higher consciousness, personal philosophies, spirituality and intuitive matters. It is your house of long-distance travel and foreign objects or places, as well as law and science. It is the house of judges and higher education.

Tenth House

Child's Tenth House: This house is also important for a child from a broken home because it is oppositin the fourth house, the child's foundation that has been shaken to the core. The child may have ego-related troubles that prevent him or her from succeeding or finishing tasks. Do not reprimand the child for an unfinished task; rather, encourage the child to finish it and then acknowledge a job well done. On a positive note, this is the house where the child learns to shine in the outside world. It is the house of authority and how the child will relate to authority figures or learn to be an authority figure. It is how the child will try to be noticed. This house also represents a parent, traditionally the mother, but today it can be either parent. Look at this house for how the step-child relates to parents and authority and how he or she will handle authority.

Adolescent's Tenth House: This house suggests ways your teenager can shine, show off and truly feel good about himself or herself. It is the house that shows if your teenager is a shy and retiring teen and, if so, the planets in the house and the sign on the cusp of the house show you how you can encourage your teen to shine. This house also suggests how your teen learns ways to cope with authority and become an ego-strong person. The teen years are the years when the individual quits thinking that being a firefighter would be fun because of the big red truck and begins to think about what will be fulfilling for other reasons. It is a time to explore many avenues and try all types of things, perhaps leading to college or learning a trade; this lasts into the early twenties, and this house can be read this way through that time period.

Adult's Tenth House: This is the house of career, profession, fame and honors. It is a house of responsibility and shows how you handle career and home life individually and with regard to each other. It suggests how you make your mark in the world. Areas within which you excel are suggested here. It also shows how well you handle authority or how well you handle a position of responsibility. Thus, how you handle the responsibility of the opposite fourth house as a positive contribution to that house in your step-parent role can be suggested by this house. It is also how you relate to your parents, which probably influences your parenting skills.

Eleventh House

Child's Eleventh House: This house shows how the child learns to relate to friends and develop social skills, as well as what groups the child will be interested in. It is also the house of wishes. Look here for clues for how to help your child fulfill his or her wishes, and perhaps what types of group activities may interest your child. If there is a strong Leo influence, perhaps your child would want acting, music or dance lessons. If there is a strong Sagittarius influence, perhaps your child would like a lot of sports activities and want to play on a sports team.

Adolescent's Eleventh House: This a very important house for the teenager. It is the house of friends and is very influential in your teenager's life. It shows where peer pressure is coming from and how your child will handle it. It also shows an expansion of dreams and wishes for the future. The child's eleventh is a good house to look at for extracurricular activities such as music, acting, sports, clubs and things your child will like and that will help your child develop a strong sense of self in a group setting.

Adult's Eleventh House: This is a major house for step-parents because it is the house of step-children. Look to this house to help understand your step-children and to relate to the people they are; this is in addition to the understanding that comes from your spouse's natal fifth house. The fifth house can be strong if you have no children of your own and look upon your step-children as your own children, or even if you have your own children but look to your step-children as your own. However, the eleventh house is the true house of step-children and is a very enlightening house for you. This should be one of the first places you look if you have problems, and do the same during good times; check for planets transiting (current position of the planets in the heavens rather than where they were at birth) this house and also which planets are in synastry. Also, this is the house of dreams, wishes, friends and groups. The fifth and eleventh houses are opposite each other. Is there any wonder why so many step-parents have a totally different experience from their spouses concerning the same children? Learning to balance these two houses is key to your success as a step-parent. Look at your spouse's fifth house to see how your spouse relates to his or her children, and at your eleventh house to see how you relate to your step-children. You both may see the same child in a very different light.

Twelfth House

Child's Twelfth House: This house suggests things the child keeps to himself, often because the child is not mature enough to express feelings verbally, which is even true for some adolescents.

Look here for hidden problems due to the broken home. This house represents things the child does not wish to share with anyone. What happens in childhood goes deep into the subconscious here. It suggests your child's desire for unqualified love.

Adolescent's Twelfth House: This house more than any other shows where your teenager escapes into his or her own teen world as a retreat from either growing up or growing up too fast. Sensitive teens who suffer at the hands of other insensitive teenagers' remarks or deeds will bury hurts very deeply here. On the other hand, when something wonderful happens (which it often does) and your teen is elated, this also goes into the subconscious and helps develop a strong feeling of self-worth. This house suggests how you can deal with your teenager on a deeper level and indicates ways to offer helpful suggestions.

Adult's Twelfth House: This house points to things hidden (unknown to you), secret enemies, hospitals or institutions, jails or restraints and, most importantly, your subconscious. Look here to see what your motivations may be in helping to rear children. Your unconscious often directs your reactions to others and you may find a great deal of personal insight into yourself which will help you be a better parent or step-parent.

Other helpful hints on the houses:

- Houses ten to three represent personal control.
- Houses four through nine suggest influence by others.
- Houses one through six are more private.
- Houses seven through twelve are more public.

Therefore, a majority of planets in houses ten through three indicates personal control, while a majority in houses four through nine indicates influence by others. A majority of planets in houses one through six tends to be more private, whereas a majority in houses seven through twelve is more public. These are considerations to look at when viewing your step-child's chart that may lend insight into the child. If the child is more private, perhaps the child does not want his or her creations on exhibit, or perhaps putting a creation on exhibit would be just what is needed to begin to develop more confidence. Determining this is child by child, case by case.

Astrological Signs

The twelve astrological signs indicate personality traits and are discussed below from the perspective of the child, adolescent and adult. Again, as you read the traits you can see how the child and adolescent develop into an adult.

Aries, March 22-April 20

Aries Child: This is the child who approaches life with zeal and fearlessness. This child never slows down and is the one others follow. Keeping up with this child will wear you out, and he or she gets very frustrated when things do not move quickly and thus may move from task to task, only finishing some. He or she needs sports and games and constant motion. This is the child who will not sit still in your lap.

Aries Adolescent: The Aries adolescent seems to have more energy than the average teenager who seems to sleep a lot. The full thrust of the Aries fire energy is put into everything this teen does and this teen may be very impatient when things do not go fast enough to suit him or her. If something does not pan out, this enthusiasm can quickly become anger or acting out. It is a good idea to have a lot of physical activity, dance, sports and the like so this teen has someplace to vent frustration. Again, as a teenager, this is the person the others will follow.

Aries Adult: The Aries child develops into an adult who is a self-starter, enthusiastic and quick to act. Fearless and eager to try something new, they are competitive and should watch for Mars combativeness since Mars rules Aries. Use Mars energy to push forward at a rapid speed.

Taurus, April 21-May 21

Taurus Child: This child may exhibit stubbornness, but is so charming you do not care. He or she wants a lot of constant comfort, loves possessions (toys) and likes a lot of "stuff," and needs a private place to hide his or her allowance. This child is very sensitive, creative and patient (or impatient) and will stick to tasks and see them to completion. This child is very persistent so hobbies that take a long time to finish or possibly learning a musical instrument which takes years will not put this child off. This child wants to sit in your lap.

Taurus Adolescent: This is the teenager that definitely needs his or her own room and possessions that siblings do not touch. Since Taurus is a sign that loves physical comfort, push this child toward physical activity, and do not let him or her sit in front of a computer or TV and eat sweets all the time. Once started in a sporting activity, this teen will find he or she really likes it and that it feels good. Even as a teenager, Taurus can be over-indulgent. The Taurus adolescent may show signs of artistic interest, and is very dependable, even as a teenager.

Taurus Adult: The teenager grows into a dependable and patient or impatient person, and one who is creative, methodical and will plod endlessly to get a job done. The Taurus adult also wants lovely surroundings and possessions. The Taurus charm that is demonstrated as a child can be lost at times as an adolescent, but returns with a vengeance in the adult. Difficulties with a Taurus concern any kind of change and it is necessary to learn to adapt. Taurus practicality and stability more than make up for inflexibility.

Gemini, May 22-June 21

Gemini Child: The Gemini child, like the adult, must have variety and keep busy at all times. There may be a lot of nervous energy, and do not be surprised at what this child says since the mind is incredibly active. Something new will develop almost on a daily basis with this child.

The Gemini child will be very bored if not doing several things at one time and may not finish projects. This is another one that is very hard for an adult to keep up with. This child may talk early.

Gemini Adolescent: The Gemini adolescent will probably communicate more with adults than other astrological signs. The Gemini cannot help but be lively, talkative and chaotic. Gemini is a dual sign and this duality comes out "big time" in adolescence. This is another sign that does not appear to be lazy, so involving the Gemini teenager in lots of activities is very good; but they should be quite varied such as the school newspaper, a team physical activity and perhaps the debate team. As long as this teenager is busy, he or she will be happy. This one is quite clever and probably one step ahead of you and not easily fooled by consoling words.

Gemini Adult: The teenager grows into a quick-minded, talkative and versatile adult. Just as the child and teenager, the adult must be doing more than one thing at a time. The Gemini adult is often high strung and also needs a place to use up the excess, nervous energy. It should be fairly easy for a Gemini adult to relate to a child since they go from one thing to another in a short period of time. Gemini adults can have more than one career going on at a time, and there may be a tendency to more than one marriage.

Cancer, June 22-July 23

Cancer Child: This child is very intuitive and picks up on feelings of others. Thus, this child will be very sensitive and hit hard during a divorce as security and home are most important. This child may either be overly emotional or try to crawl back into his or her shell to hide the emotions. A lot of nurturing is needed and, when provided, this child will grow in a very positive way. In turn, the child may nurture and be empathetic, and become an even more nurturing and empathetic adult. The child may feel a need to nurture the divorced parent. Thus, when the step-parent comes along and takes over a parental role, this child may feel displaced.

Cancer Adolescent: The Cancer adolescent is usually home a little more than the average teenager. They may be more reliable at watching younger siblings. However, in adversity the Cancer retreats to its shell and this child may not express problems as easily as other signs of the zodiac. You may need to coax this child to speak about things going on at school and with friends, but this child will remain helpful as a teenager. The teenager is a romantic and daydreams about the future. This teen needs to feel secure even while doing the teenage act of breaking away.

Cancer Adult: The Cancer adult can also feel insecure, especially when family problems arise. Dealing with step-children can lead to feelings of "does the spouse always take their side or I am just a third wheel in this family." This is exactly what Cancer should not do. Rather than exhibit difficult Cancer traits, use the Cancer trait of nurturing and the feeling of family importance to relate to everyone and you will find your insecurities lessen. You are very sympathetic and empathetic and your step-children will relate to this. You can really make the ideal home you dream about.

Leo, July 24-August 23

Leo Child: The whole world is the Leo child's stage. This child is definitely the show off and the actor, but as confident and optimistic as this child is, he or she is also warm, compassionate and generous. This is another child that all the other children will follow. This child's approach to everything may be overly-dramatic so this child needs outlets for creativity and exuberance, and any activity where he or she can be on stage or achieve recognition will be welcomed. This child will not take criticism lightly and positive suggestions will get you much further. He or she is more likely to act out rather than hold emotions in when parents divorce.

Leo Adolescent: Take the Leo child's traits and multiply them. Add to this someone who actually jumps at the chance to take risks and show off. This teen is like a magnet and others will go along with whatever he or she says, without question. This teenager needs direction in a positive way for all of this pent up energy and enthusiasm and, just as the child, this teenager needs activities where he or she can be the center of attention. Since this is an innately stubborn sign, learn to give a little more, listen to opinions and passions and offer positive advice. Leo does not take well to negativity. Leo's generosity really begins to show in the teenager who may be tempted to give away CDs and the like to friends because he or she loves giving gifts.

Leo Adult: The Leo child/teen grows up to be the energetic, passionate, generous and persistent adult. The Leo adult has a lot of confidence and also a magnetic personality, but may be a lot for a water- or earth-sign child to cope with so take care to see what each child in the family is like and respond appropriately. (Water signs are Cancer, Scorpio and Pisces; earth signs are Taurus, Virgo and Capricorn.) Leo's generosity is abundant and children will love that. The Leo adult also likes a lot of physical activity and this is perfect for the step-parent who loves to bike ride and skate with the children.

Virgo, August 24-September 23

Virgo Child: The cautious and shy adult stems from this cautious and shy child. Virgo is a sign that can play alone and prefers structure over chaos. Suppose for example this child has an Aries sibling with whom he must share a room. This is a recipe for disaster. The scattered Aries would drive the structured Virgo child crazy. The Virgo child is born with an established work ethic and feels it necessary to work hard and prove himself or herself. Words of encouragement and positive input go a long way into making this Virgo secure and self-confident. This is the child who will be mad at himself when he does something wrong. A strong analytical mind shows up at a very young age and this child should be proud of his or her mental abilities. This child also may be fearful of new foods or things perceived as harmful, such as insects. You will not have to encourage this child to save, and he or she will lend siblings money with interest.

Virgo Adolescent: The Virgo adolescent is a blessing compared to other signs of the zodiac. The Virgo trait of extreme neatness and tidiness does not fully leave this teenager and his or her room is not quite the disaster of other teenagers' rooms. This is a hard working adolescent who strives to achieve, and is health oriented. Also, the trait of practicality will stand even through the trying teen years. The Virgo teen needs to be encouraged to cut loose a little. If the Virgo teen appears to "teen-like," it is probably because there are a lot of planetary placements that counteract the Virgo Sun. The Virgo teen may be self-critical and needs positive encouragement.

Virgo Adult: The Virgo adult is meticulous, analytical, cautious, shy, concerned about health and works in a step by step fashion. This pragmatic adult will find practical ways of dealing with any problems, and Virgo's calm is truly soothing to any family chaos. Thus, a Virgo step-parent may be very calming. However, the Virgo trait of criticism is not welcome in a step-parent.

Libra, September 24-October 23

Libra Child: This child is the charmer, and will make a lot of friends, each one being very special. This child likes peace and probably won't be as argumentative as other signs. However, indecisiveness is a problem for both the child and adult. They weigh things over and over and over trying to make a decision, and often just do not make one at all. Encourage your child to be rational and fair but to then make the decision. Because of this child's distaste for discord, a broken home is especially hard to deal with. Artistic endeavors are a good distraction to get through tough times, and your child may find a musical instrument or an art field that is a life long love. Like Taurus, which is also ruled by Venus, home and comfort are very important to Libra.

Libra Adolescent: The Libra teen is also charming, just like the child, and even-tempered and non-aggressive. This is the teen who wants to adapt and be everyone's friend, the one who will express himself or herself and listen as well. The Libra trait of weighing one thing against the other is firmly established and part of how this teen will develop into an adult. Libra is ruled by Venus, so appearances are very important, and this teen wants nice clothes, his or her own room and perhaps a nice car. Whereas a Taurus, a sign also ruled by Venus, wants nice things, it is a Taurus trait to save while it is a Libra trait to spend. Manners come easy to this teen, and they are rarely rude. However, the trait of wanting to please everyone, including peers, may get the teen into trouble.

Libra Adult: The Libra adult can also be indecisive, weighing one thing against another, over and over, often not making the decision, and this is really the greatest difficulty for the Libra adult. If the child and teen are encouraged to make a decision, this trait will be much less difficult for the adult. The Libra is nonaggressive, artistic, adaptable, temperamental and charming. Work in partnerships is very strong for Libra, and working with the spouse on matters of the home is thus very beneficial.

Scorpio, October 24-November 22

Scorpio Child: The Scorpio child is headstrong, searching for self at an early age. Like the Scorpio adult, the child tends to be self-sufficient (or will do anything to be so) and may want a lot of time alone. This is actually very good since as a parent, you may have some peace you would not have with another sign. Also, the child is very intuitive and the sixth sense may be very disconcerting. You cannot hide family problems from this child. This child will persist until a goal is reached and is naturally motivated; it is hard to sway his or her opinion. A loyal friend, this child loves a mystery and will be very good at research. It is a must to have secrets and privacy.

Scorpio Adolescent: The Scorpio teen is a little more quiet than most teenagers, strong-willed, secretive and may be suspicious of adult motives. If you invade Scorpio's secret places, you will probably not be soon forgiven, if ever. As with the child, this teen needs privacy, a trait that seems to strengthen rather than diminish with age. This teen may enjoy reading about the darker side of life. A lot of discussions are involved with a Scorpio teen even if you really do not know why you are talking about something. Scorpios like to be challenged and will find it very rewarding to work hard toward something. In fact, working hard makes the thing worth having. This trait will grow and carry over to the adult. Jealousy and revenge are Scorpio traits that may start to really show in the teen years, so helping this teen learn to direct this negative energy into something positive is very important for the step-parent.

Scorpio Adult: The Scorpio adult is very intense, suspicious and magnetic. He or she can also be sarcastic and jealous. Intuition is one of Scorpio's greatest traits and will serve you well when working with step-children as you will be able to determine their motives and agendas. As with any fixed sign, the Scorpio adult will work hard and long to finish a project. The Scorpio adult is just an older version of the Scorpio child and teen, and hopefully has learned to turn revengeful or jealous energy into something positive.

Sagittarius, November 23-December 22

Sagittarius Child: The Sagittarius child is restless and must feel a sense of freedom even at an early age. This is the child that chases rainbows and dreams of exotic places, especially made-up places. The Sagittarius child is enthusiastic and seeks adventure from day one. As the child grows, so does his or her social consciousness and a sense of right and wrong. This child will speak without thinking about the consequences, so what is said at home may not stay at home. Because this child thinks in the whole, not in detail, mundane tasks may not be the best choice. Early on, this child is the humanitarian and will always fight for issues important to him or her.

Sagittarius Adolescent: This is the teen who works tirelessly on projects that help others, such as food banks or club-sponsored charitable activities. They speak their minds without thinking and this can get them into trouble at school. This teen really wants freedom and you probably will not know where this teen is half the time. But this is also the teen that will probably follow his or her idealistic heart and do good works rather than hang around with the wrong crowd. With a little encouragement, this child will go far; but you must learn to deal with scattered activities, some of which will be finished and some of which will be finished much later if at all.

Sagittarius Adult: The Sagittarius adult can be idealistic but can also self-righteous, so you should try to make sure the idealistic side is demonstrated to children. You desire freedom and you must do things so that you do not feel tied down. You are optimistic and giving, and may also be restless, which would be a good match with more energetic children. Be cautious about being too dogmatic since your ideals are not necessarily those of everyone else. You are versatile and open-minded but may tend to extremism or irresponsibility.

Capricorn, December 23-January 19

Capricorn Child: This child is born with an innate sense of order. The adult trait of self-discipline tends to show up at an early age, and along with seriousness comes a sense of security, or insecurity if his or her world is shaken. A parental divorce would be devastating and even more so since it is not the proper order of things. This child needs reassurance from you for personal security and needs to be told it is okay to be frivolous, that the world won't come to an end. Once this child learns to let loose a little, he or she is almost the perfect child for an adult—well behaved, self-disciplined, a good worker and well mannered. In fact, this child may often be more adult than the adults in the situation.

Capricorn Adolescent: The Capricorn teen is practical and serious, but may tend to worry. This teen may go nuts over a school project or about something not being perfect, and needs a less serious and more teenage approach to life. This is the one who needs approval to feel he or she has done a good job. On the other hand, like the child, this is a teen who is easy for the adult to relate to. Helping the teen be organized, as well as helping him or her to have fun will make you a very strong influence and be fulfilling for both of you. This teen is reliable and dependable, but may be pessimistic.

Capricorn Adult: The Capricorn adult may be serious, self-disciplined, cautious and responsible, and must watch for rigidity and cynicism. The responsibility will be well received by your step-child, but you must try for a lighter, less serious touch in order to relate to the child. You must be proud of what you are doing, even step-parenting, and thus you will try very hard to be a good step-parent. You will also take pride in your step-children's accomplishments. If your step-child is a very outgoing, energetic sign such as Aries or Leo, you must really try not to be too rigid and let things roll energetically along rather than trying to control situations.

Aquarius, January 20-February 19

Aquarius Child: This is the child who truly travels to the beat of a different drummer. He or she is a bit different and a rebel, begins to form personal ideals early in life and will listen even if at odds with you. This child will want all the latest gadgets and be very interested in technology, and will also make a lot of friends even if often appearing detached. This is a very fun child, but if you are an extremely stable and reserved person, you may find it disconcerting.

Aquarius Adolescent: The teen will continue and improve upon the child's spirit of rebelliousness, but often in a good way. This child sets high standards and is quite honest with those around him. The adolescent is learning to accept philosophies of others while starting to develop his or her own higher consciousness. This teen will be accepting and tolerant as long as he or she is also accepted. A strong sense of humanitarianism is being developed, and the Aquarius trait of detachment is very strong in the teen years. Let this teen go (within reason) or you will butt heads because this teen must feel a sense of freedom. Technology is also very interesting to the Aquarian teen and you can find common ground exploring the latest in computers, cameras and the like with your teen. This teen is unpredictable.

Aquarius Adult: The Aquarius adult is the humanitarian and visionary, but just as the child and teen, still the rebel and reformer. There is still a sense of unpredictability, and you are the inventor and a wonderful teacher. Your strong points with regard to a step-child are that you stimulate imagination, teach and help the child explore new worlds. You give a child a sense of the macrocosm and high ideals.

Pisces, February 20-March 21

Pisces Child: The Pisces child is extremely sensitive and often picks up the emotions of others, thereby appearing moody. Thus, when the adults are having problems, this child is extremely affected by their problems. This is the child who needs a lot of reassurance that he or she is not the problem. On the other hand, this child wants approval and will be very helpful and try to do what you want in order to gain approval. This is a sweet child that tries too hard to please and should be encouraged to do his or her own thing even if everyone does not like it. This child may escape into a world of his or her own imagination and this is a very good release, as is an artistic side that should be encouraged. This child may seem a little shy and distant at first but will easily grow to care and trust if encouraged.

Adolescent Pisces: The teen also has a strong need to escape when upset, either into his or her own imagination, dreams or through the use of stimulants or depressants. Make sure your teen has a release during troubled times so he or she does not succumb to peer pressure for escape. This is not to say every Pisces teen will use these other forms of release (or that some other signs may also have a tendency to need escape). Make sure your teen does have outlets for insecurities, as well as his or her imagination. Because Pisces is so sensitive, this teen will feel the weight of the emotions of those around him or her and definitely needs release. Music and the arts are wonderful for Pisces, as is enjoying time in the country. Pisces likes to feel needed, so as a step-parent it is important to make sure this teen feels this way. Also, help your teen develop the intuition while encouraging him or her not to feel horrible about the plight of others.

Pisces Adult: You are trusting, humble, adaptable and empathetic and can be easily influenced and moody. You are also very intuitive. You like to help others and can relate very well to the emotions of your step-child since you probably feel the same emotions. A good use of your empathy and a way to become even closer would be to help create artistic or musical outlets for your step-child in order to deal with emotions. You must learn to keep you feet on the ground when dealing with younger members of the family.

When discussing the Sun signs, you must keep in mind that other placements in an astrological chart may strengthen, lessen or deny the traits described above and that the entire chart must be considered.

The Planets

Each planet has its own qualities and is the ruler (associated with) of an astrological sign. The qualities run true to form for the child, adolescent and adult, and the planets in a child's chart are very important, as are the aspects the planets make to each other and other points in the chart. The child's planets and their aspects in synastry to the adult charts are extremely important in step-parenting. (Aspects are geometric angles that will be explained later in this chapter.) The planets are as follows:

The Sun, Ruler of Leo

The Sun suggests your ambition and drive, and is where your child will learn to shine and where you will shine as an adult. It has both positive and negative qualities. If you help your step-child achieve recognition via the Sun sign, he or she will be proud of these accomplishments. The house the Sun is located in gives clues as to where your step-child/teen may shine and be proud. It is where strength lies.

The Moon, Ruler of Cancer

The Moon suggests emotions, fluctuation and sensitivity. It is where your child/teen will learn emotional lessons and lessons of change, as well as how to deal with other people's emotions. The transiting (current position in the zodiac) Moon is where to look when you want to help your child/teen change things. The monthly New Moon is the time to help you child/teen start something new and the monthly Full Moon is a time to help your child/teen get through emotional times. If the New Moon is in a fire sign, it is a time to be active, take initiative and be bold. If it is in an earth sign it is a time for practical measures and to acquire material goods or work toward material matters, and a time for physical comfort. If it is in an air sign, it is a time for open lines of communication and social activities, writing, talking and generally connecting with people. If it is in a water sign, it is a time to deal with feelings and emotions, security comfort, romance and home. The Moon is one planet I use a lot in step-parenting, and later in this book I will discuss the use of lunar returns (defined in later chapters) to solve problems.

Mercury, Ruler of Gemini and Virgo

Mercury represents your ability to communicate with others and your thought processes. It is where your child develops rational thought and communication skills. The Mercury placement suggests how your child will grow into a communicating adult and where your teen will probably tend to try not to communicate or will push forth his or her ideas.

Venus, Ruler of Taurus and Libra

Venus represents relationships, consideration and temperament. It is where your child learns about love and trust and where artistic temperament comes into play. It is where your teen may first fall in love, and the child's musical or artistic abilities are suggested. You can learn to relate to your step-child's security issues in light of his or her Venus placement.

Mars, Ruler of Aries

Mars represents your energy, drive and combativeness. It is where your child learns about anger and how to control it, as well as how to direct energy in a positive manner. It is where your teen will be combative and aggressive in becoming independent. It is where you can help direct your child/teen's energies in a positive manner.

Jupiter, Ruler of Sagittarius

Jupiter suggests confidence, optimism, expansion and opportunity. It is where your child feels he or she can expand horizons and anything is possible, and where optimism shines best. It is where your teen will seek to really expand and where your teen's unbridled enthusiasm may come through. The Jupiter placement is where you may help your step-child/teen develop optimism and grow, developing the confidence that he or she can be and do anything. The Jupiter placement and Jupiter transits are a lot of fun and important to your relationship with your step-child. For example, if your personal Jupiter in synastry sits in your step-child's second house, you may help the child learn to make money, develop personal values or feel secure.

Saturn, Ruler of Capricorn

Saturn represents responsibility, restriction, obstacles and self-discipline, as well as life's lessons. It is where your child learns to work hard for future reward or, in other words, learns to work and to have some patience in getting what he or she wants. It is also where your child learns to deal with obstacles and sometimes defeat. Saturn is also one of the most important planets when dealing with a step-child. Saturn's placement is where you can help the step-child work hard, gain responsibility and become a responsible and mature teen and adult. Since it represents obstacles, its placement suggests where your child will become frustrated; expect this and help your step-child to go beyond his or her perceived limitations and boundaries, most of which are probably in the child's mind. Saturn is also the planet between the personal planets and the outer planets of Uranus, Neptune and Pluto. By helping your step-child with Saturn lessons, he or she will develop a higher consciousness and ability to deal with the world. Karmic ramifications of Saturn will be discussed in later chapters.

Uranus, Ruler of Aquarius

Uranus represents the rebel, the unconventional and the reformer. Uranus is where your step child/teen will really "feel his oats." It is where actions will be unsuspected and unusual and where the child will rebel. It is probably a placement that, unless you are an Aquarius, you will have the most difficult time with your step-child because you will not know what to expect.

Neptune, Ruler of Pisces

Neptune represents intuition, inspiration, deception and fantasy. Neptune is where your step-child/teen will be very intuitive, creative and emotional and where his or her artistic side may be revealed. It is also where your child may exhibit confusion, as well as tremendous and mature insight. Look at this placement for where your step-child/teen may take on the burden or emotions of those around him or her or may succumb to peer pressure. Use the Neptune placement to help your step-child/teen develop his or her musical and creative side as an outlet for emotions. Also, if your child is prone to psychic ability, Neptune's placement is where to help develop it.

Everyone has Neptune and Pisces somewhere in the birth chart. When I refer to a potential for drug or alcochol problems in the context of the Neptune or Pisces placement, it does not mean there is abuse. A potential may never manifest, and probably won't, in the individual's life. This should be remembered in all of the example charts in this book.

Pluto, Ruler of Scorpio

Pluto represents upheaval, dramatic change, reorganization, transformation and the nonconformist. Pluto is where your step-child will have secrets, where he or she will be intuitive and a natural detective, and possibly show what groups your child will be drawn toward. Pluto is where you can help your step-child/teen develop a sense of society and gravitate toward groups of interest. Because Pluto has a generational influence, it will suggest the collective psyche of your child/teen and how this generation will relate to the world.

The Signs Applied to the Planets

The planets will either reinforce or contradict the traits of the astrological signs within which the planets sit. Some planets are personal and some are generational or at least tend to relate more to the macrocosm. The following suggests how the planets apply to the astrological signs:

The Sun: The Sun is the most personal planet because it symbolizes your personal drive and where you will shine. It takes the Sun one year to move around the zodiac (one month in each sign). The placement of your step-child's Sun suggests where you may help him or her to shine and develop his or her strengths. As the Sun transits a chart, each house it enters is a time to work and shine in the areas the house represents.

The Moon: The Moon is very personal as well since it represents your emotions. However, the Moon moves from sign to sign every two and one-half days. When transits (current positions of the planets) are discussed, you will see how crucial the Moon is as a tool for change and timing. Your step-child's Moon suggests where you can be of help emotionally and areas where he or she may change again and again.

Mercury: Mercury is also very personal. It indicates your thoughts and communication skills and style. Mercury stays in an astrological sign about two and one-half weeks (up to two and one-half months at times, when retrograde). Mercury suggests your step-child's thought processes and communication skills and the placement suggests where you can help your child learn and grow.

Venus: Venus is also a personal sign representing your emotional and creative natures. It takes between one year and thirteen months for Venus to move around the zodiac. Venus suggests your step-child's creativity, artistic tendencies and love of nature. It also deals with security or insecurity issues and finances.

Mars: Mars is also a personal planet because it symbolizes your drive, personal and sexual desires, and combativeness. It takes almost two years to move through the zodiac. Mars suggests where your step-child must learn to control his or her temper and gear individual energy to positive action.

Jupiter: Jupiter is a transitional planet from the personal to the outer planets. It spends about one year in an astrological sign. During the time it is in a sign, it offers great benefit and personal opportunities. When Jupiter transits (current position in the zodiac) a sign, it is a very good time to take advantage of opportunities. Jupiter's placement in your chart indicates your philosophy of life and your belief system, and because it is in a sign for a year, your peers tend to agree with you. Thus, you can see where your step-child's beliefs will form. Jupiter takes twelve years to move around the zodiac.

Saturn: Saturn is very important because of its importance as the most transitional planet between the inner, personal planets, and the outer, generational planets. It is personal regarding karma and as an indicator of areas of hard work, obstacles and rewards for a job well done. But the rewards may be in the future, so Saturn is a place to begin to work toward something. This placement is where your step-child will learn patience—waiting for a reward for work done—and where your step-child will learn the meaning of overcoming obstacles. Saturn transits the zodiac in about twenty-eight to twenty-nine and one-half years. With Saturn's signs you share common issues with those close to your age. Saturn returns (when Saturn reaches the exact degree and sign of your natal Saturn) are crucial benchmarks in life.

Uranus: Uranus is an outer planet; it takes eighty-five years to travel through all twelve signs of the zodiac, or about seven years in each sign. You thus share the eccentricities of your peers, as does your step-child with his or hers. House positions will give some individuality to Uranus in the chart.

Neptune: Neptune is an outer, generational planet. It takes one hundred sixty-five years to travel around the zodiac, or about thirteen and three-quarter year in one sign. The house within which Neptune sits will indicate your personal reaction to generational issues. On a personal level though, it can suggest intuition, substance abuse tendencies, your artistic nature, dreams and psychic abilities.

Pluto: Pluto is an outer planet that takes two hundred forty-five to two hundred fifty years to travel through the zodiac. It marks generational issues. When Pluto was in Cancer from 1913 to 1938, there were two world wars. Pluto was in Leo for those born in the 1940s and early 1950s; the Korean War was in the early 1950s. It is easy to see how those born in the late 1940s and early 1950s became the "flower children" of the 1960s since the recent history of war was a powerful lesson. This generation also saw the onset of the United Nations to avoid further wars. The house occupied by Pluto will suggest how you will personally deal with generational issues. On a personal level, Pluto suggests power and control issues, and issues of reform.

The Ascendant

The Ascendant is the sign on the cusp of your first house. A cusp is the dividing line between two houses, so the Ascendant is the dividing line between your twelfth and first houses. The Ascendant suggests how you appear to others. Thus, it will suggest how you appear to your family, who may define you by your Ascendant traits. Planets in the first house may somewhat modify this appearance. The Ascendant suggests your persona. Since this is how family members perceive you, they will react to the nature of your Ascendant as you begin to see the initial family interactions with yourself. As you develop, the traits of your Ascendant evolve and so does your relationship with the family. This is also very true of step-children and step-parents. When you first meet your future step-children, you are probably reacting to traits of the their Ascendants (and they to yours) and as they mature and as your relationship develops, your reactions will also evolve. This is a very important placement when looking at relationships with others.

Aries Ascendant: These are the leaders, the independent souls. They are energetic, ambitious, courageous and confident. They may anger quickly but also calm just as quickly. You will have to work to keep up with them and probably, unless you have a heavy Aries influence, won't ever be one step ahead. People with an Aries Ascendant tend to be very intense. The family may not be able to relate to everything the Aries wants to pursue, but the Aries will probably go after his or her goals anyway. The Aries Ascendant person often encourages the family to try new directions.

Taurus Ascendant: People with a Taurus Ascendant appear to be very self-sufficient, capable and hard working. They will plod along toward goals, but can also be very impatient; usually gentle, when prodded they become very angry. The Taurus Ascendant may be either very secretive or very open. They have very good earning potential and since they are viewed as hard, efficient workers, they make a good impression on the employer; if self-employed, they do very well. They enjoy luxury and must have beautiful surroundings. Feelings are deep and lasting. People with a Taurus Ascendant are lovers of beauty in the home and love all those in the home.

Gemini Ascendant: These people are curious, mentally active and can be nervous. The Gemini Ascendant must have a lot going on or will become bored, and because this is a dual sign there may be some indecision. This is the cheerful conversationalist at the dinner table, always ready to share or hear a new idea. On the other hand, often the Gemini Ascendant has secret thoughts that are not shared despite the amount of conversation carried on with others. Gemini minds can be very creative as well and Geminis tend to be quick-witted. Physical activity is good for excess energy. As with any dual sign, there may be a tendency toward more than one marriage.

Cancer Ascendant: The Cancer Ascendant is the typical nurturer. They are very sensitive to others and may actually take on the emotions of others who are under distress. They also have a very good imagination, are sympathetic and have a very good memory. In fact, they don't forget a thing—good or bad. They really cannot take criticism very well and it is important to find ways to encourage rather than criticize them. A Cancer Ascendant also tends to be very intuitive, so it will be hard for family members to keep secrets.

Leo Ascendant: Leo is the actor of the zodiac so these people tend to be very dramatic, as well as good-natured, outspoken, impulsive and adventurous. This is the family member that others look to for fun. A Leo Ascendant also has a lot of strength beneath the fun-loving exterior. They tend to be even-tempered, but are also quick to anger and quick to forgive, and generous. They are the ring-leaders others follow, so don't expect them to follow you.

Virgo Ascendant: People with a Virgo Ascendant are conservative, industrious, detail oriented and not extremely adventurous. There may be a tendency to be critical and if a family member has Virgo Ascendant, try to help him or her learn to say something constructive rather than critical; this will go a long way in enhancing family relationships. Virgo Ascendant people are very discriminating and can also be tactful if they put their minds to it. Anything connected with business or commerce will be of interest to them. Health and hygiene are very important, and this is the family member who really needs a pet.

Scorpio Ascendant: People with this Ascendant appear reserved, tenacious and intense. They have both constructive and destructive tendencies. Luxury is appreciated. Perhaps the most unusual trait in light of the Scorpio tendency to secrecy is that they are actually quick-witted and verbal. There is a tendency to action and forcefulness, but bluntness can be a problem. They are also very intuitive and will often know what is happening in the family. Anger may be extreme and they may not cool off easily. Although they will remember what angered them long after others have forgotten, they also remember the good. These people will accomplish a lot due to their enterprising nature and they do not give up. Intuition is strong, and the dark side of life may fascinate them.

Sagittarius Ascendant: This is the freedom-lover, happy, optimistic, charitable and spiritual. They are the dreamers, and the world needs the Sagittarius foresight and enthusiasm. They tend to be frank or outspoken but are good-humored and sincere. This is a restless Ascendant. These people set high standards and enjoy positive input from family when they reach their goals.

Capricorn Ascendant: Like Virgo and Taurus, the Capricorn sticks to it, is serious about getting things done and is very focused. This is a sign of accomplishment and thus these people may actually disregard others in order to achieve their goals. It is a business and commercial sign, but that is not to say that Capricorn traits do not lend themselves to all walks of life. They respect philosophies and religions but are self-contained with regard to their place in them. Because they are not especially demonstrative with regard to feelings, this carries over into the family.

Aquarius Ascendant: These are the people others probably cannot figure out. Change is important to their well-being, along with a tendency for patience and quiet. They sit back and take it all in. Everything mental will probably be appealing, and the career will follow what is new and different in the chosen field, no matter what the actual work is. They are future-oriented thinkers, and also have a stubborn streak. Although mentally motivated, they also take erratic action at times. This is the family member no one may not know how to deal with.

Pisces Ascendant: These are affable people who are intuitive and may take on the problems of others and assimilate their feelings into their own. This means they can be drained of energy when around people who are needy and demanding. They may lack confidence. Home is important and they like a peaceful environment where they can flourish and build up their self-esteem. They will probably know about family secrets but may be confused about them. Their feelings are very intense and it is important for family members to remember just how sensitive they are. These people are the "pie in the sky" dreamers who motivate others to experience events outside of their practical worlds. Some Pisces Ascendant people are creative or artistic.

Planets in the First House: As an example of how first house planets influence the Ascendant and may somewhat change perception, suppose you have a Taurus Ascendant. You appear steady, hard working and dogmatic. But suppose you also have Mercury in Gemini in this house. You will appear to be mentally quick in addition to being steady and hard working. This influence adds positive connotations to the Ascendant and further rounds out the personality. Suppose you have Uranus in the first house with the Taurus Ascendant. You appear steady and dependable, but you probably also shock everyone at times by doing something totally erratic and unconventional. All of the first house influences, along with the Ascendant, suggest how others and, specifically for this book, your family, sees you and how they react to you.

Elements and Qualities

There are also elements and qualities to consider when interpreting a chart and these are somewhat the same for adults and children. The elemental signs and their corresponding houses are:

Fire Signs and Corresponding Houses: Aries (first), Leo (fifth) and Sagittarius (ninth). Fire signs represent drive, ambition and action. They are the go-getters. As children and teens, they are the ones you cannot keep up with and they often seem uncontrollable.

Earth Signs and Corresponding Houses: Taurus (second), Virgo (sixth) and Capricorn (tenth). The earth signs are the practical ones, the ones who work and cope on a day-to-day basis. They are the steady plodders. They are the loving, dependable children and teens who want a lot of security and toys.

Air Signs and Corresponding Houses: Gemini (third), Libra (seventh)and Aquarius (eleventh). The air signs are the thinkers and the communicators. They talk at an early age and often surprise others by what they say. Even as children and teens, they are the thinkers of another planet.

Water Signs and Corresponding Houses: Cancer (fourth), Scorpio (eighth) and Pisces (twelfth). The water signs are the emotional ones. They are empathetic and often deal on intuitive or subconscious levels. They are very loving children and teens who want friends and yet who want time alone to ponder their thoughts. They can be very sensitive, so watch not to hurt their feelings.

The sign qualities and their corresponding houses are:

Cardinal Signs and Corresponding Houses: Aries (first), Cancer (fourth), Libra (seventh) and Capricorn (tenth). These houses and signs represent action. Look to these houses to help your step-children develop personally.

Succedent or Fixed Signs and Corresponding Houses: Taurus (second), Leo (fifth), Scorpio (eighth) and Aquarius (eleventh). These houses and signs represent stability. Look to these houses to help your step-children feel secure and stable.

Mutable Signs and Corresponding Cadent Houses: Gemini (third), Virgo (sixth), Sagittarius (ninth) and Pisces (twelfth). These houses and signs represent mental activity and systems of belief. Look to these houses to help your step-children develop their mental processes and communication skills.

Aspects

Finally, the aspects the planets make to each other or perhaps to the Ascendant or the Midheaven (the cusp of the tenth house), the lunar Nodes or Vertex (defined in later chapters) play a very important role in delineation of a child's chart and even more importantly in synastry when dealing with family situations. The traditional aspects are:

Conjunction: The planets are next to each other, usually in the same sign, within about nine or ten degrees.

Opposition: The planets are opposite each other, or 180 degrees apart, within about five degrees.

Square: The planets are ninety degrees apart, within about five degrees.

Sextile: The planets are thirty degrees apart, within about three or four degrees.

Trine: The planets are twenty degrees apart, within about five degrees.

Inconjunct or Quincunx: The planets are 150 degrees apart, within about six or eight degrees.

Other aspects are:

Quintile: 72 degrees (within three or four degrees).

Semisextile: 60 degrees (within five degrees).

Semisquare: 45 degrees (within three or four degrees).

Biquintile: 144 degrees (within three or four degrees).

Sesquisquare: 135 degrees (within three or four degrees).

The number of degrees on either side of an aspect is called an orb. For example, a conjunction is 180 degrees. If a five-degree orb is used, there is a ten-degree range for the aspect from 175 to 185 degrees. As a general rule, I use a five-degree orb, but the closer to the exact degree, the more powerful the aspect. I may narrow or slightly expand the orb depending upon other indications in the chart. For a sextile, I use a three- or four-degree orb.

The conjunction, sextile, semisextile, trine and biquintile are considered harmonious aspects where the drives and desires indicated reinforce each other and egg each other on (perhaps too much).

The opposition, square, semisquare, sesquisquare, and quincunx or inconjunct are more difficult aspects to deal with and they point to inner conflicts or drives that compete with one another but are beneficial as you work your way through them. In fact, the easier aspects are sometimes too easy and thus opportunities can be missed. The more difficult aspects can indicate areas where we develop strength through challenges, like resistance training when building the muscles.

Figure 1, astrological outline; Figure 2, major aspects outline; and Figure 3, solar wheel demonstrate the above.

Figure 1, Astrological Outline

Sign	Symbol	Ruler	Symbol	Element	Quality
Aries	♈	Mars	♂	Fire	Cardinal
Taurus	♉	Venus	♀	Earth	Fixed
Gemini	♊	Mercury	☿	Air	Mutable
Cancer	♋	Moon	☽	Water	Cardinal
Leo	♌	Sun	☉	Fire	Fixed
Virgo	♍	Mercury	☿	Earth	Mutable
Libra	♎	Venus	♀	Air	Cardinal
Scorpio	♏	Pluto	♀	Water	Fixed
Sagittarius	♐	Jupiter	♃	Fire	Mutable
Capricorn	♑	Saturn	♄	Earth	Cardinal
Aquarius	♒	Uranus	♅	Air	Fixed
Pisces	♓	Neptune	♆	Water	Mutable

Figure 2, Major Aspects Outline

Aspect	Degree	Symbol	Property
Conjunction	Within 9°	♂	Energy flow enhanced
Opposition	180°	☍	Energy flow inhibited
Square	90°	□	Energy flow inhibited
Sextile	60°	✳	Energy flow enhanced
Trine	120°	△	Energy flow enhanced
Inconjunct or Quincunx	150°	⚻	Energy flow inhibited
Quintile	72°	Q	Energy flow enhanced
Semisquare	45°	∠	Energy flow inhibited
Semisextile	30°	⌄	Energy flow enhanced
Biquintile	144°	Bq	Energy flow enhanced
Sesquisquare	135°	⚼	Energy flow inhibited

Figure 3, Solar Chart Indicating Houses and Signs on the Cusp of Each House

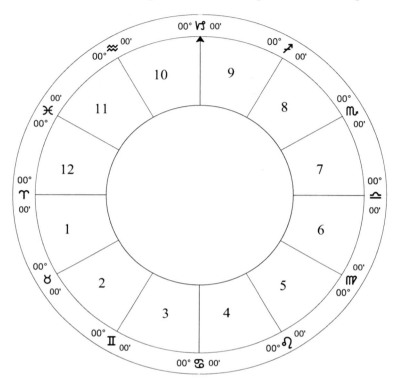

Chapter 2

Putting It Together

A NATAL CHART IS your personal guide, but only a guide, offering insight into personal choices. Rarely, if ever, is anything set in stone. In fact, that is the fun of a natal chart—it can indicate options you may not be aware of or that you thought were unattainable. This is true of your step-child's chart as well. You may get insight into facets of the child's personality and the choices he or she makes. You also may get insights into how to best help your step-child handle being the product of a broken home and how to help your step-child cope with a step-parent. You may help the child with his or her strengths and help the child find ways to improve on weaker areas, as well as fun, creative ways to bond.

There are basic steps to follow when interpreting a natal chart. Those listed below may be applied to all natal charts, adult, child and adolescent.

1. Begin with your Ascendant. This is how you appear to others, your persona and how you will appear to family members. The Ascendant suggests the first impression others will have of you. Planets in the first house may modify the motifs of your Ascendant somewhat. The Ascendant also suggests your direction in this lifetime and will underscore how you handle situations.

2. Look at the Midheaven (tenth house cusp). This is where you ego is, where you will achieve honors and recognition. It is where you identify with yourself.

3. Look at your Sun sign. It is where your drive and ambition lie and where you will shine. This is the place to start when looking at the strengths of an individual.

4. Look at both the Descendant (seventh house cusp) and Nadir (fourth house cusp) to see how

you relate to partnership (seventh), marriage (seventh) and family (fourth) situations.

5. Go around the astrological wheel and interpret each house cusp. Look up the meanings given for each house and the meaning for the sign on each house. Any house on an astrological chart may hold clues to how you handle step-parenting in a creative manner.

6. Look to the ruler of the sign on the cusp of the house for further help in interpreting that house. For example, if the seventh house of partnerships and marriage has an Aries cusp, the planetary ruler is Mars; so you would look to the house where Mars lies for clues into your marriage. Suppose Mars is in the eleventh house, which is the house of your spouse's children. Then the step-children would greatly affect your marriage. If it were in the eighth house, which is the financial house related to your marriage, possibly money would have a great effect.

7. You must also look at the qualities and elements of the sign. For instance, Aries is a fire sign and placed on the cusp of your seventh house, you would approach marriage with a tremendous amount of fire and energy. Aries is also a cardinal sign, and placed in the seventh house, a cardinal house, it represents action.

8. As you go from house to house, when you come upon a house that contains planets, look up how the planets add further information to the cusp meaning of the house. Some planets may re-inforce the motifs of the astrological sign on the cusp, while other planets bring in conflicting themes to be faced. This is also very, very important in synastry, which is discussed in a later chapter. Some planets are more personal and others symbolize society. Mercury is personal, indicating how you think and communicate. Pluto is slow moving and often indicates world conditions. If Pluto is in your eleventh house, you may be more concerned with working for the good of humanity than concentrating on your step-parenting (your step-children are represented by the eleventh house). Or you may have power struggles and control issues with your step-children.

9. A stellium of planets (four or more planets in a conjunction, or grouped together) is an obvious indication of your strengths. You must look at a stellium with a view toward how such a concentration of planets can help you or your step-child. Stelliums may also include points in your chart such as the Ascendant, Descendent, Midheaven, Nadir and the lunar Nodes or asteroids.

10. Also, consider the aspects the planets make to each other for their further significance through the chart. This is very important and will give you clear clues. The aspects made from one chart to another are crucial in creative step-parenting. An unaspected planet is quite significant since its energies are not harnessed in any way. When an unaspected planet is subject to a transit, a tremendous opportunity is created to use this planet constructively.

11. The lunar Nodes are also quite important. The Nodes are derived via the intersection of the Moon and the Earth's orbit. These points are called the North Node and the South Node, and they are always in opposition aspect. The South Node is a karmic point. If you are uncomfort-

able with the concept of karma or do not use it, think of it in terms of a metaphor. The South Node is a good place to look for your own motivations, and your step-child's South Node is a good place to look for his or her motivations. The North Node indicates what you are intended to do in this lifetime and a good place to look for what will fulfill your step-child. Nodal contact between two charts is a karmic placement.

12. When dealing with a step-child, there are specific transits I feel are quite beneficial. Transits are the actual position of the planets on any specific date and time. The transiting Moon is crucial since it changes signs every two and a half days throughout a month. The Moon helps you find opportunities to work on areas of trouble or on areas of joy, depending upon whether you look at the glass as half full or half empty. Sometime during the month there will be a time for bonding in art, music, sports, through communication, helping with school work and other activities that can create positive change in your relationship with your step-child. Thus, even though the Moon can represent high emotional tides, it can be a great asset to you.

A Mars transit can suggest tension and anger, but more importantly it can suggest places where energy and a lot of activity can form a strong bond. Use the Mars energy to start projects with your step-child, attend or participate in sports activities, begin school projects that require a lot of work and so forth. Also, you can help your step-child learn to use Mars energy constructively.

Jupiter is also important since it opens doors of opportunity for you to bond with your step-child. You can help your step-child dream big and begin to realize his or her dreams with a Jupiter transit. It is your job as the adult to help direct energy in a positive manner and, as with Mars, if there is combativeness or anger, let it come out in constructive ways and burn itself out.

Even Saturn transits can be beneficial. Learn what your step-child wants and then help him or her begin to learn about the benefits fo working hard. It is a time to help the child understand there will be obstacles in life but that they can be worked through. Saturn is a beneficial teacher for both of you. If you have an affliction (difficult aspect) between either your Saturn and a planet in the step-child's chart or vice versa, this is a place that really needs work to overcome negativity.

Transits of the outer planets (Uranus, Neptune and Pluto) tend to take on generational themes but may also be personal in the natal chart. If any of these planets transits a planet, changes that occur will probably take longer to completely manifest themselves. These planetary energies will act as they always do: Uranus may cause a period of chaos and confusion, unpredictability and the like; Neptune may cause a period of insight, confusion, dreams, intuition and the like; and Pluto may cause a period of reform and reorganization, power and control issues. In looking at a child's chart, I try to look more at the personal planet transits because they can help change occur more quickly. Outer planet transits tend to affect a particular house during the course of the transit, changing a particular area of life represented by the house, not just the planet in the house.

You should get a feeling of what each house represents by continually weighing planets, house cusps, rulers and aspects to determine which motifs are repeated by several factors and which motifs are minimized.

By using the above method, the houses come alive. There is a constant flux of information until a vivid picture is formed. It is critical to interpret the entire chart as there may be certain elements which are not apparent at first glance but which can be very helpful.

Then look at the synastry between your and your step-child's charts to see how you will bond, where tension may lie and how you can help create a strong family relationship with your step child.

Critical: If you do not have a professional license in counseling, it is always important to refer children and step-parents who are having difficulty to a professional with skills to counsel them. Astrology may be insightful but it is not a license to counsel.

In following chapters, I delineate one extended family's natal charts, including step-mother, the step-children, the charts of father, step-sister and the father's ex-spouse. I will put the charts together in synastry to show how comparison of the astrological charts may help you become a better and creative step-parent. I will explain how astrology can help bond the "new" family and create a happy atmosphere for everyone. These methods work as well for parents as they do for step-parents, but step-parents really can benefit at the onset from this book.

Chapter 3

Stages of Development

IT IS IMPOSSIBLE TO fully understand creative step-parenting without understanding how the child grows and develops.

I am not a psychologist, but I have a background in education, including the pertinent social and psychological foundations. If I see a situation where I think a child or an adult may need counseling, I do not try to do it astrologically but refer them to a state licensed professional. An educational background and research only provides clues; it does not make one a viable counselor. At times, professional counseling is the best method. Astrology affords options but does not heal per se. Always leave counseling to the professionals!

Following is an outline of child development I find very helpful. If you know the stages of growth of your step-children, you can compare their growth to their astrological potential and really have a leg up in helping to create a growth-oriented, positive relationship. This outline focuses on mental and psychological development.

The Baby Stage: By four months, the baby will begin to really notice things. He or she will follow things with the eyes and hold them in a fixed position. The baby will explore with hands, find toes and react to voices, light and color. He or she will begin to communicate with sounds, smile and begin to play.

By eight months the baby will know its name and begin to recognize situations that can cause harm, such as height. The baby may be shy, will begin trying to imitate and will recognize himself or herself in the mirror. If you are stressed, the baby may become stressed. The baby will begin to communicate by crying in different ways for different things. He or she will focus on smaller objects and begin to play by finding a hidden toy or rolling a ball. Tasting, touching, banging and shaking are ways the baby learns through exploration. This is the age the baby throws food off the high chair.

By twelve months the baby may start to be weaned and this is a first stage toward independence. He or she will speak and imitate even more, and still enjoy looking in the mirror. The baby may become a little clingy and want mom or dad around all the time. Picture books are favorites, and the baby knows some words and gestures such as waving goodbye. He or she may begin stacking or placing objects in a pattern.

Twelve to Eighteen Months: The baby may not be able to dress, but can undress and this may be a game. Since babies this age are walking, they explore more and become very tactile. They will experience separation anxiety but also will play alone on the floor. He or she can follow simple instructions and will begin tearing things apart, as well as handing toys to adults to play. This is the time to hold and read to the baby, who enjoys praise.

Eighteen to Twenty-four Months: This is a time when you will have to run after the child but he or she may not be very coordinated. This age-group is able to feed themselves and gets into everything. They also like large ride toys. Twenty-four months begins the terrible two's and the baby is now beginning to get there with "no." They will become a little selfish and do not like to share, wanting attention and continuing to enjoy pictures and books. The baby knows his or her name and may be aggressive by hitting at someone. He or she also wants hugs and kisses, and this is when the baby becomes attached to a blanket or stuffed animal.

Two Years: The child is now mobile, and will begin to enjoy rhymes and tunes, know the name of a toy, enjoy books and try to sing. They want to be around other children but may not know how to play. Again, imitation is very strong. They will become very frustrated if they cannot do something. A toy may be offered, but then the child wants it right back—self centered.

Three Years: The child becomes coordinated enough for beginning sports and dressing himself. Directions can be followed and choices made, and the child wants to help out around the house, becoming a clown to make you laugh. The child is becoming very observant, and enjoys play time with others but has not yet learned the art of sharing. He or she recognizes gender. It is a time to think about pre-school.

Four Years: This child may begin learning, i.e., knowing sizes and recognizing the alphabet. Now the child can learn to spell his or her name and is beginning to count and speak in complete sentences, singing and rhyming. This is a verbal age and anger can be expressed verbally now. It is an age that begins to understand rules. It is an age of imagination and sometimes fear, such as fear of the dark. This is a training wheel bicycle age. This child will begin to play more with other children but still may not like to share. *At this age (three to six years, actually), it is important to remember that even though children do not express it, they blame themselves for the di-*

vorce of their parents. It is a very egocentric age so you must help this child understand that it is not his or her fault.

Five Years: This child knows colors, stories and how books are read. He or she enjoys drawing, coloring and making jokes, and understanding of the alphabet and numbers is growing rapidly. They may be somewhat better at sharing and will organize games with others, although they may only play with a best friend. The vocabulary may also be colorful in order to gain attention. The child is beginning to be sensitive to the feelings of others, and also understands what is right and what is wrong, and the difference between giving and taking.

Six to Eight Years: Reading abilities are evident, as is the construction of things, and the child begins to understand simple math and solve problems. This is the age where the child tells time and knows he or she must be on time to school. It is the age where groups and clubs become important. But it is not a flexible age and there is not a lot of middle ground in feelings.

Nine to Eleven Years: There should be signs of interests and hobbies, reading, daydreaming and the beginning of goal-setting. There may not be a lot of follow-through, but the ideas are there. Since children of divorce seem to not complete tasks, the lack of follow through may be very pronounced with your step-children. Although they are not criticizing you yet, they will begin to notice your mistakes. There is increased activity in team or competitive sports. They may prefer to be with friends and ignore you. They are better at controlling emotions now and are starting to notice the opposite sex. Again, there is little room for flexibility and things still are black or white. They may start showing some defiance and also may begin to harshly tease peers.

Adolescence: These are the years that children are moving toward complete independence. Their friends become very important and they now are able to fully express themselves. They may be rude and really point out your faults. There is an inherent moodiness in the adolescent years, and they sleep a lot due to physiological reasons. They will test rules and limitations. They have now developed abstract thought processes and will surprise you with their thoughts and ideas. Things are no longer black or white. This is the age of experimentation, be it religious or philosophical, sex, drugs, alcohol, cigarettes or danger. While you have to give them more freedom, you will have a lot more to worry about.

This is an age where astrology really helps you get a grip. There is an interest in careers and what they will become. This is the age when they first fall in love. For girls in particular, everything is either the most wonderful occurrence or is the end of the world. Teens will gain identity during these years. They have the ability to compromise but may not do so too often. They are also developing their ideas toward humanity and the greater good at this time. They are thinking about their role in the world. They will develop their adult capacity for tenderness and love. They may either accept or not accept traditions. This is the last step toward adulthood and you must let them begin making their own decisions, within reason, handling money and also taking consequences for their actions. It is time to learn from their own mistakes.

Chapter 4

Retrograde Planets and the Effects of Progressions

THE NATAL RETROGRADE PLANET is tantamount to a karmic placement, while transiting retrograde planets work on current situations. Transiting retrograde planets work differently than non-retrograde transiting planets and I often use the transiting retrograde planets to help clients take an opportunity to make corrections in their personal lives that may not be as easily done at other times. When a retrograde planet transits a particular house in your chart, it is a time to use this planet's energies in a different manner than you usually do for a deep and personal level of change. Even the outer planets that are not necessarily considered personal can be used on a very personal level for inner change. However, for purposes of this chapter, I use the natal retrograde planets to observe past conditions that affect your step-child and that give you insight into how to help this child make his or her life easier, more productive, more secure, and the like. Look at the planet and house placement far more than the sign the planet is in. However, rulership is also very important with the retrograde planets. If karma is not something you feel comfortable with, again, please use it metaphorically in terms of the definitions below.

Consider retrograde planets in the natal horoscope and how they act in development. If you look at a natal retrograde planet, it appears to be moving backward in the sky. Retrograde motion is observed only from Earth and the planet only appears to move backward. However, if you consider that retrograde planets work differently from direct planets, you may consider that this apparent backward motion is a way to look backward or into the past. Thus, a natal retrograde placement will have keys to past life conditions that affect you in this lifetime. The natal retrograde planet is two-fold: a look into the past, and its effect in the present. The retrograde planet works on a deep inner and personal level. It is this natal retrograde planet that can help you understand your step-child. Remember that we all choose when, what and who we come back to. Your step-child has chosen you (and vice versa) to be part of his or her life for some reason. As these retrograde planets progress (secondary progressions) you may get some insight into how the karma will be worked out. If you put your planets with your step-child's planets in synastry, you will see how you can help your step-child, times of opportunity and how to better relate to this child on a deep and personal level. Retrograde planets can be very important in understanding your relationship and helping that relationship to grow positively. You have come together to work out past conditions. If you are lucky enough to have a step-child with retrograde planets, you have a head start on this work.

I find retrograde planets very helpful and they give me a lot of insight into step-parent/step-child relationships. I do not find retrograde planets to be a problem but a guide. Remember that with retrograde planets, feelings are innate. They are just there and you may see no present fundamental reason for them. However, you may see a pattern of the child directing actions so that his or her feelings are self-fulfilling. If so, you can be very helpful by suggesting alternatives that would also be fulfilling. You may act somewhat as a friend rather than a parent so the child does not resent your suggestions. Maryanne Kremer, in her article "Retrograde Venus: Reincarnation," describes retrograde planets as giving you karmic response to a tendency to do what you have done in the past. She also states that positively aspected retrograde planets suggest traits developed in only a few past incarnations and negatively aspected retrograde planets suggest patterns repeated over many incarnations.

Steven Forrest, in his book *The Changing Sky*, describes secondary progressions as a type of inner growth, development and maturity whereas transiting planets suggest external forces. It is in this light that I use progressed retrograde planets to find opportunity to bond with your step-children as they grow and mature. Whenever a retrograde natal planet goes direct by progression is a good time for growth and development. This is a time to really work on past conditions. It is almost a double dose of internal growth since progressions work on the inner being and retrograde planets show insight into past conditions and what makes the inner being. Also look at the aspects the retrograde planet makes to other planets or points in the natal horoscope for further influence on this karmic kind of condition. In later chapters you will see that the family examples I have chosen have a lot of retrograde planets with which to work. I find there are often a lot of retrograde plants in charts of families with step-parents and step-children.

Mercury Retrograde

Mercury has to do with thought processes, communication and speech. It is the planet of logic. Retrograde Mercury would tend to internalize these facets of your being, and a retrograde Mercury person may be a slow and deliberate thinker or someone who tends to act without thinking. There are two sides to every retrograde planet just as there are two sides to every direct planet.

The Mercury retrograde person may feel unsure about giving the right answer or speaking out. On the other hand, the person may be a very deep thinker and only wish to speak when sure he or she is right. Whichever way retrograde Mercury seems to manifest itself with the person, you can be assured that probably in a past life this person got into trouble speaking out and one of the life lessons is power over his or her own communication skills and thought processes.

Look at the house retrograde Mercury is in for further insight into this placement and also, and as important, the rulership of the sign that Mercury is in. For example, if Mercury is in Cancer and the Moon is in the fourth house, there is a double dose of Cancer associated with this retrograde Mercury. Perhaps this person was not able to express himself or herself around the family or ideas were ignored by the family in a past life, and the individual is vying for attention every time he or she speaks. This person may feel insignificant intelligence-wise around the family. This is the person you should encourage to speak his or her mind and to think for himself or herself. Never say or infer that this person is lacking in mental skills (although you should not do this with anyone, it is doubly important with this person).

Retrograde Mercury Through the Houses/Signs

First House/Aries: You tend to be a quick thinker and respond quickly or perhaps hold back responses because you have been in trouble in the past for your responses. The child is action oriented.

Second House/Taurus: You are seeking comfort that may have been denied in the past or must try to make others comfortable for your own security. Personal values are important but you may be reluctant to express them. Financial security is also very important to your mental well-being.

Third House/Gemini: You try to avoid trouble with siblings and need quiet time to work out your thoughts. You are a very deep thinker even if you do not realize it. Again, you are a rapid thinker who may have gotten into trouble in the past for expressing yourself. You may not feel comfortable expressing yourself now. Or, you may have a learning problem stemming from past conditions. These manifest themselves in various ways from a short attention span to perhaps the small child who needs distance glasses but does not yet realize it.

Fourth House/Cancer: You feel you may get into trouble every time you try to express yourself. Although this is probably not true, it is probably how you really feel and even felt as a child. You need quiet at home to compose your thoughts. Praise is needed so the child will be willing to share and communicate, and praise as a child will help to develop your communication skills as you grow up. Mental security is tied to a nurturing home life. Make sure the individual knows his or her ideas are important.

Fifth House/Leo: Thoughts of creativity are strong but it may take time for the child to feel comfortable with what he or she creates. The child needs a lot of positive feedback for self-esteem, as does the adult. Writing stories or telling stories will help work through insecurity in artistic or creative endeavors. Speculation or gambling could be a problem in later years.

Sixth House/Virgo: There is a seriousness about doing a good job. This child/adult is a hard worker demanding a lot of himself. This stems from either demanding too much of others in the past or too much being demanded of the individual in the past; either way, the work ethic is very strong. Praise the child's efficiency and do not let the child be too hard on himself or herself; watch for nervousness or health issues brought on by this. One caveat is that the child or adult is so much the perfectionist, that he or she may shut down rather than fail. Again, praise for a job well done will counteract this.

Seventh House/Libra: Retrograde Mercury here suggests that there may be problems in partnerships or relationships that have to be worked out. Communication with a partner is the key and the ability to truly express self rather than being afraid to do so. The time to really focus on a good partnership or marriage is when Mercury is direct. At a young age, this would be a best friend type situation. Through all interactions with people, retrograde Mercury suggests a need to work on truly communicating your feelings openly and trying not to be afraid of what others may think about it.

Eighth House/Scorpio: Retrograde Mercury here is really great for in-depth research, psychotherapy and the occult, as well as handling other's money. This house placement is a good one because the retrograde Mercury person thinks deeply and goes over each detail. This is a house where retrograde Mercury may shine. Perhaps in the past the person has not performed research or done homework well, but this time can make up for it big time. Thus, the child early on should be encouraged to develop eighth house skills.

Ninth House/Sagittarius: Issues of religion, ethics, philosophy and education have to be worked on with this placement. Again, a lot of deep thought will be in these areas. Perhaps education will be interrupted and you will have to go back to school, maybe several times, to earn a degree. This is one house that suggests that perhaps the retrograde Mercury child was in trouble for speaking out about religion or some important ethical situation and now may be afraid to do so; he or she must learn over the years that it is now okay to speak up.

Tenth House/Capricorn: The one thing this person wants is to be conscientious and very reliable. This may be making up for not being so in the past or for expecting too much from employees in the past; but this is a very good trait now. This is a work-oriented and effective person. You feel a sense of responsibility and if you make mistakes you are too hard on yourself. You will continue to always learn on the job. This house also suggests the child may have things to work out with his or her father and later with authority figures.

Eleventh House/Aquarius: Retrograde Mercury here suggests a conscious attention to new technologies, humanitarian issues and social causes. You may have a very strong sense of these things in order to make up for not being so socially minded in the past. You may even internalize the conditions of others intellectually and have a great empathy for their causes. Your approach is original and when Mercury turns direct a rebelliousness against the norm may grow, or in other words, you will intellectually grow into yourself. Thus, when the child's Mercury turns direct, expect some forms of rebellion. Generational issues may also be really important to this child.

Twelfth House/Pisces: Retrograde Mercury here can be a little tough, but like the eighth house placement, is very good for a therapist. There are deep-seated thought patterns that have no rhyme or reason and often come out in dreams or cause sleep disorders. The ruler of the sign is very important to ferret out what areas need work with this placement. You may overcompensate for your own fears or guilt by being overly kind or understanding to others. On the other hand, once this placement starts to work itself out, the kindness and understanding are truly who you are. This placement also lends itself to a great imagination. You may thus have a very imaginative child who tries too hard to please.

Retrograde Venus

Retrograde Venus suggests possible feelings of isolation, that you are unlovable, or perhaps you cannot relax during social situations. Thus, you probably have a difficult time functioning in an intimate relationship, often to the point of sabotaging that relationship. In past lives you may have had external problems that kept you from a relationship you wanted, and by this incarnation, you have learned that you cannot relate to others in an intimate and mature way. As a child you probably feel that your siblings are more loved than you, perhaps your parents have told you that you were a "mistake" or something similar.

Socially, this would be a shy child or one who would prefer to be with one friend at a time and feels uneasy at parties. Teens are probably uncomfortable at the school dance or in large groups or clubs. The reverse of this is the child or teen who tries to be accepted and may try too hard to please or get involved in the wrong crowd if they feels they can belong. This is a child whose peers can really influence him or her. Try to steer this child to positive groups and clubs and to places where the child can feel of value. An example is an organization that helps in some way, perhaps one that visits the elderly, where this child will develop a sense of self-worth. Again, the house placement and rulership are very strong keys to where you can help this child work to feel loved, accepted and of value.

Retrograde Venus Through the Houses/Signs

First House/Aries: Help the child focus on personal relationships and to develop a sense of security. For the young child this would be friendship relationships or family relationships, and as the child grows into adulthood, one-on-one romantic relationships. This lifetime is to develop understanding and self-understanding. Beautiful surroundings will help with inner peace.

Second House/Taurus: Venus here suggests a love of beauty and perhaps artistic talent. These traits are innate and development of them should help the child feel good about himself or herself. He or she may want to earn money to give to friends to solidify friendships and should learn that friends like the child for himself or herself.

Third House/Gemini: Venus direct suggests pleasure in communication, whereas Venus retrograde suggests a desire for solitude. This desire is strong and this is an area where perhaps you got into trouble for speaking out and now wish to remain silent. The life lesson is to learn to communicate freely but tactfully. The negative of a retrograde Venus here suggests a laziness about mental activities. The positive is a very deep thinker.

Fourth House/Cancer: You need solitude. Also, with Venus direct you may have a nurturing mother, but if retrograde you may have the opposite, one who actually gives you the solitude you desire. The retrograde Venus child needs to learn to be open with family and to communicate. The child and the adult may overindulge in physical gratification for emotional security.

Fifth House/Leo: This is a good placement for retrograde Venus. Artistic endeavors come naturally, and you have been an artist, musician or creator of some kind many times before, so this is a very comfortable place. Working with children is good if the retrograde Venus can communicate openly. The retrograde Venus person will feel secure and comfortable when creating, so encourage and praise these activities. Also, the adult and the child may feel very deeply about a relationship but be unable to express their feelings. The lesson here is to feel free and comfortable to share your creations and your feelings.

Sixth House/Virgo: You may not feel your self-worth at work or you may be insecure about your abilities. These feelings are very deep and hard work and achievement will help overcome them. For the adult, the trick this time is to learn to feel secure about your ability to earn money and about your job; then you will begin to feel fulfilled. For both child and adult, over-indulgence can affect health and often occurs when they feel insecure. Pets help you to open up to emotional security.

Seventh House/Libra: You may feel unworthy of a great partner or not expect as much as you should in relationships. You may look for harmony and security but undermine your own efforts to find same. Because of past conditions, your lesson is to learn that you are worthy of a great relationship and to set your sights high. You may also go for someone who is a "little different" from usual family members. With the child, this may be insecurity about a best friend. If the child is a product of a broken home, it may take long into adulthood to feel secure in relationships.

Eighth House/Scorpio: Venus direct here suggests you are looking for an intimate relationship and that you must learn to share assets as well as emotions. You want an intense relationship but must try not to be manipulative or to be manipulated. With Venus retrograde, these feelings are very deep and you may not know your own motivations. Retrograde Venus here suggests past troubles in finding appropriate intimacy and gives you a great chance to do so this time. Help the child with this placement to share his or her feelings so that pitfalls as an adult might be avoided.

Ninth House/Sagittarius: You are innately attracted to foreign matters and foreign individuals. Higher education is important and since retrograde motion tends to internalize things, you will probably be very good at higher education, philosophy and the like; but there may be a delay in education. Your innate ability to relate to foreign things suggests that you may not be as comfortable with what should be familiar. You will only be satisfied with your partner after you become satisfied with who you are and feel comfortable relating to all those around you. This will probably come a little later in life. The child will like learning and probably be drawn to social organizations or places of worship, and also question what you mean when you say something.

Tenth House/Capricorn: Your career goal is to have security and beauty around you, but you also need to look within for security. Retrograde motion is deep and innate and it will take time for you to feel comfortable with recognition. Superiors may be able to take advantage of you. The goal here is to balance your hard work and desire to please with the feeling that you are truly doing a good job and deserve what you are entitled to. These same traits apply to the child who needs support and recognition and may feel undeserving.

Eleventh House/Aquarius: Retrograde Venus here suggests an innate passion for new technologies, perhaps an unconventional occupation or way to make money. The key is to become comfortable with a group setting rather than shy away. The child should be encouraged to join a club, scouts or another group in order to share unusual ideas with friends. Then both individual friends and groups will prove to be a benefit.

Twelfth House/Pisces: This is a tough placement. The manifestations of Venus retrograde here are buried very deep. You may be a harsh judge of yourself or undermine your own efforts to succeed. The child may be self-critical and thus insecure. Also, as with Neptune, problems such as drugs and alcohol may occur. On the other hand, working with Venus retrograde can be a great benefit in therapeutic dreams; perhaps a lot of nature walks and outward expression of beauty is the goal for this placement. Take the child camping and help his or her confidence grow while exploring nature.

Retrograde Mars

Retrograde Mars suggests a problem in directing energy and anger. This may be the child who seems calm most of the time, but at times explodes at the least provocation. Karmically, there may have been a military background with a lot of violence or perhaps some act of traumatic violence in the past, and the feelings of uncontrollable anger and misdirection of energy are deep. The child will not know why he or she feels this way while others are happy.

The other side of this placement is a child who has a very deep level of drive and is very successful, one who channels these feelings of anger into energy, almost over-compensating. He feels he must always be the high achiever. A balance between the two is where the child needs to be. Sports are very helpful at a young age, and pounding clay is a positive outlet. By the teen years, if directed positively, you will have an active teenager. Although temper may always erupt at odd times, this can lessen over the years.

The house where retrograde Mars appears and the house of the ruler of the sign that Mars is in show where this tension may come from. If the houses are the third or fourth, perhaps there was a violent or angry family/sibling situation or perhaps some trauma happened to the family. If there is a twelfth house connection, anger or inability to direct energy will be very deep and relaxation techniques could be helpful.

I once read that young persons killed in WWII or the Korean conflict were the students of the 1960s, who reincarnated very quickly, still traumatized souls, and then vehemently protested the Vietnam War. Although most protest was peaceful, there was a lot of anger and energy directed to the anti-war sentiment. There was also some violent protesting at that time.

This example reminds me of a retrograde Mars placement. Although not everyone who protested the Vietnam War has a retrograde Mars, the manifestation of the anger into the anti-war sentiment is very retrograde Mars. This is a good example of directed anger and energy into a cause rather than into self, which can also happen with a retrograde Mars.

Retrograde Mars Through the Houses/Signs

First House/Aries: This is a tough placement. You either let anger go, explode, or try to mask anger somehow just to have it explode even more violently at a later time. Since the planet is retrograde, the fact that energy and anger are suppressed is very important. The trick here is to learn to express anger in a positive way and to get things out into the open quickly and helpfully. This way the Mars energy can be directed for personal advancement and good. For both the child and adult, sports is a very good release for this placement. If anger is controlled, personal action, willingness to take risks, self-confidence and courage will develop.

Second House/Taurus: Mars direct here suggests work and energy directed toward beauty, monetary security; you are driven by your values. With Mars retrograde you may be driven to achieve and accumulate only to self-destruct by going on a spending spree when under conflict. The child may save toward something he or she wants, only to get angry at a sibling and then purchase candy with the money and eat it in front of the sibling; the motive is to get even, but the child only hurts himself or herself by going without the initially desired item. The very positive side of this pattern is a deep drive and this is the child who will work long and hard for what is personally of value; this is the trait to emphasize as the child grows into a determined adult. Self-indulgence may also present a problem here. It will not appear all the time but you may go through periods of indulgence, especially when Mars is afflicted by aspect to a transiting planet.

Third House/Gemini: Retrograde Mars here suggests possible trouble with siblings and may even lead to a feud situation. Also, as the child grows and Mars turns direct, he or she may act out based on feelings hidden in the past. Mars direct suggests a good and solid mind, good powers of concentration, and Mars retrograde can make this trait deeper or sabotage it, depending upon aspects and how the child grows into the Mars direct position by progression. Communication is a very important trait to develop in order to facilitate the quick mind and deep thinking. There is a restless mental energy suggested by Mars here, and Mars retrograde may suggest a tendency to scattered mental patterns.

Fourth House/Cancer: Just like the third house, Mars retrograde here suggests you may have trouble with those at home to the point of a feud. It also may suggest a tremendous amount of insecurity and need for actual physical comfort from parents. Either way, as Mars turns direct, the child should learn to deal with anger toward family members and grow into a positive situation. Mars retrograde suggests push-pull situations with family members; you need them but want to push them away at the same time. A lot of your energy may be directed toward family situations due to past life conditions. The key here is positive direction and avoiding the energy drain of fighting old situations, which you may not even recognize.

Fifth House/Leo: Mars retrograde here suggests a very deep, innate sense of creativity and also a lot of pent up energy, so things such as sports, dance and creativity are important. Help the child express creativity and use this great energy early in life to steer the retrograde Mars in positive directions. If you do not recognize your Martian creativity, your children or lovers will probably have a lot of energy and creativity in order to pull you along. Also, there is a suggestion of arguments or violence coming through this placement, but again, this energy can be positively directed with your children or lovers into creative endeavors enjoyed together. Also be cautious about speculation and gambling, as this placement suggests you could really get caught up in the excitement and think you will have that big score if you just place one more bet. It is a nervous, frenetic energy. Passion comes quickly and is felt deeply.

Sixth House/Virgo: You need to feel efficient and productive in the work place. However, with Mars retrograde you may feel you do not live up to your standards. Karmically, you may have had problems in past lives, being told you were not a good enough worker, so you may even try to overcompensate for this. Mars suggests a strong self-will so if you feel you are not appreciated you may shut down and not work at all. Thus, the child with Mars retrograde needs a lot of praise for a job well done and just trying his or her best. Getting this child a pet to care for will greatly enhance self-esteem because the child will feel needed. Mars retrograde here can really be a good placement since it represents a lot of energy to get the job done, and with appropriate responses for a job well done, the child will develop a good work ethic. With regard to health, nervous energy may cause anxiety. Again, sports is a good outlet for Martian energy.

Seventh House/Libra: Mars retrograde here suggests you may feel you are not as powerful as your partner or that you cannot assert your power. This comes from past conditions where you faced anger or hardship for asserting yourself. The key here is to know that equality and balance is what is best in a relationship. If you let others take power, you will eventually erupt and rebel in the relationship. Remember, often you feel powerless because of innate feelings and not because of what your partner is doing. Be careful not to blow up for no reason. The child must also learn a balance of power, and giving the child a little more freedom or power than necessary may help him or her gain that balance prior to getting into teen or adult relationships that could be volatile. If the child does not learn the balance, this may also lead to abuse of power as an adult.

Eighth House/Scorpio: Mars retrograde here can be a little tough. Since this is a house of intimacy, it suggests you may feel inhibited in intimacy and have a lot of pent up energy directed toward intimacy. This leads to difficult times, either trying to be intimate or blowing up in order to sabotage intimacy. There is also a problem with shared resources as you may feel a need to control but may also feel controlled with regard to joint finances. Again, Mars retrograde is about balance of power and not exploding because of pent-up issues. Your feelings are innate. Perhaps you were not allowed to have a say in resources or were made to feel ashamed on intimate issues previously and the key is to find a balance this time. Mars going direct is the time for the child to learn to compromise. Perhaps the child can have a part of his or her allowance to spend in any way. Mars retrograde also deals with psychological issues and can suggest a very good therapist in the making. It also suggests a lot of energy directed toward in-depth research whereas Mars direct could act too quickly and miss points.

Ninth House/Sagittarius: Mars Retrograde here suggests you may feel more at home in a foreign place than the place you were born. You have an innate comfort with foreign places and things, and a deep desire to travel. This is also the house of your spiritual being, your personal philosophies and higher education, which may be delayed. You have a strong belief system, and may have encountered trouble in the past for your beliefs, prompting you now to keep them to yourself. The child with Mars retrograde will probably show a keen interest in science. As Mars turns direct, it is a time to encourage the child to express and own his or her own beliefs and to acknowledge spirituality without preaching; the goal is to help the child learn to be secure in his or her own beliefs. The Mars retrograde teen may be tempted to run away to foreign lands in search of self.

Tenth House/Capricorn: Mars Retrograde here is another placement that suggests past problems with authority. This may translate into a current feeling of lack of respect for authority, that authority figures are picking on you and the like. The Mars energy should be used to balance authority and your own limitations. Also, retrograde Mars suggests that your identity stems from career and achievement. Therefore, if you feel conflicted with authority and limitations, you may not feel you are living up to your potential. The trick here is to help the child learn to deal with authority in a positive way and learn to overcome any of his own personal limitations. For example, perhaps the child would really like a career in law but does not want to work for a large firm where life is controlled by the job. Perhaps a law job in something like environmental lobbying would be a good idea. Take whatever the child or teen is interested in and help combine it with a type of career that would be a viable way to express the retrograde Mars. Also, Mars retrograde here suggests that either the mother or father may have been critical in the past and the child needs praise for attempts and well as successes.

Eleventh House/Aquarius: Mars retrograde here suggests a strong, innate tie to groups, causes, technology and friends. Wishes may be realized a little later in life. Retrograde Mars here is not too difficult. You have a lot of deep energy associated with whatever groups or causes you belong to and feel an almost zealous energy to promote them. Those with Mars or Mars retrograde here would make good politicians since they are tied to causes and, among other things, the eleventh house represents the legislative side of government. This is the house of step-children, and thus with Mars retrograde in this house, you have a very strong tie to the step-child and there may be a lot of tension between you. There is a lot to be worked out. Activities with groups that are fun are a good way to begin working out previous situations. Also, make a home where this child brings friends and where they are always welcome. Make home fun with lots to do. If you have both children (fifth house) and step-children (eleventh house), try to balance the fifth and eleventh house energies so they feel equal in order to eliminate some of the tension that may result.

Twelfth House/Pisces: Mars retrograde here is a tough one. It suggests subconscious resentment, and is deep-seated from lifetimes of behavior. You may be gentle, compassionate and deeply courageous or may be assertive, aggressive or volatile; whichever way you go, you are working out past resentments. Help the child learn to search for reasons for why he or she displays this behavior. If the child comes unglued at the slightest teasing, perhaps he or she was teased mercilessly in the past and must learn to avoid persons who tease or learn to laugh at self; it will take the edge off and people will not find it so fun to tease if they do not get a rise out of the child. There may be a tendency for passive and aggressive behavior from the child with which you also must deal. With a retrograde Mars there may have been a past condition such as a jail or an institution where the person was either the victim or the tormentor. Either way, this child feels guilty and this is another situation where you must help the child overcome guilt. Everyone makes mistakes, but it is not the end of the world. The child needs help to learn to move on. Sometimes escapism is a very good way to deal with a retrograde Mars, such as meditation, retreats and the like. There needs to be balance.

Jupiter Retrograde

Jupiter direct is expansive and connected to religion, higher education and philosophy. It is where opportunity is expressed, where doors open. This positive outlet for Jupiter is the antithesis of Jupiter retrograde. Jupiter retrograde suggests that in a past life you may have been very religious and spiritual and have encountered trouble for it. So now you are cautious about any organized religion or perhaps even show disdain for those you feel need it. You may refuse to hear that inner being who needs to be a part of something greater than the self. Thus, you may always be searching for something to give your life meaning or on the other hand may only strive for material or tangible things that do not in the end give you the meaning you are looking for.

For a child with this placement, you must help the child look into the importance of the intangible and the true meaning of value, not just the tangible object that has physical value. This child's lesson is that things are of value when the child feels he or she is also of value, and that inner beauty is important. Again, the house and rulership are very important.

Jupiter retrograde in the fifth house suggests that creativity is a way to show the child personal value. Romance does not give value itself; the person you are with should find value in you. Jupiter retrograde in the ninth house is a very strong placement so the child must dig deep down and reestablish feelings of faith and personal philosophies and look outside himself or herself for value. This is a tough placement because the important factor is to work on what Jupiter retrograde tries to shun. You must come to a place where you are happy because of higher beliefs and not necessarily because of things or other people. You must learn to be happy with you. On the other hand, the feelings of ethics, religion, etc. may be so deep that the child still follows this path despite what others think. There may be an almost martyr-like quality to such dedication.

Retrograde Jupiter Through the Houses/Signs

First House/Aries: Jupiter here suggests the child needs to learn to look inside for what is really important. If the child grows into the adult who has a quest for material success, he or she must also achieve a balance of the spiritual and material in order to be truly happy. This can begin at an early age. On the other hand, this is the person who may only seek the spiritual side of life and needs to learn that the tangible is also necessary. Whether or not Jupiter is retrograde, this will be an expansive, curious child. This is the child with a lot of innate self-trust or the child who was criticized and has trouble trusting self. There may be a tendency to be dogmatic.

Second House/Taurus: Jupiter retrograde here suggests a deep belief in security. Pleasure and comfort are very important. Thus, your need to overindulge may be so ingrained and deep that it is a hard habit to break. Perhaps you were deprived previously and are making up for it now. On the other hand, you also have a deep and expansive sense of values and may overcompensate in all you do based on these values. Again, as with all retrograde planets, the key here is balance and temperance. You may use physical comfort as a healing alternative. The child needs help in understanding rather than a cookie to assuage hurt feelings.

Third House/Gemini: Jupiter retrograde here suggests there may be sibling tension. The child wants an expansive and nice relationship with siblings and achieving it now is a better choice than doing it as an adult. Also, with regard to lower education, the child may be a late bloomer but will do quite well. For both the child and adult, communication is very important and there is a desire to share your ideas even though you may be reticent to do so. You are very mental but may have a difficult time expressing your expansive ideas. Expression will come as Jupiter turns direct and you mature.

Fourth House/Cancer: You have a very deep feeling of family, and if there is conflict you will be the one who tries to reconnect with family. It is very important to you. You may feel like going far from home and probably will do so; but you will always want that feeling of security and connection. Protection afforded by your home is important for both the child and adult, and you will want it no matter where you are. You may be the teacher of family issues to your family.

Fifth House/Leo: Something way down deep makes you want exciting and expansive romance. You will put a lot of energy into a relationship to make it so. You may have a fear of not having enough excitement for the relationship to last. You will also be the natural gambler, always optimistic that the next bet will be the big winner. Unlike Mars retrograde, there is not so much angry energy; rather, it is optimistic energy. You demand a lot of yourself and in turn may tend to demand too much of children. If your step-child has Jupiter retrograde here, the child may be very demanding and insist that his or her values and agenda are most important. This is a good place to push any creative interest the child may have because the child can be as demanding of himself or herself as necessary while creating.

Sixth House/Virgo: Jupiter direct suggests a very strong belief in a work ethic. In the past you may have been criticized or reprimanded for your work and now you are actually too hard on yourself with regard to your work ethic and productivity. You should concentrate on expansion of your job in a positive way and not be afraid of being criticized for what you do. Over-zealousness can lead to burn out. You need to reign it in a little and be pragmatic. You probably do not want to be too critical of a child with this placement since the child will really take it to heart and be hurt or just give up. Positive suggestions are the way to go. Once unafraid of criticism, Jupiter here will be very good for you. Your work opportunities should be plentiful. Also, you have an innate sense of healing so a healing profession would be good for you; you would be inspirational in new methods. The child will innately know how to help pets.

Seventh House/Libra: With Jupiter retrograde here, you believe in relationships and want a philosophically compatible partner; but you may fear a relationship and it may take some time to achieve this. You may almost want too much of an ideal world and need to find a balance of sharing ideals with a world that is not always perfect. Jupiter here suggests that the child is naturally a social being, but because of past conditions may be shy. This child should seek a lot of friends, as these relationships will lead to a future with a positive mate. This is a good placement for someone who counsels others regarding marriage or partnerships.

Eighth House/Scorpio: Jupiter retrograde here suggests that at previous times you may have been overly expansive with regard to intimacy issues and now may have trouble letting Jupiter express its energies here. The key, as Jupiter turns direct, is to analyze what you really want and to expand with your partner in a mutual relationship. You may almost trust too much. With Jupiter retrograde you may have a tendency to get swept away and turn your mate into something on a pedestal rather than a human being. The same is true with shared resources. You may be up-tight about sex or overly expansive in sexual experimentation. Again, balance is the key. An uplifting relationship is what you really want. Emphasis should be placed on shared and balanced intimacy. Also, you may really desire to dig deep into the human psyche or occult matters. This is a very fulfilling part of retrograde Jupiter. Let a child of any age explore issues of the mind, as this will interest and free the child's mind. The child will probably like witches, Halloween, ghosts and the like. You may be overly expansive with joint resources or, because of past conditioning, be afraid to share in joint resources. The child may have trouble with intimacy, even being wary of family members, so you should help the child overcome this when Jupiter turns direct by progression. Otherwise, the child may be afraid to venture out on his or her own. The child will be interested in research and investigation as he or she gets older.

Ninth House/Sagittarius: Jupiter here suggests that because of past conditions, you may now be on a continual quest for something to believe in. Your beliefs in the past may have been so strong in that you were severely disappointed in them or encountered trouble for your zealousness. You may either get hooked to the point of a cult organization or try to go overboard in rejection of beliefs. The balance of understanding and purpose is very important with retrograde Jupiter here. Also, you may tend to begin higher education over and over, seeking something new and different each time rather than settling down for something that really would satisfy you. The child also exhibits this innate quest for knowledge and for something to believe in. Help the child keep on track as he or she grows in order to make full use of higher education. Also watch a tendency toward over-commitment to a cause.

Tenth House/Capricorn: Jupiter direct here suggests many career opportunities and a belief in structure, authority and the work ethic. You expect the utmost of yourself with regard to your career, and your identity is closely tied with honor and recognition. If Jupiter is retrograde you may have to go back to college or graduate school at a later time in order to fulfill your career potential and to feel happy about what you eventually end up doing. You also feel a need to constantly expand your career horizon. The child also thrives with structure and has a constant desire to improve; success is very important. This is not a bad placement for Jupiter retrograde.

Eleventh House/Aquarius: Jupiter retrograde here suggests you have a very open and humanitarian view of the world. However, this open thought process may have been a problem for you in the past so it takes a little longer for you to really feel free about your thoughts and to relate to groups and friends that share your humanitarian outlook. You may also enjoy technology and the most current trends. The caveat with Jupiter retrograde here is that you may always feel restless and have a need to expand your circle of friends or groups, rather than expanding with them. Since this is the house of step-children, Jupiter retrograde here suggests you may want to expand their horizons and become friends with your step-children but may push too hard and too fast. Let things develop over time and Jupiter will help expand your relationship. Do not push like you probably feel like doing.

Twelfth House/Pisces: Jupiter retrograde here suggests a deep commitment to idealism or faith. The problem is that you may actually turn this faith into something extreme on a very large scale. You must distinguish between faith and dogmatic absolutism. Perhaps in the past you had trouble because of your beliefs and now you bury them so as not to get into trouble again. Your dreams are very real and meditation would be good for you. The small child may actually have nightmares because of past events. Creative dreaming and suggestions of nice dreams will help the child create a positive nighttime and as the child grows, creative dreaming will help him or her cope with life. This is a very good tool for Jupiter, whether direct or retrograde, in the twelfth house.

Saturn Retrograde

This is a tough retrograde to deal with. Saturn is a karmic planet, and when retrograde, there is a double dose of what has to be worked on or worked out this time around. However, as difficult as it might seem, remember that you have chosen this time, place and people, and Saturn retrograde. Retrograde Saturn suggests many things from the past to work out, things that have been done again and again. Now is the time to really take hold and work on this placement. For the child, Saturn retrograde suggests a time of difficulty with following the rules. This is a past of difficulty with authority.

This is a child who will continually push the envelope, and will be impatient with the rules. As the child grows and enters adulthood, boundaries are an issue, whether they cannot say no to anyone or whether they cross the boundaries of others. This placement suggests abuse of power, either by you or by others who were over you. Thus, power is also a very important issue with the Saturn retrograde.

If retrograde Saturn is in the seventh house, for example, perhaps you had an abusive spouse in past lives or perhaps there were difficulties with a business partner. You thus have to be careful not to now do the same things to others. Also, you have to be very careful not to repeat patterns that led to your abuse in the past. The lesson of Saturn is to learn patience, to focus and to learn to work long and hard toward your goals. This steady plodding will help you stay focused so you do not fall into the same patterns.

I always look at Saturn as a good thing because the lessons you learn from Saturn benefit you over your lifetime even though Saturn retrograde can be difficult. If this is a placement of your step-child, this is a place to really help that child focus, work hard and bond while you work together. This placement, depending upon the house placement, may suggest that the child feels obligated, that he or she owes others. The child may try to take on too much responsibility in order to forge a connection with others.

Lynn Koiner, in her article "Retrograde Planets," quotes Pat Geisler that Saturn retrograde can suggest the absence of a father or an uninvolved father. So if you are dealing with step-children and there is a retrograde Saturn, check to see if there is father involvement with the child.

Retrograde Saturn Through the Houses/Signs

First House/Aries: This is the house of the child who will feel he or she must work very hard and be responsible in order to achieve. The child feels unwanted and must learn in this lifetime to say no and not take on too much responsibility in order to prove himself or herself. This child seems to have a lot of inhibiting factors in life. This is the child you must teach to let go and just have fun and not to be self-critical. The child seeks everyone's approval. There is a tendency to be on over-drive to achieve and yet at the same time actually block oneself from this achievement—a kind of self-sabotage because you feel you don't deserve to achieve. Achievement may occur a little later in life. Hopefully, by adulthood, these feelings will have lessened.

Second House/Taurus: This is actually not as difficult as other Saturn retrograde placements. You tend to be very structured and financially responsible; perhaps a parent declared bankruptcy or something similar happened so you overcompensate. On the other hand, you may also structure or try to control personal pleasure rather than just let it happen. The child may feel responsible for the parents' money problems and needs to learn to separate love given and financial responsibility. Parents with a strong work ethic are a very good influence. According to Bill Tierney in his book *The Twelve Faces if Saturn*, Saturn here suggests that both the destitute and the affluent can have this placement. Both stations are symbolic of inner personal worth.

Third House/Gemini: Saturn direct suggests structure in thinking, but retrograde suggests early problems with school. This may cause the child to be self-critical. The mind will develop methodically and mental structure will come along—maybe just not as quickly as desired. However, the child may end up being more thorough in learning. Also, criticism from authority figures can be very hard for this child. Make sure to phrase your comments as positive suggestions. This child must prove his or her mental ability to himself or herself and may be anxious until that occurs; and, the child may feel insecure about his or her abilities in comparison to siblings. The adult will be a structured thinker but may have trouble expressing thoughts.

Fourth House/Cancer: The child feels he or she must please the family and is responsible so may never say no, even when he or she does not want to do something or just does not have the energy. Again, self-worth is important to instill in the child as a way to learn to say no. The child feels an innate sense of responsibility or that he or she owes the family, rather than just being loved because the family loves the child. It is very important to help the child make this distinction. This is a tough Saturn retrograde. As an adult, there will also be difficulty saying no to family and you may take on too much responsibility and possibly care for an older family member. Since this is the house of psychological roots, Saturn retrograde may suggest an insecurity from past family experiences and try to block feelings now. Early mothering or lack thereof makes a big impact now. A water sign Saturn retrograde tends to be very karmic. If Saturn retrograde is in a water sign, coldness may be a defense mechanism.

Fifth House/Libra: As a parent you probably will have trouble saying no to the child, feeling you are not doing enough. You want the child to love you and just cannot deny him or her. For the child, Saturn retrograde is not as tough and the child will probably work in a very structured way even when creating. This is the child who gets frustrated if he or she cannot stay in the lines when coloring. The child may also turn to the other extreme and express too much confidence as a front and perhaps run over others. The Saturn retrograde person in the fifth house is the innate risk-taker or gambler in order to prove himself or herself; this individual is afraid of being seen as average. As with the other houses of Saturn retrograde, this child needs direction for work and to know that creativity is not what endears the child to others. With regard to a teen or young adult, this may indicate looking too hard for love or possibly going for an older, parental type. The adult will have trouble saying no to his or her child. I feel this inability to say no is so that the child will really love the adult; it is an insecurity. Saturn retrograde here suggests obstacles in love but also a realistic if not pessimistic attitude toward love and also wanting love to be perfect. There also may be issues of control. Thus, the adult with Saturn retrograde here has a hard time finding the right love.

Sixth House/Virgo: There is an innate feeling of insecurity with anyone in authority at work. Therefore, you tend to be very structured and dogmatic so as not to make a mistake. This is an anxiety-producing placement, and you will do almost anything to feel secure with your job, so your boss may take advantage of you. Your need for security may lead to workaholic problems or problems with bones or teeth. This placement also suggests the child may try to work too hard to please superiors and perhaps be careless while trying to do too much. This is the placement of the perfectionist who cannot see boundaries between what should be done and excess. The lesson here is to learn to work without feeling like you owe others more than honest work for honest pay. Do not feel you have to clean up everyone else's mess.

Seventh House/Libra: Saturn retrograde here can be quite difficult. It suggests past difficulty with authority even to the point of abuse, whether you are the abuser or the abused. Thus, you may tend to repeat this when looking for a partner. The key to working out this placement is to find partnerships of equality, whether in responsibility or authority. The child may tend toward friends who pick on him or her or who can be bullied. Help your step-child learn the balance and equality lesson early in order to avoid serious pitfalls in adult relationships. On the other hand, if your child's father or step-father is a positive role model, this will go a long way in working with the retrograde Saturn. Once the child works with this placement, careers which require some sort of a contract such as management, attorney or counselor may be viable choices to positively work with this placement. These are positions of power and authority that can be abused or used for positive purposes. With regard to adult relationships, watch for those wherein one party tends to be the authority figure almost to the point of parenting. Saturn retrograde suggests marriage in later years, an older spouse and a karmic partnership. Fear of failure is also a problem here.

Eighth House/Scorpio: Saturn retrograde is also very difficult here. It suggests an innate fear of intimacy issues or the feeling of control or of being controlled by your partner. You may innately doubt anyone who gets close to you. Shared resources are also a problem. You feel insecure about them, either because you believe you are unworthy of the assets or that they are yours and you do not want to share. One way to work through this placement is to find a career that lets you work out Saturn-eighth house issues. For example, working with other people's money, i.e., investment counseling, gives you power and control to a limited extent and you may be comfortable with this. Also, investigation or counseling or therapy of some sort are helpful career choices. This is a positive way to use the Saturn retrograde in the eighth house. As the child grows, hopefully there will be a positive role model to create feelings of security so intimacy won't be such an issue as an adult.

Ninth House/Sagittarius: Saturn Retrograde here suggests a deep, feeling of faith or lack thereof. You will work hard to come to some sort of life philosophy that is right for you, but during this work, you may experience many feelings of doubt or overwhelming guilt or take on too much responsibility. Possibly in a past life you were persecuted for your beliefs. In this life you may be reared in a household that is too strict regarding religion. The trick here is to find a philosophy, faith or something related that is comfortable for you, that you are not too dogmatic about and that you do not try to make others follow. On the other hand, if you find comfort with ninth house issues, you may find travel, education and philosophy good outlets for you and things that give you a sense of fulfillment on a very deep level. This would be karmic fulfillment. You would also be very comfortable working behind the scenes of a major company, being a critical cog in the wheel but not expecting a lot of limelight. The child will have an innate sense of faith that will either grow or be rejected for another esoteric concept. Education will be important and there is a natural curiosity for foreign places and things, but the individual may not travel as much as desired in adulthood and may lack understanding of the reality of other cultures.

Tenth House/Capricorn: Saturn retrograde here suggests a very deep, innate need for stability and a need for personal control with regard to career. You may take on too much at work in order to control everything yourself. Also, authority figures may be a problem, either those over you or perhaps you are too hard on those under you. Criticism is also a problem, and you may be overly sensitive to it. Often people with Saturn retrograde here feel a sense that they must do something, that they have a real sense of purpose; this is a driving force and a positive outlet for Saturn retrograde. Just do not take on too much because you feel you somehow owe it. This can be a useful and positive placement for Saturn Retrograde once you learn the lessons of control and criticism. The child with this Saturn retrograde placement by sign and by aspect suggests what motivates him or her to succeed and what control issues may exist.

Eleventh House/Aquarius: With Saturn Retrograde here, your friends are probably karmic in nature. This suggests a strong tie and sense of obligation to them. Also, you will be strongly attracted to groups that share your karmic sense of justice. Again, as with all Saturn placements and especially with Saturn retrograde, control and authority are issues whether it be friends or groups. You will be attracted to inventive and original groups and feel innately comfortable with them. On the other hand, with Saturn retrograde you may feel insecure with friends and try too hard to please. The lesson is to learn to enjoy your karmic friends but not feel overly indebted to them—the equality issue. Social issues and politics may be important and working in these areas is a good way to use Saturn retrograde; you will feel a sense of giving back and this will go a long way in assuaging your sense of indebtedness. Also, you will probably be the pragmatist in the situation. With regard to the child, organizations that emphasize service are good sources of fulfillment. According to Lynn Koiner, children with this placement tend to be reared in a world of adults so they often do not fit in with peers. The key is to help this child go from the retrograde influence to the comfortable feeling of Saturn direct.

Twelfth House/Pisces: This is a tough placement for Saturn retrograde. You have a very deep sense of debt to society, and this will underlie how you live your life. You will try to find ways to pay this debt, often to the point of self-sacrifice. You may also have an innate sense of anxiety or fear due to past conditions you are unable to recognize and deal with. As you grow and mature, hopefully you will learn to use this sense of obligation positively without sacrificing all in order to do something worthwhile. You will always strive to feel worthwhile and may be very structured in the order in which you do things. Mistakes may leave you devastated and this is a problem place for the child. Help the child to understand that everyone makes mistakes and it is okay to do so. Working alone is also another possibility; however, you should try to work with others rather than demand too much of yourself while alone. Your father in past lives really did a number on you, either positively or negatively, and you must learn to deal with your innermost feelings and fears. Thus, a child with this placement may have fears that cannot be expressed. A fatherly, protective type attitude toward the child will go a long way in helping him or her feel secure and able to express fears and in turn grow.

Saturn is somewhat the bridge from the inner, personal planets to the outer, generational planets. Thus, Saturn retrograde affects you as an individual vis a vis you view of the world, and your innate karmic sensitivities are punctuated. Saturn retrograde is almost a calling to work on issues larger than yourself. It tends to make you go beyond what you can be to what you need to be for yourself and the world.

The following planets are the outer, generational planets that can be used either personally or for the whole, while Saturn may be used for the universe but is also very personal.

Uranus Retrograde

This placement suggests the rebel. Each child rebels in his or her own way, especially in the teen years, but this child really does so big time. Rebel is written all over this child from the start. Uranus retrograde suggests a past life expert at fighting the establishment. This is the lifetime revolutionary. This revolutionary feeling is quite innate and probably the child thinks everyone feels the same way. The lesson here is to find a way to help the child learn to give in a little in order to gain a lot of what he or she is striving for. Compromise and conformity are hard lessons for this child to learn. When Uranus is direct it is a time for the child to understand and be able to give a little. If the retrograde Uranus is in the third house, this child may rebel at having siblings or in school. Learning that school can really help one get where he or she wants to go is a hard lesson to learn. Again, the house and rulership shows where the lessons come from. This is a very exciting and fun child, albeit a hard child to rein in. A good example of this are those born with Uranus in Leo from 1956 to 1962. They challenged life and love relationships, and it was the hippie era of free love and communal living. Freedom and breaking loose from the establishment were very important. The lesson for all Uranus Retrograde placements is that of compromise so that you may retain your freedom, rebellious ideas and activities but still function in the real world. This is a difficult lesson to learn and is a strong carryover from past lives.

Retrograde Uranus Through the Houses/Signs

First House/Aries: This is the ultimate rebel. He or she probably was in trouble in the past for rebellious and revolutionary ideas; but it is so innate that the individual keeps on doing the same thing. This is the spontaneous child and possibly the flaky teenager. Uniqueness is very important. Along with an innate sense that you must be free, as an adult you are also tolerant of others. Independence and a pioneering spirit are deeply routed. This is really a fun house for Uranus or Uranus retrograde but you cannot tame the child or the adult. The key here is to help the child learn to express individuality and a sense of freedom in somewhat acceptable terms to society. Help the child gear his or her energy to social causes that are important.

Second House/Taurus: With Uranus Retrograde here you may have an innate sense of insecurity that you try to assuage with financial security and independence. Your way to achieve this would be unusual and you may feel afraid to take rises or you may be willing to take a lot of risks. You will probably not be comfortable working a 9-to-5 job and must have irregular hours as well as irregular, independent work. Security and nice things are very important even if you appear unusual in your approach. You are more than willing to earn money in inventive ways. A child must be allowed to do jobs that one would not necessarily think a child would want to do; this is necessary in order to feel satisfied while earning an allowance. A teenager's part-time job may not be what you expected but the teen will do things his or her own way. This is the rebel with a cause.

Third House\Gemini: Uranus Retrograde here suggests past life conditions that were unusual or unorthodox with siblings or relatives. Perhaps the child now must learn to give a little in order to maintain sibling relationships. Also, the conscious mind works in unusual ways. Your way of thinking or viewing the world does not match up to the norms. This is not bad but something you must realize is often unique to you. Your mental tendencies are rooted in past conditions and early schooling may be difficult just because it is too structured for you. You may either have exciting friendships with your more unusual peers or feel you are an outcast. The child will learn to live in a normal world with not so normal thoughts with this placement, and will probably have trouble in early education.

Fourth House/Cancer: You have a past history of rebelling against the household and continue the tradition. Your lifestyle has its merits, but your family probably does not understand you. You may have a tolerant and far-thinking parent, but the other one may be a little distant and unable to relate to you; or your parents may be alike. In any event, with Uranus retrograde, you are always looking for unconditional love in strange and unusual ways. Lynn Koiner says Uranus retrograde here suggests early home life may appear normal but probably is not. As a step-parent of a Uranus retrograde fourth-house child, your challenge is to let the child express restlessness and an unusual approach while helping the child realize that he or she can be different but still live in the real world.

Fifth House/Leo: With Uranus retrograde here you have a deep-rooted inventive and artistic nature. You also have an unusual approach to romance and child rearing, and must have a sense of freedom, even from your children, in order to express your creative nature. The lesson here is compromise. Rather than be erratic, set times and places for you alone and do the same to be with your children. If your step-child has Uranus retrograde here, help the child be a revolutionary through art, dress and the like, and help him or her understand the principal of compromise. Adults feel normal but others probably do not see you that way and you must seek your place in the world that meets your unconventional manner.

Sixth House\Virgo: Any type of routine in work is innately abhorrent to you. This is true of the child as well; structured chores or studies will not be tolerated. Do not fight this child; try to find creative outlets since repetition will lead to immediate boredom. Freedom is very important and you, or a child, will not be able to complete a job without it. The problem with this placement is that rebelliousness in the workplace is not often tolerated and, again, compromise is the key. Also, health problems may be caused by the feeling of being trapped in a work situation.

Seventh House\Libra: Uranus retrograde here suggests a past pattern of unusual or unorthodox relationships. Thus, you now seek a relationship that is unusual and has variety, or you may need a variety of partners. There is an innate eccentricity about those you choose, and you are drawn to all types of people, especially those very different from you since they present a challenge. You will probably not be happy unless your partner is a challenge and keeps you guessing; although you may have a good relationship, your partner must continue to surprise you throughout the years. This can be a tough placement for stable, steady, and what are considered to be normal relationships. The key here is to find a relationship that gives you a sense of freedom. Not easy. You may tend to fall in and out of love quickly.

Eighth House/Scorpio: Uranus retrograde here suggests past difficulties leading to challenges with intimacy during this lifetime. Unusual sexual situations may exist. There is a push-pull between wanting a deep, committed relationship and wanting complete independence. There is also an unusual approach to handling joint finances. On the other hand, this placement speaks wonders for creative accounting in the handling of other people's money. Investigations and psychology would be very good callings for you, Death plays an important role in your own psyche, and the child with this placement may seem preoccupied with death and hidden matters that are psychic in nature. The trick here is to help the child feel okay about being unusual but to learn to live in the real world. The child should be very good at study and research and this could develop into a career for the adult.

Ninth House/Sagittarius: Your desire for intellectual freedom is very strong. You feel like an outcast because of revolutionary ways of thinking and revolutionary life philosophies, and you are drawn to humanitarian causes. You may not attend institutions of higher learning in a conventional way but you will acquire an education, possibly in intermittent segments that fall between other intellectual pursuits. The child with this placement will innately be adverse to any type of dogma, and patterns of learning will not necessarily benefit the child. Learning must be challenging and never the same two days in a row. As the child grows, ideas regarding spirituality will also be revolutionary. Again, compromise is the way to get through the Uranus retrograde placement. You may still be revolutionary in your thoughts, but when Uranus is direct you will be able to relate more to other people's way of thinking.

Tenth House/Capricorn: This can be a little tough. Status quo is not suited to you so you must find a career that affords you freedom and the ability to invent, achieve and progress in unusual ways. You are the reformer and may do very well in a company that needs reorganization. With this placement you feel an innate need for power and authority and probably an innate need to rebel against anyone in authority. Again, you need something that affords stimulation, probably irregular hours and a non-routine job. The child will look for praise and acknowledgment for something he or she has invented or an unusual activity. This can be a creative placement; however you must learn to compromise a little within the context of what society sees as normal in order to achieve and advance.

Eleventh House/Aquarius: You innately challenge the rules and any groups you belong to, as well as your friends. With Uranus retrograde here, you may get involved quickly and fall out quickly with a group or with friends. Anyone you are associated with must be stimulating and inventive. Freedom is very important to you, along with issues of equality and humanitarian ideals. As a child, you may go your own way and seem different from the other children; but you do not have to be an outcast as you can inspire those around you. You may tend to change your goals quickly, as well as over and over again.

Twelfth House/Pisces: Uranus retrograde here suggests very deep, psychologically erratic thoughts and feelings. You are the rebel but may not even know what you are rebelling against. This is probably the toughest Uranus retrograde placement. You may even feel as though you are insane. You will break the rules for no reason you can see. What is important is a sense of a good world and you may constantly change in order to achieve that goal. Freedom is innately important and this may suggest a loner or someone whose actions are chaotic. With Uranus direct, it is easier for you to go deep within yourself to find out what you really want. With Uranus retrograde you may act erratically but not understand that you are looking for yourself, and you may experience sudden bursts of insight followed by confusion. The key is to allow your erratic feelings and thoughts to surface and deal with them without letting them rule who you are and what you are doing. For this child, confusion and perhaps even tantrums may occur, and as a step-parent you should cut this child a little slack and give him or her space to work out the confusion.

Neptune Retrograde

Neptune direct is the planet of dreams, psychic ability and creativity, but also that of escapism, drugs and alcohol, confusion and taking on the problems of others as your own without even knowing it. If Neptune is retrograde, the negative qualities of Neptune may be even harder to deal with. On the other hand, creativity may be so natural that it just flows. Neptune retrograde is a receptacle for all of the problems of the world and often deals with this by escapism in a variety of forms. The trick, and this can be done far more easily through progression when Neptune turns direct, is to help the child direct energy into the creative realm, going after dreams and even psychic ability with the need to escape and without the confusion often associated with Neptune. Appreciation of creativity and psychic phenomena is important rather than trying to escape from it.

Look at the house and ruler to see how to work with Neptune retrograde. For example, if Neptune is retrograde in the fifth house, relationships may be an escape for the person; but since Neptune also suggests deception or self deception, the person may be disappointed with his or her relationships when they do not turn out as hoped. If escaping through creativity, you probably will not ever think your projects are good enough. Thus, in a relationship or creatively, you will keep on trying new things without really appreciating the persons around you or what you have done. Help your step-child understand this insecurity with others, or insecurity with what he or she creates, and learn to deal with it and to appreciate self. Neptune and Pluto both are considered generational planets and often Neptune retrograde will manifest itself with the themes of the generation, so look to your step-child's peers and generational commitments to help this child grow positively. Again, the retrograde planets are where you can really make a difference and create a strong bond.

Retrograde Neptune Through the Houses/Signs

First House/Aries: Neptune retrograde here suggests psychic abilities that may not be understood and, therefore, may cause fear and anxiety. The receptivity of this placement to surroundings is very strong. Help the child to express the artistic and creative side of Neptune and to learn to set boundaries and say no to others who may drain his or her energy. Also, addiction is suggested and anything potentially addictive should be avoided. One major caveat is that although addiction may be suggested, it does not mean someone will become an addict. In fact, most people have addiction suggestions somewhere in the chart and do not become addicts.

Mysticism and psychic abilities may be developed and understood over time and used wisely. This placement is also difficult because of self-delusion about situations and people. Learning to see things for what they are is one lesson of this placement.

Second House/Taurus: You innately want comfort and connections to others. However, Neptune suggests looking at things with self-deception or perhaps even being deceived by others. Since Neptune is retrograde, you must really watch for this problem while seeking connection and comfort. Neptune retrograde here is a very good placement for earning through mysticism, psychic ability and spiritual endeavors. However, you must watch that others do not take advantage of you or that you take on their problems as you own. With Neptune retrograde you may tend to a mentor/student relationship with the student draining you. A child with this placement should be encouraged to use the imagination to find his or her security and place in the world. The generational themes, things outside yourself, are very important and also places to look for potential earnings and for personal growth.

Third House/Gemini: Neptune retrograde here suggests a child who is very dreamy, possibly daydreaming his elementary education years away. Encourage this child to bring the dreams into reality and use them in communication and learning. This child may feel like a stranger in school or with siblings. As an adult, hopefully you will have learned how to use this imagination and creativity positively. If not, you can go through adult life in a cloud. If you learn to deal with the cosmic milieu you can be very effective with mysticism and spirituality, sharing information with others.

Fourth House/Cancer: The largest problem for children with this placement is that if the home is not calm and peaceful, they will have to find an escape, be it through friends, substance dependency or some type of cult group. Neptune retrograde here is tough since the child will take on all the problems of the household as his or her own. If you are a step-parent, go out of your way to make sure things are serene. If the household is calm, this imaginative child may be a pleasure. The home will be seen as a place to shut out the harsh outside world. As an adult, you may take in strays (animals or people) and will have a very nurturing home.

Fifth House/Leo: This is a tough placement for romance since you are looking for the perfect romance and probably are not very realistic about people. Disappointment usually follows. An adult or teen may have this is a problem. When something is painful, there is a tendency to rush to escape it rather than work through a problem. This is a great placement for creativity and imagination. A child with this placement will be very creative and seek security in knowing that you approve of his or her imagination and creativity.

Sixth House/Virgo: It is hard for people with Neptune retrograde here to know what they really want from a job. Again, since Neptune is often dreamy and unrealistic, the perfect job does not exist and you may have a lot of job changes searching for something that is just not there. What you do need to look for in a job is a creative and personally sensitive work environment; this will help you cope. With the child, school stress could lead to perceived illness, and with the adult, job stress could also lead to physical problems. Jobs in healing or spirituality will be fulfilling, as will working with animals. In the sixth house setting it is very important to look for something that fits with your ideals and also to be sure you are realistic about what you are doing.

Seventh House/Libra: Like the fifth house Neptune, you want the perfect partner, but he or she does not exist. Learning to cope with the real person rather than your idealized version of him or her, just to be disappointed later, is the lesson here. You may also need to learn to handle someone who uses escape mechanisms. You cannot take on your partner's problems. Learn empathy without becoming that person. This is also a placement that could suggest a higher calling at the expense of an adult partnership, a priest or nun, or someone who is so involved in spirituality and giving that he or she does not have time for a relationship.

Eighth House/Scorpio: You have an innate need to ferret out the hidden and to understand death and psychic matters. It is much stronger with Neptune retrograde here than with other planets, except perhaps Pluto or Pluto retrograde. The longing for a soul mate is quite strong and you may spend your lifetime again seeking that which is perfect. The key here is to learn to look realistically while still owning the ideal. Mysticism is very strong and helpful, and there may be a tendency to look at the dark side of life. There is also a possibility of deception or self-deception around shared resources. Learning to use retrograde Neptune positively without "going to the dark side" is a lesson of this placement. An example would be to use this placement for matters of healing rather than matters of dependency and escape. This is one of the placements that suggest perhaps therapy would be beneficial and may help in self-understanding.

Ninth House/Sagittarius: You are probably seeking utopia, but nothing is perfect and disappointment will occur. You may literally travel to the ends of the earth seeking the perfect place or thing. On the other hand, there is an innate feeling of wonder at the world, and compassion is strong. Therefore, your place may be in healing but with a world view. If the world disappoints, however, this is another placement of abuse or dependency. The key is to learn the lesson of compassion without taking on the weight of the world and becoming bogged down, disappointed and perhaps addicted. The child will look at the world in wonderment and should be encouraged to express his or her imagination. There is an intuitive bent toward higher education, philosophy and travel, all of which are also very important for understanding.

Tenth House/Capricorn: With retrograde Neptune here, you know there is something you should be doing, some career that will be fulfilling; but you will have a hard time pinning it down. You feel you have a mission. Again, the perfect career is not feasible and you must set your sights realistically in order to feel you are accomplishing your mission. Your imagination and intuition are strong assets to what you choose to do. As a step-parent, help the child deal with imagination versus reality and encourage the artistic nature while avoiding extreme actions or extreme wants, often expressed by the child as needs. The child has an innate desire for recognition, but is also shy.

Eleventh House/Aquarius: This placement suggests that the teenager will seek groups or persons expressing high ideals but may not really know if they are his or her ideals. There is confusion on what is the teen's own and what is not. The child, teen and adult will sometimes be really clear about what they want for the future and in the next minute will be confused and imaginations may run amok. Friends are important in helping ground this placement as long as the friends truly share the same ideals. With this placement, working in generational and social endeavors would be very fulfilling. Freedom may be idealized and at the same friendship ties are sought. Alcohol or substance abuse problems with friends or needy people can create problems for someone with this retrograde placement.

Twelfth House/Pisces: Your inner imagination is so strong and vivid that this placement may be difficult; but, it is really a wonderful placement for creativity and spirituality. The caveat is that you may be so perceptive, psychic or mediumistic that you have a difficult time coping with the real world. Reality just may not make sense to you, and your ties to reality may be very tenuous. This is a placement of the artistic or the addict. Obviously, the higher is what you must strive for and what you must encourage your step-child toward. Dreams and utopia are wonderful and you strive for them, but reality can only accept part of the dream. Spirituality is important for this placement, but you must watch fanaticism. Miracles seem natural. If your step-child comes to you with something outlandish that he or she has seen, it is probably true.

Pluto Retrograde

Pluto is associated with power and reformation. Pluto retrograde is associated with inner power or psychological transformation. This is also a very good placement for investigation. With regard to past life conditions, Pluto retrograde suggests you were probably singled out from the group, perhaps even a scapegoat. Thus, you probably have a low level of trust. Regeneration of your psyche is what you need now. You may be a loner. You also have a lot of intuition with regard to what motivates others, having been the subject of their negative motivations in the past. Your lesson now is to learn to believe in the group once again and to work with others. This means that the distrusting child who may be afraid to join a club or who is shy needs help in getting out and learning to trust and share with others.

Pluto retrograde is a good placement for all kinds of work for the benefit of the group, reformational ideas with regard to work and generational ideals. Pluto retrograde progressed to Pluto direct is a very strong placement. Look to the house that contains the Pluto retrograde for where strong powers of reform or of regeneration may occur. Although Pluto retrograde works well in all houses, the child must learn to cooperate with others in order to gain full benefit. For example, perhaps the child has Pluto retrograde in the eighth house and decides to save with his sibling for something they both want and can easily share. The Pluto retrograde child may have trouble because he feels he will pay more than his share or that his sibling really won't come through after all the sacrifice the retrograde child has made. Suggest that they both put their money in a clear jar each week so they can each see what the other is doing. This will strengthen the trust. Pluto retrograde in the twelfth house is great for the therapist, and it gives an intense sense of self-preservation. (Interestingly, Christian Dior and Bob Mackie both have Pluto retrograde and constantly reinvent not themselves but the styles they create—classic for Dior and outrageous for Mackie.)

Retrograde Pluto Through the Houses/Signs

First House/Aries: With Pluto Retrograde here, you may reinvent yourself over and over again. You are very intense and innately seek control, and you have a fear of ostracization and need to control situations at all times. You have a strong desire to understand the human psyche and investigation and healing are good areas to feel fulfilled. The child will want to be everything, one thing after another, and constantly reinvent himself or herself. This is done with a view to not only be accepted but to have control over others. As an adult, this is a strong placement since no matter what happens, you will get back up, regroup, reorganize and go on.

Second House/Taurus: This placement suggests a real fear of not controlling money and resources. There is a fear that without total control over the tangible, you are vulnerable to the will of others. There is a confusion of mental control with control of the tangible, and also a compulsive or addictive nature. This is probably one of the toughest placements of Pluto retrograde since you are dealing with the tangible versus the intangible and equating the same weight to both. On the other hand, this is a good placement for economic understanding that can help you acquire great wealth. The lesson here is to learn to share resources equally and not to equate money with personal power or use money for personal power. The child with this placement has a deep core need for his or her own possessions and room. Even if a room must be shared, the child must have a section of that room entirely his or her own.

Third House/Gemini: Mental control is of utmost importance and mind games may occur. Since mental control is so important, this is a good placement for a teacher. You should be very good at any kind of game that requires mental prowess or language skill. Chances are, you are very organized. Past life conditions with siblings may lead to the child's attempt to control siblings. Perhaps you were the runt or the picked-on sibling and now you are trying to make sure you are top dog. You will try to organize them in all they do. If your step-child has this placement, it is important to let this child organize his or her room and participate in mental games to work the retrograde placement rather than try to control siblings.

Fourth House/Cancer: With Pluto retrograde here, you may be coming from a position where family was either too organized and rigid, thus stifling you, or where there was a lack of organization and you now feel insecure and in need of safety and protection. Thus, a child with Pluto retrograde needs a positive, nurturing role model in a parent or step-parent. On the other hand, you cannot be smothering since this too can cause control issues. As Pluto goes direct or as you grow, you need to learn to share control over domestic issues. This is also a placement where the child will try to find out all of the family secrets and may be considered nosy. Remember, understanding these secrets gives the child a sense of emotional ties or roots. Give the child detective stories and games where he or she has to use mental skill.

Fifth House/Leo: You have an innate sense of art and creativity. This is from many past times of being the creative one. You also have a past condition of vying for control in love issues. You are the innate risk-taker and gambler. This is the child who has no fear and thus must be closely watched. As the child grows, he or she will become more secure and less of a control freak if the creative side is allowed to flow. Issues of control in love will probably always be with you but you can take steps to help lessen this trait by learning to receive as well as give. The constant giver may do so because he or she feels the other party will owe a debt and this way the giver can control the relationship. Learning to receive and share helps lessen the control issues.

Sixth House/Virgo: Pluto retrograde here also suggests deep-seated control issues related to work. Rather than subject yourself to conflict, you may prefer to work alone. Control over what you do and how you do it is of utmost importance, and with retrograde you feel it is crucial to who you are. Power plays and manipulation can be a problem. The child must feel mastery and control over school work or the health may be affected. The lesson with this retrograde is to let go a little, let the chips fall where they may and realize not everything has to be perfect. A good manifestation of Pluto retrograde here is jobs in the health field, including reorganization or reformation of procedures, and this will be quite fulfilling. This is a placement of the child who brings the hurt bird home and tries to nurse it back to health.

Seventh House/Libra: This placement suggests past problems with partners or a spouse and issues with regard to power and control. You probably either overpowered your mate or were a victim and, either way, you may have difficulty now in establishing a cooperative relationship. You may also look to a partner as a source of ending or causing all of your problems. This is a tough placement for Pluto retrograde. However, the lesson here is to learn to share equally and when Pluto is direct, you have a lot of time to do so. Also, the lesson of never forgetting past sleights of your partner is a tough one. Again, there is plenty of time to master your relationship as you grow. As you learn to get on and over past occurrences, you will work through this placement. So, although it is a tough one, it is a practical one that can be worked through with conscious effort. If you help your step-child learn the art of compromise, it will go a long way in his working out the seventh house retrograde before reaching adulthood.

Eighth House/Scorpio: With Pluto retrograde here you probably have an innate desire to understand that which is hidden, death or any dark side of life. If you are not grounded in other areas, this could control you rather than you controlling your compulsions. Again, there are deep-rooted issues of power and control. This time power and control issues may concern shared resources. The lesson again is to learn to cooperate and share rather than either being the control freak or letting someone else control because of past issues. The child must learn to share and not expect all to be given when he or she wants it. This will lead to the adult who actually does control his or her own desires rather than letting them run wild. Control issues may also be over intimacy or sexual matters, or running the show. This is a wonderful placement for investigation and research, and you also may be very good at handling other people's assets, i.e., financial advising.

Ninth House/Sagittarius: Your principals, religion and personal philosophy have great control over you. This is based in past conditions that have occurred over and over. Morality or ethics are as important to you as your most important goals and dreams. You cannot separate yourself from your beliefs. One way to keep from being too dogmatic is to travel and expose yourself to different cultures and beliefs, even if only through reading. You will then be able to reorganize yourself into someone who may have strong beliefs but who also understands others and has a more worldly view of life. This is a great placement for a professor or a minister. Expose the child at a young age to other people and cultures and he or she will be ahead of the game as an adult.

Tenth House/Capricorn: Pluto retrograde here suggests issues of power and authority stemming from parental control or lack thereof. Past conditions may have been intrusive, or there may have been a role model who was irresponsible and just not there. Either way, you now have issues of control and authority stemming from that situation. These issues will probably spill over into your career, promulgating issues of power, reorganization, manipulation and control. The key is to feel like you have mastered the skills you need so that you are secure and can neither be controlled or feel the need to control others. Once this happens, your powers of organization, research skills and structure in your work will take you a long way. One of your strong points is to see and eliminate that which is not needed; efficiency is the goal. When Pluto is direct, and especially when direct through progression, personal power issues can be resolved. Also, helping your step-child feel he or she does have some power will go a long way toward helping to resolve retrograde issues prior to adulthood. Let the child have power over what spending the allowance on as long as part of it is saved, and TV choice within certain parameters. There are a lot of ways to empower the little one, who must feel important in order to deal effectively with retrograde Pluto.

Eleventh House/Aquarius: You feel an innate draw toward what is new, technologically, as well as the avant garde. You are also drawn toward groups, not so much as a part of the group but to reorganize the group into something fitting the current times. Pluto retrograde here is a positive manifestation of control and reorganization. Your power is deep and often the group will not realize it before you have reorganized it. Just as with Pluto direct, you may develop friendships but also eliminate them quickly and easily. You will cut out what is not right. For the child, this means something like trying to get the scout troop to do something other than sell cookies as a fundraiser. This is a good placement for Pluto retrograde for both the child and the adult.

Twelfth House/Pisces: This is also a strong placement for Pluto retrograde. It suggests a role of counselor or someone who does deep analysis. But this is also the person who can pick out weaknesses and play upon them. With Pluto retrograde, you may not realize your own motivations. Faith or lack thereof can be a problem, either by being too dogmatic or waving in the wind trying to find something that makes you feel empowered. Intuition and visions are common with this placement. The caveat here is to be careful of doing anything that could put you in a position of incarceration. If Pluto retrograde has difficult aspects, watch out. The real strength here is the person who is a good counselor, whether professionally or just for those around him or her. Pluto retrograde is very deep thinking.

When any retrograde planets becomes direct through progression, it is a time for work in the areas where the retrograde had the greatest impact. This is a time to grow and move on. This is a time to become what you want to be rather than relying on the old comfortable feelings of the retrograde.

Again, if you do recognize the concept of reincarnation, look at the retrograde explanations as a metaphor. The retrograde placement still has the same affect.

One reason I have chosen the example families presented in the following chapters is that each child has some good retrograde planets with which to deal and they are very good family examples of how retrograde planets can help in understanding. I also often find that extended families do have a lot of retrograde planets with which to work. It just makes your job easier when trying to find clues into working out relationships. The retrograde is a good source of where work is needed, and it gives you insight into the inner workings and inner needs of the child.

Chapter 5

Using the Lunar Nodes

LUNAR NODES ARE POINTS, not planets, and thus have a more esoteric meaning. The Nodes are points where the Moon crosses the ecliptic. As the Moon moves north, the point at which it crosses the ecliptic is the North Node, historically called the Dragon's Head. As it moves south, the point at which it crosses the ecliptic is called the South Node, historically the Dragon's Tail. The Nodes tend to move in a retrograde fashion. Thus, already, you can get the idea that there is some sort of karma involved. There are times when the Nodes are both direct or stationary but they are retrograde more often than not.

Like the previous chapter on retrogrades, if you do not feel reincarnation is valid or if you are ambivalent about it, use the descriptions metaphorically. You do not have to believe in any theory to use the definitions. Thus, I will not go into the philosophy of karma to a great extent. Suffice it to quote Isaac Newton (although he did not mean it karmically): "For every action there is an equal and opposite reaction." Whatever you do or even think has a result, sometimes an immediate and tangible result, sometimes a result far, far down the line. We are all born with karmic baggage, be it positive or negative, and we choose when and with whom to work it out.

Nodes are looked at in terms of karma (past and present), perhaps how your environment may affect you or in such limited terms as "good luck" for the North Node and "bad luck" for the South Node. Looking at the Nodes in a karmic sense, it stands to reason that the South Node would be bad luck because it represents where you are coming from regarding the past, the focal point of past energy coming into your natal chart. The North Node is good luck since you are given an opportunity to work out the manifestations of the South Node. The South Node suggests where you are coming from. According to Mohan Koparkar in his book *Lunar Nodes*, you work out the South Node placement through a grand trine; if the South Node is in the first house, you will work with the first, fifth and ninth houses. These are the people who are the intellectual or creative impetus for society. If the South Node is in the second house, you will work through the second, sixth and tenth houses; these are the people who contribute to the business and economic growth of society. If the South Node is in the third house, you work through the third, seventh and eleventh houses; these are the people who protect society and contribute peace and harmony.

I look at the North Node as the place where the individual works out the South Node energy on a more personal rather than societal level. Also look at the ruler of the sign that the Node is in to learn further places of personal effort to work with the Nodes. Look closely at the dispositor of the Node. Say the Node is in Cancer, its ruler is the Moon. If the Moon is in Aries and Aries is ruled by Mars, then Mars is the dispositor of the Node. This is a very strong place to work on Nodal energy. Nodes are opposite each other so the goal is balance. Thus, if the North Node were in Aries and/or the first house, the South Node would be in Libra and/or the seventh house and the work would be personal energy directed and coming from partnerships or spouses. In this case there may be too strong a tendency to give in order to obtain harmony and thus a need to be a little more selfish. To stand up for oneself is the lesson to learn.

One of the most important uses of the Nodes is to look at them in synastry with the charts of step-children. The South Node contact shows past connections or connections that must be worked out. North Node connections may also be karmic, but South Node connections are tougher and stronger. North Node connections are easier to work through. Nodal connections with any luminary, the personal planets and especially Saturn suggest a very strong past tie. The Nodal connections are the ties that bind. When looking at charts of couples who are going to marry, I always look for these binding ties since they will get you through the hard times. If these ties are not there, there is a tendency not to work through tough times. The same is true with family Nodal and planetary ties. They do bind the family, so if you have North Node or South Node connections with your step-children, you (and they) have chosen to come together. An understanding of the Nodal contacts goes a long way in helping you work with your step-children. One and probably both of you have chosen to be together. Deal with it now or do it again.

Nodes in Signs/Houses

Aries/First House North Node with Libra/Seventh House South Node: The North Node is where you are working this lifetime in order to process the opposing South Node energies. Thus, the North Node in Aries or the first house suggests your lesson is to learn to stand up for yourself, to assert yourself, to use your fire energy not to promote yourself ahead of others but to be your own person. With the South Node in the seventh house or Libra, you are coming from a position of perhaps seeing yourself through your mate, perhaps giving in to keep balance and harmony, perhaps being dependent on others. The key here is to keep balance and harmony while being able to also be yourself. You may tend to attract partners who are dominating because of past experience and your lesson is to use the Libra diplomacy so they do not rule you, or to learn to detect this trait in yourself and to go for someone else. Heavy North Node influence could lead to self-advancement or possibly even aggression. You must learn to be yourself and not totally sacrifice for others. You are a combination of sensitivity and artistic versus the energetic fighter.

Taurus/Second House North Node with Scorpio/Eighth House South Node: North Node in the second house suggests personal resources are important versus being dependent on another for the same. It is personal worth versus seeing your worth through your mate. It is practicality and industriousness versus sensuality or hedonistic tendencies. The key is to keep resources and personal strength while being able to share with a mate or to keep a balance of power in the relationship. A heavy emphasis on the North Node could mean unusual financial situations. There may be a defensive attitude toward relationships due to an abundance of past difficult endings. Relationships may tend toward intensity and crises.

Gemini/Third House North Node with Sagittarius/Eighth House South Node: This suggests knowledge from past conditions brings about strong intellectual ability. It also suggests conscious thought versus higher conscious philosophies. This is a good placement for a teacher of children. You will bring another world to them. This also suggests strong relationships with siblings. You are a good communicator, and a strong or well-aspected North Node suggests disbursement of knowledge and possibly short moves or trips. This is a good placement for the North Node without bringing difficult baggage from the South Node. However, you may have a fear of expressing your personal belief system because of trouble in doing so in the past. On the other hand, you may not appreciate other points of view or be objective about your personal actions. You may have a wild side. You will probably have nervous energy whether used positively or negatively. The goal here is a syntheses between learning yourself and teaching others.

Cancer/Fourth House North Node and Capricorn/Ninth House South Node: Perhaps you were so career oriented in the last life that family was discounted and now family is the most important thing. Family will take priority over career. There may also be a close tie with the mother and breaking away from parents may be difficult. You will probably be more private than public. The key here is to really place an emphasis on your roots for your feelings of security as well as your feelings of doubt. Once you understand this, you should be able to achieve balance between family and career. Try to make sure you act practically and not just emotionally. You have worked hard for self-esteem and honors and feel a great sense of pride but also must be less selfish and work for the benefit of family. Do not take a self-righteous attitude toward family or be too self-absorbed. You do not have to control; let family life and life in general play out.

Leo/Fifth House North Node and Aquarius/Eleventh House South Node: This placement indicates that children are important and success in romance is also suggested. However, you may bring to these relationships some far out ideas, including ideas about social issues that seem a bit strange. Creativity is important to you and may be considered "out there." There may be conflict between social issues and obligations to children, for which the key is to balance the two. This time around you are developing personal strength, taking action rather than wishing about things. You are also learning to be your own person among friends.

Virgo/Sixth House North Node and Pisces/Twelfth House South Node: This placement suggests an emphasis on tangible or work-related activities rather than deep personal growth. It seems almost a respite from personal turmoil of the past. Physical health may also be an issue. When you learn to deal on a deep, subconscious level, some physical maladies will fade away. The key is to balance work and health with inner, spiritual growth and to be willing to work with others rather than behind the scenes or on your own. Work is actually very important for your mental well-being. This placement suggests a need to work in a confident manner, as well as discarding the unimportant and reinforcing important values. There is a lesson of dependence versus independence, idealism versus self-confidence.

Libra/Seventh House North Node and Aries/First House South Node: This is a partnership versus personal situation. However, in the past personal issues have taken the forefront to partnership ones, and this time, the partnership is emphasized. Marriage and partnerships are extremely important even to the point of self-sacrifice. The partnership itself has a good public image. The key here is to look at both yourself and partners and how you respond and promote yourself as an individual and find the balance between the two. Try not to interfere with your partner's individuality, and watch the tendency toward vanity. Also watch a tendency toward short-term allegiances and changing your mind, partly based on not looking at the realities of a situation up front, or because of idealizing things. You may have to learn the hard way not to be jealous or critical. This placement suggests you must weigh head-on action versus consequences.

Scorpio/Eighth House North Node and Taurus/Second House South Node: This placement suggests you are coming from a place where you handled your own resources and that your values were utmost to you. Now you must learn to cope with joint resources, which may or may not be plentiful. Also, the occult, death or hidden matters will occupy your attention and may even be an escape when in conflict over shared assets. This placement is very strong for your values versus another's values. The key here is to balance the responsibility for shared assets and try to integrate both sets of values into a working relationship. Disregard of this placement may cause sexual difficulty or a misunderstanding of your partner's needs based on his or her values. This placement suggests a tremendous need of security but an inability to break past behavior patterns so you drudge along toward a sense of security rather than plowing ahead rapidly and embracing what would give you a sense of security. You may limit your spiritual being. You may have been decadent in the past and now must compensate for that.

Sagittarius/Ninth House North Node and Gemini/Third House South Node: This placement strongly emphasizes the rational, logical mind versus the philosophical, intuitive mind. The North Node placement suggests coping through higher education and intuition, while the South

Node suggests difficulty with siblings and logical or mundane thinking. Over time the North Node may cause moves or at least a lot of dealing with foreign matters or cultures. This tendency may cause loss of contact with siblings. The South Node suggests past difficulty and things to work out with siblings, and the North Node tends to pull away from working this out. This is a much more involved placement than its opposite, and is one of duality versus loyalty. It suggests a person terrified of commitment, which is the lesson, whether with other persons or in other areas of life. There also may be a lack of discrimination and need for acceptance. The positive side of this placement is energy and a desire for higher truth, spirituality and knowledge. Meditation would be very good with this placement.

Capricorn/Tenth House North Node and Cancer/Fourth House South Node: You are coming from a place where domestic life probably took precedence over career and public honors or recognition. Thus, you are goal-oriented and your career takes most of your time. You may have had a difficult childhood regarding the mother or father and domestic life does not appeal as much as professional life. It may be as if you have to prove yourself to your family. Authority and power are very important issues for you to resolve. The key is to balance public life, career and activities in the community while maintaining a strong sense of family. Even if you are not home a lot, you can still have a good family life. You may have even been publicly remanded for loyalty to family in the past so family seems to be a trap for you. This placement suggests maturity and scrutiny versus immaturity and idealism. You may be wrestling with wanting to be taken care of versus being the care giver. It may take a lot of practice to grow up and this may frustrate those around you, primarily family members. Another tough lesson is that of letting go, be it persons, places or things. You also must learn to have values based on what is good for the whole of society, not just personal needs.

Aquarius/Eleventh House North Node and Leo/Fifth House South Node: Past dealings with children suggest problems with dealing with them now. Emphasis is on friendship and achievement through the help of friends or associations rather than parenting. There is an imbalance with regard to love relationships versus friendship. The key is to find a balance, and if children are involved, to learn to deal fairly and patiently. Developing some sort of creative endeavor helps achieve balance. Since the eleventh house is that of step-children, any Nodal contact here is crucial in your relationship to step-children, be it the South Node or the North Node. This placement suggests working toward a higher ideal for humanitarian reasons versus falling into patterns of self-involvement. But with step-parenting, it suggests a tremendous involvement in giving to step-children and often your own children may be a problem because of this. You are walking a tight rope and must really balance. If you do not have children, it may be easier but still difficult in learning to give and be less selfish. This is a tricky placement for step-parenting.

Pisces/Twelfth House North Node and Virgo/Sixth House South Node: This placement is just plain dealing with karma. You are concerned with insecurity and proving yourself at work. Perhaps you were a difficult boss and now must learn how to be a sacrificing employee. Health may suffer under affliction. Working behind the scenes in hospitals or some type of institution, psychic ability and unusual working hours are all part of this placement. The ideal is to bring sub-conscious misgivings to the forefront and integrate a strong work ethic to balance them out. This is a tough Nodal position. Over time you may realize past and harmful patterns but just cannot seem to give them up. Old patterns such as sex or manipulative games versus understanding and giving come into play. If you do not strive toward understanding, life situations will bring it home big time. You may actually become ill because of the stress of life. Quickly reaching human compassion will take care of this placement, but it is tough to do.

Importance of Nodal Contact

Now that you have an initial understanding of how the Nodes work, their importance in step-parenting is apparent. Nodal contact from one chart to another explains why individuals often act and react together when there is no apparent planet/sign placement relationship in their charts to suggest such action. When there is nodal contact between charts, there is a need to act and react with each other that transcends rational explanation. I always refer to the Nodes as the ties that bind. For example, if you have a couple with doubtful chart comparison but they have the Sun or Moon in conjunction with a Node, they will probably last longer than the couple whose charts seem compatible but do not have strong nodal ties. The karma just insists on being worked out. No matter the relationship or the gender of the parties, karmic manifestations are there and must be worked through. Perhaps the parties have an easier time working through problems with their roles now as opposed to the past. Any contact to the South Node brings your inner needs into being. Thus, while you may need to work through the North Node, you are prone to repeat the old habits of the South Node placement. Herein lies the rub. If your South Node is conjunct someone's planet, that person will probably react to your South Node and vice versa. For example, suppose your South Node is in the sixth house and a boss or employee has Mercury conjunct this South Node. Perhaps the boss or employee will help you work through whatever needs to be done. If you have contact with someone's North Node, the person may not feel as strong a contact but a core feeling of investment in each other's lives, present or future. Either way, the South Node and North Node are both very strong ties. It is these ties that really help in dealing with step-children. If the nodal ties are there, you are ahead of the game since you both will want to work out life situations. The nodal contact is very strong.

The synastry of the nodal contacts, either by conjunction or by other aspects, in step-parenting can be very enlightening. For purposes of this book, I use the nodal contact with another person's chart and not the nodal contact to your own planets.

Nodal Contacts in Synastry

Nodal contact is very important in synastry. Remember, the South Node is where you are coming from. Thus a conjunction within a couple of degrees of one's South Node to another person's planet is very strong. It is a place to work through. A contact with the North Node is what you are doing now to work through and so a planet contact to another's North Node is also very strong. North Node contact is how you have chosen to work, not necessarily the baggage you bring to a relationship but how you choose to work things out. Any nodal contact by aspect between two charts can be very important in any relationship and is a key to where to work with your step-children in order to enrich both your lives. The conjunctions are the strongest contact with the Nodes and where to look for help, but aspects to the Nodes may also be very helpful.

Sun/Nodal Axis

South Node Conjunction: Luminary conjunctions are the strongest Nodal contacts. The Sun conjunct the South Node suggests a coming together to work very hard on yourselves, a strong core connection that is felt immediately. No matter how much trouble you may have with the other person, this is a tie that really binds. I look for Nodal-luminary contact in charts of persons marrying each other, as these are the couples that make it over the rough spots. If there is a Sun-Node tie to a step-child, you may have trouble, but deep down you recognize each other and will work together, even through the rough times. Chances are the South Node person gave a good deal to the Sun person and now the Sun person has a turn to reciprocate. This is not necessarily a negative situation since you have learned a lot in the past and some lessons must just occur again.

North Node Conjunction: You have chosen each other to work together. You may not have as much past contact, but chose for your own reasons to meet and work now. You have chosen to grow, create and stimulate each other. This is an easier contact to work with than the South Node. Although traditionally the South Node suggests past contact, I feel that the North Node also may suggest past contact as well and a positive way to grow. The charts I have worked with all seem to indicate that the Sun-North Node parties also have that innate recognition of each other. This placement often suggests the parties will go way beyond the past, trying something new and different.

South Node and North Node Opposition: If the South Node is conjunct the Sun, it is opposite the North Node and vice versa. Therefore, any opposition, either South Node or North Node, is a strong connection and a place where you may have difficulty working through the aspect and thus working through the relationship. However, this is a very worthwhile placement for growth and mutual influence. An opposition may be difficult but is not bad. It is the place to work together. Aside from the conjunction, this is the next best place to grow.

South Node Trine: This is a beneficial aspect and where energy flows easily for growth and harmony. If the South Node is in trine to the Sun, there was probably some past contact but not as much baggage as one would think.

North Node Trine: This is a very motivational placement. It suggests a lot of energy and activity, be it creatively, socially or emotionally. You work well together. This placement will help bring you close to your step-child.

South Node Sextile: This position suggests you may have trouble overcoming past conditions since the relationship is so natural you just go with the flow rather than trying to grow. Thus, although a sextile is easy, you tend to just let things continue. Look at how to grow.

North Node Sextile: There is a lot of motivation to grow and excel. However, because the South Node is opposite, you may tend to fall back into the easy patterns represented by the South Node. Thus, use the energy of the Sun and really work together.

South Node Square: This creates an inhibition on growth between the subjects. It is difficult for the South Node person to work with the Sun person even though the work must be done. Look for positive areas in the chart that are easy to work with at the beginning and then move toward and work through this placement. There is a lot of core tension between the parties.

North Node Square: This is a good place to work hard even though it is difficult. A feeling that you can work hard and accomplish is there and should be explored.

South Node Quincunx: This is a difficult and inhibiting aspect. Growth is difficult at best.

North Node Quincunx: This aspect is somewhat lighter than the South Node quincunx but still suggests difficulty in growth. This is not the close contact of the conjunction but still an area where work is needed in order to grow.

Moon/Nodal Axis

As with the Sun, the Moon is another place where karmic contact is very important. Moon aspects with the Nodes:

South Node Conjunction: There is a strong, innate emotional flow between the parties. The Moon person may feel the need to give emotionally to the South Node person. Emotional and family situations are very strong. If you have a South Node conjunction with the Moon of the step-child, you both feel deeply that you need to work on emotional well-being.

North Node Conjunction: This aspect allows more emotional freedom and less sensitivity. There is a mutual attraction between the parties and a friendship or social feeling along with the need to nurture. This is a very strong and good aspect, and a rather motherly placement; so if it is your Moon conjunct your step-child's South Node, you are part way home.

South Node and North Node Opposition: The opposition of either Node to the Moon suggests emotional difficulty and areas to work on. There is a difficult flow of emotions stemming from past conditions. Whether you are bringing baggage or choosing to work on this placement, you need to have patience and the Moon person may tend to be drained by the Node person. This placement suggests future work will be needed.

South Node Trine: This is an easy flow of energy so the South Node will not drain the Moon person so much. The problem here is that the flow is easy and emotional problems that could be worked on may be ignored just to flare up again and again when there is a transiting planet affecting this placement.

North Node Trine: You have a relatively easy time of expressing your emotions with each other. It is a good placement to work on emotional security. However, the easy flow of energy of a trine suggests you may miss opportunities because things are just flowing along. Look at the transits to see where work here would be beneficial.

South Node Square: This is an emotionally difficult placement. Growth may be inhibited because one party, probably the South Node person, is afraid to stand up to the emotional situation and grow. On the other hand, nurturing may also be affected and the Moon person must watch and make sure proper nurturing is attained even in the face of difficulty. This is a strong placement so just do not throw your hands in the air and give up.

North Node Square: This placement suggests inhibition on emotional growth as well. Although not as difficult as a South Node square, it nonetheless suggests obstacles. However, this placement is strong and the square is often beneficial since its difficulties are where lessons can be learned and where strong, successful growth can occur.

South Node Sextile: This is not too hard a placement, but it does suggest work is needed on emotional support and emotional growth. However, with the sextile, positive energy from the parties should help each other.

North Node Sextile: This is a nurturing placement for the Moon person and a help to both parties in emotional and creative growth. This is a very positive placement to work with a step-child and make him or her feel secure with the family structure and have fun in a creative way.

South Node Quincunx: This suggests inhibitions in emotions with regard to the parties and a lot of excess baggage to work through in order to gain emotional security and trust. Look at the house placement to see where areas of activity may spur emotional security. This is on the part of both the South Node and Moon person, as they both need reassurances about each other. On the other hand, once worked through, it is a very satisfying experience.

North Node Quincunx: You may not have the difficulty that is suggested by the South Node-Moon placement; however, you feel as if you do. This is also a difficult aspect to work through, but you should find opportunity to do so.

The luminaries (Sun and Moon) are very strong when combined with a nodal axis placement. Although the other planetary placements are also very important in light of the Nodal axis, their actual house placement expresses where work is needed or can be very beneficial but not necessarily the same intensity as the connection of the luminaries to the Nodes. The luminaries, no matter what house they are in, are the strongest placements with which to work with your step-child or anyone in a personal relationship. The other planets must be looked at in light of the houses they are in and whether the aspect suggests an easy flow of energy or a difficult one.

For this reason, I will define the contact between the planet and the Node and you may apply the aspects/houses learned in previous chapters to them. For example, if you have a trine with your Mercury to your step-child's fifth-house South Node, you have a strong feeling of communication, perhaps through the arts or perhaps in a parent/child manner; this is a good place to start relating to this child. Help your step-child with creative projects or play games together and have fun in order to grow and gain mental trust and respect.

Mercury/Nodal Axis

There is a mental link, often teacher/pupil in nature. There may be a mentor relationship or business relationship. Idea exchange and sociability are important. Under affliction, mental growth can be hampered by single-mindedness.

Venus/Nodal Axis

You may feel there is unfinished romance if this is an adult relationship. With step-children, this is a feeling of financial security for the child and with the step-parent, a feeling of needing to afford that security. This is a very strong tie, and luxury around the house is also indicated. There may be trouble adapting to new circumstances with a South Node placement and according to Donna Van Toen in *The Astrologer's Node Book*, Venus-South Node suggests people from divorce or where the home is broken. Thus, if you have a Venus-South Node placement in synastry, you probably have a great empathy for each other in light of the broken home situation.

Mars/Nodal Axis

Assertiveness versus quarrels and over-compensation is the key here. Growth comes from the positive assertiveness rather than the arguing to get your way. The Mars person may tend to pick at the South Node person. Sports and game competitions are a good way to use this energy positively. Then both parties can express their enthusiasm and grow. There are a lot of male-female roles with this placement for adults, but I am limiting this to how to develop a good relationship with step-children. This is a challenging relationship. You must both adapt to grow.

Jupiter/Nodal Axis

This is a nice, friendly situation that can lead to growth, or the opposite if one person is a fanatical zealot. There are probably material rewards to the Node person but there can be greed if afflicted. There should be a philosophical exchange that leads to positive growth if not afflicted. Group activities are a good way to relate to your step-child. Get involved in something you both feel is worthwhile. This is also a teacher/student situation. If the child's Jupiter aspects your node, you will learn more from him or her than you think.

Saturn/Nodal Axis

Since Saturn is karmic in nature, Saturn with a node is doubly karmic and a very strong placement with which to deal. However, since both have karmic ramification, they can be quite complimentary. There is a tremendous range of response to each other, and a lot of learning and teaching. Both parties can limit each other. There is a lot of past baggage, as well as a complementary outlook on life. The upbringing of the step-child will play a major role in how these placements mesh. There is a lot of exchange of attitude and philosophies. Growth comes through hard work achieved together. On the other hand, if afflicted, opportunities for growth may be ignored or may be outrightly rejected. This is a placement of work toward growth at its best or else feelings of regret over the relationship may occur, in turn leading to stagnation.

Uranus/Nodal Axis

This placement suggests actions that are unusual, unique and abrupt. There is probably a lot of intensity. With this placement, look for generational themes that can help your relationship grow. You each have your own special way and there will probably be a lot of unexpected things happening over the years. All in all, this is a good placement to work together and gain a mutual respect.

Neptune/Nodal Axis

This placement suggests an innate empathy or sensitivity to the other person. There also may be a tendency to idealize the other person; you may have unrealistic expectations and then be disappointed. The key is to have empathy but try to be realistic about who you each are and not to confuse your emotions with another's emotions or confuse your individual feelings. There should be a very psychic connection.

Pluto/Nodal Axis

This is a more difficult placement than Uranus or Neptune. There is a reformational quality about the situation and it can be stimulating or there can be conflict. You are both looking to make the relationship better. However, there also can be a tendency toward jealousy on the part of the Pluto person. Rather than get bogged down in petty things, find something generational that you can both work toward in order to help you achieve a higher level of relationship.

Node/Node

According to Mohan Koparkar, this occurs with people around the same age or those who are eighteen to nineteen years apart. He feels it is not a major factor in synastry. However, if you are about eighteen or nineteen years older than your step-child, this is a good placement to look at for something you both find important and that can bridge the generation gap. It is a nice placement. If you have a conjunction, you also have an opposition, but I find the conjunction paramount.

Ascendant/Nodal Axis

There is a personal connection that is very nice and also has a very easy feeling to it. Even in opposition, this is not bad. According to Koparkar, as the South Node moves away from the Ascendant, there is an independence gained.

Midheaven/Nodal Axis

This is an almost father-child relationship with all of its ramifications. There is a nurturing aspect here, as well as strong family bonds. It is the parent-child or teacher-student feeling. This can be a good placement but also may express the usual difficulties of a parent and child as the child grows.

Vertex/Nodal Axis

This is a very strong placement. The Vertex suggests the type of people you draw to you. When combined with a node, it is a conscious karmic draw. The houses where the Vertex and Node are located show how you will work through this placement. For example, if it is in the third house, you may help your step-child with school work or help him to deal with his siblings, creating a strong bond between you. If it is in the fifth house, you may help the child creatively, sharing fun and again growing together.

Remember to look to the houses where the planet and Node are placed as a key to how to work effectively with them. I find that the house placement really tells the tale, more than do the signs of the planet and Node.

Chapter 6

John

LET'S LOOK AT JOHN (Figure 4) first since he is the oldest step-child. John has more planets in the tenth to the third houses, which suggests he will be personally in control of his life rather than letting others control him. Control is important to John. He also has more planets in the seventh through the twelfth houses, suggesting he may be a little more public than private in his lifetime. He has planets in three cardinal houses, suggesting action on his part during his lifetime. He has five planets in mutable houses, suggesting he is fixed in his ways, and only one planet in a succedent house, suggesting he is not necessarily controlled by others. He has a pretty good balance of four water, three air and two fire planets, but only one in an earth sign. Although for the most part the planets are balanced, there is a lack of planets in earth signs, suggesting emphasis on money or possessions. As you read further, you will see where control over money may be an issue. Two cardinal planets are in the house of money so there is definitely an emphasis here. There are two fixed planets and the remainder are mutable so there is a balance with the planets as well.

Ascendant/First House

John's rising sign or Ascendant is 0 Virgo. First of all, zero degrees suggests he is coming into this lifetime to begin something new or to learn the lessons of Virgo. With zero degrees, he has no direction or innate base from which he feels comfortable to begin this lifetime. There is nothing in past experience giving him a sense of direction for this time around. The Virgo lessons are that of practicality, responsibility, doggedness, attention to detail and attention to health issues.

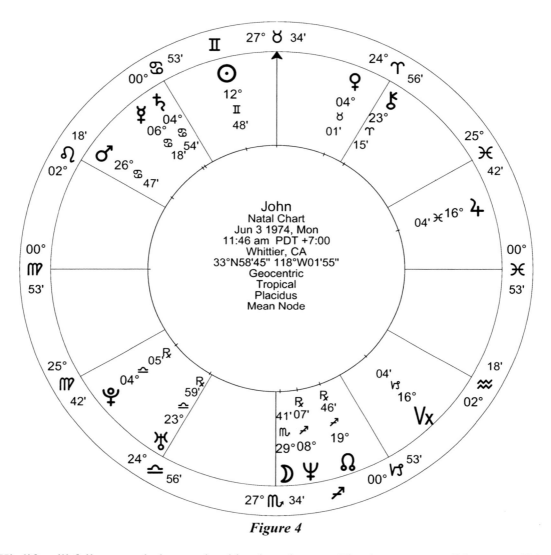

Figure 4

His life will follow a path that teaches him these lessons. That is not to say all lessons will be hard to learn; life is a learning experience, both difficult and fun. Since the Ascendant is how a person appears to others, John will often appear to the outside world as though he is paying attention and is responsible, even as he is learning to do so. As he grows, he will begin to learn how to own his Virgo rising and, hopefully, will learn it early rather than later. He wishes to be known for his competence.

Mercury rules John's rising sign and is located in his eleventh house of dreams, wishes, friends and groups. Thus, matters important to John personally would be those of the eleventh house and he would wish to appear responsible to any group he is associated with; his friends and wishes will have a practical quality about them. Mercury (ruler of Virgo) is in Cancer and he wants his family recognize his Virgo qualities as well. He also wishes to appear practical, responsible and dependable in the finances of any company or career he chooses.

The Ascendant is square the Moon in the fourth house or foundation, so we know a divorce will be more personally devastating for John than possibly for other children. It causes his emotions to creep in and undermine his logic and practicality.

The Sun and where John will shine is in the tenth house and this is a good placement with his Virgo Ascendant. His appearance of organization and competence is an asset in his career and will take him a long way. Since the Sun is in Gemini, he has the mental adaptability to go along with his practical nature to really succeed. As a step-parent, helping him recognize these strong points goes a long way in cementing the relationship. He may also have more than one career or one job at a time. He is mentally restless and this is a good thing for the tenth house since he will constantly be using his mind to improve his career or conditions around his career.

Second House of Money, Assets, Possessions and Personal Values

John also has Virgo on the cusp of the second. He will take a practical, responsible approach to these matters. His values are often reflected in his peer group or he has generational values with Pluto in the second house.

Pluto is in Libra. Learning to share is an important lesson. With Pluto here, control over money and assets is very important to John and he needs to lighten up just a little. Pluto is the first of the retrograde planets in this chart. Because it is in the second house, it suggests a core need for control over resources and a core fear of being vulnerable, either through lack of funds or psychologically. Money is a psychological control for John. He wants to do with his allowance as he sees fit and probably will spend it on a best friend as well as himself. But control is the big issue here. This is not a child to punish by taking away his allowance. As he grows up and marries, this trait of total monetary control will be very important and may be a big issue in the marriage. Also, with Pluto here, his personal values will be that of his generation and this reinforces the Ascendant placement. Pluto retrograde suggests his values or power through resources may have caused him trouble in the past and that he has lessons to learn this time around.

However, Pluto is square Saturn and Mercury in the eleventh house of friends, and since these signs are in Cancer, it suggests possible family obstacles with his friendships or with his wishes for the future. Pluto in Libra is ruled by Venus in the ninth house of higher philosophies, foreign matters and higher education. Thus, as a child he may be interested in foreign places or have a pen pal, and as an adult he may travel or be involved in finances with a foreign entity. Something foreign may be a fulfilling hobby. Also, higher education is very important to his self-worth, as well as something to help him acquire wealth. Since Pluto is square Mercury and Saturn in the eleventh house of dreams, wishes, friends and groups, he may feel frustrated with what is important to his value system in light of the group or friends. He also may feel frustrated about finances and his career. Pluto is also quincunx Venus in the ninth house so he may feel frustrated by his higher ideals and what he feels he should be doing. (Difficult aspects are where you have to work harder for what you want. Working through a square or opposition may actually be good for development and give you a sense of satisfaction.) Also, with Pluto in the second house, John will be very good at reorganizing finances and this ability may be a big help to him as an adult.

Uranus, his second retrograde planet, is also in the second house in Libra. This retrograde planet may suggest that he has a fear of commitment whether to things or people. His values will change throughout his lifetime. Since his Sun and the cusp of his tenth house is Gemini, a dual sign, there will probably be career changes. Uranus is unpredictable and changes may be sudden, as will changes in his commitments. In Libra, it suggests a need for balance and trying to change in order to keep balance in his life. Uranus in the second house suggests chaos and turmoil around finances. As a child he may spend on unusual things and it's unlikely anyone will be able to tell him how to save. Uranus is unpredictable so John may acquire money in unpredictable or unusual ways, or he may have windfalls followed by tight periods. Uranus is not bad though, since unexpected funds and change in personal values may be very good.

As a child, where other kids will have a lemonade stand, he will take a wagon to the store, get the lemons and sell them to the children, taking the rest of the day off while they work. His concepts are unusual. As an adult, financial independence will be very important and a sense of well-being may be tied to a sense of security. This is coupled with the Pluto desire for control. Fortunately, both Uranus and Pluto are in Libra so John will be charming in all ways he earns money. With Uranus retrograde there is a core inability to see his own need for unconventional ways. Thus, he has a karmic need for control and a karmic need to be different that, as a child, he probably does not grasp. This makes for inner conflict in both values and finances and is a lot to work through. When he learns to hear his inner, unconventional self, he will do well. He almost has an innate sense of insecurity that he may try to assuage with financial independence.

Both Pluto and Uranus are outer or generational planets, suggesting that as an adult John will feel fulfilled when doing something important to his generation, and as a child he will feel fulfilled when he is encouraged toward groups, scouts, a club or sports team. This sense of belonging is very strong and helps John develop.

John's Uranus is part of a T-square with Mars and Chiron. Mars is in the eleventh house, bringing in friends, wishes and groups and Chiron is in the eighth house of shared money or resources, intimacy, sexuality, the end of the matter, surgery and therapy. Since the eighth house is also joint assets with a spouse or partner, Uranus in the second house coupled with Pluto further suggests difficulty with shared assets or the desire to control. Chiron is a place that needs healing or is the teacher. Thus, his lessons to learn or lessons to teach are sharing as a child and appropriately handling joint finances as an adult. Chiron is in Aries, suggesting a lot of energy expended. Also, there may be lessons of a karmic quality with this placement and perhaps therapy would be helpful at some point in time. On the other hand, perhaps John is the one who is leaned upon for help or the one who administers therapy to others.

With so much Libra in the second house and its ruler, Venus, in the ninth house, the one caveat with this chart is how to make sure his friends do not lead him in a negative direction. This is all the more reason for John to get involved in supervised clubs and groups for positive growth. He is one child who is very heavily influenced by his friends or by groups even though he needs to be different and unconventional by nature. As an adult, this placement will give John a real conscious sense of how to handle the finances of the company for which he works and, with Venus in Taurus, he will be an asset to any business.

Third House of Conscious Mind, Short-Distance Travel and Elementary Education

John has Libra on the cusp of the third house so as a child he will probably weigh one thing against another again and again before making a decision. This is just a strong Libra trait and a parent must have patience. Thinking on all sides of an issue is a very good trait and important, so no one should not get frustrated when John cannot decide if he wants carrots or peas with his dinner. He will eventually make up his mind. Friends in elementary school are very important to him, as is his appearance. If there is a lot of yelling or fighting in the house, it will be very difficult for John to handle. He is the kid who needs reasoning rather than argument. It may take him a long time to agree, but he will consider all sides. This is true even as a teen. However, by that time he will have developed his ability to argue his point. As an adult, Libra is a very good sign to have in this house. It will reinforce and temper the Virgo analytical traits of his Ascendant. Libra is ruled by Venus in the ninth house, bringing in higher consciousness and personal philosophies to his conscious mind and perhaps a love of travel and things foreign.

Fourth House of Home and Foundation

This house is associated with the initial foundation upon which life is based, and John has Scorpio on the cusp; this sign is co-ruled by Mars and Pluto. The influence of John's friends is apparent with the ruler of Scorpio in the eleventh house, and Pluto suggests John wants more control at home and also that his home is tied to his value system. It is where he may learn how to do what will make him happy, as well as acquire wealth. This message comes through John's chart again and again: control, friends or group influences and values versus wealth or values that do not interfere with the acquisition of wealth.

The Moon is in Scorpio at a critical 29 degrees in John's fourth house. This is a kind of tough, emotional placement, especially for a child. As a child, John may have difficulty in expressing his feelings since this is both a Moon in the fourth house trait and a Scorpio trait. He may appear to want to nurture when, in fact, he needs the nurturing. He may feel a need to take care of siblings or pets or even his parents. Home is very important. At least one parent, probably his father, is very important in John's development into adulthood. Mother or father could be very capable and exemplify the independent worker, or may be overly emotional. This also suggests a possibility of drugs (prescription or not) and alcohol. Thus, father or mother is either a positive or a negative influence with regard to John's development. But whether positive or negative, at 29 degrees, John will be heavily influenced and grow in the end either because of or in spite of this influence. Either way, he must learn to be strong. This 29 degree Moon suggests a critical happening rocking his foundation which is probably his parents' divorce. This Moon degree indicates deep emotional responses, and its position suggests these responses are to the home and foundation. The Moon is trine Mars in the eleventh house and suggests no matter what the home situation, friends will be helpful in times of stress as well as times of joy.

The Moon is part of a T-square with the Ascendant along with the Midheaven (the cusp of his house of career), suggesting difficulty in personally reconciling himself with his home or foundation and his honor and career as an adult; or that home deeply affects his ego. This one placement also suggests why friends and groups are important to John. They do not exactly show up in this placement (as with other placements), but with this T-square it shows why they are a relief. Often a parent is both nurturing and loving, while at the same time negative in other ways, and this placement may just show both sides of the parent. It is difficult but rewarding if John takes the positive to form his foundational beliefs. The Moon in Scorpio also suggests working out power issues with a parent or with another figure in place of the parent such as a step-parent. Thus, a step-parent can understand John's need for control and give in a little so he can grow. John is a loyal family member. He also sees the hidden agendas of the other family members and will have insight into the family secrets that the parents may not wish him to have. He is also a little nosy around the house. This foundation is opposition the tenth house of career and John will have to overcome some insecurity from the broken home in order to realize honor and his full career potential.

Neptune in Sagittarius is also here and opposition the Sun and conjunct, by a wide orb, the Moon. Neptune is the third retrograde planet.

Neptune in the fourth house suggests he will be dreamy and idealize home life. He wants perfection or he may be prone to self-deception in order to cope. He will also have a lot of insight into what is going on behind the scenes of his home, or may be confused about them; at times it will be both. Neptune retrograde suggests a core need for calm in the home or John will have to find an escape; this is reinforced by the 29 degree Moon placement. The home must be a place to shut out the harshness of the outside world, so a divorce is highly stressful. It will be difficult for a step-parent to comfort this child. John needs guidance toward what is of value and the validity of his dreams. He also may dream of being free of home to do his own thing even at an early age. What faith he has in the goodness of mankind or the goodness of life comes from his early years of nurturing. The Moon combined with Neptune here suggests a lot of emotion and confusion for John as a child, especially at a very early age with the Moon at the critical degree. If he is not really nurtured at the outset, it may take him a little longer to become who he is meant to be in adulthood. Thus, a step-parent must be very patient and nurturing just as a parent must be. He is definitely the dreamer.

The North Node is also in Sagittarius in this house and is the fourth retrograde placement. With the Sun in the career house, John may shine and work harder toward his career and his career was important in past lives; but this time around, he must learn to relate to a secure home foundation and work through any negatives that show in his natal chart. Since the North Node is retrograde (the Nodes often are), this is a place of work throughout his lifetime—a double dose of karma. In other words, he must work with his tough Moon and Neptune placements toward a personal strong foundation in order to be really fulfilled. He may have to work long into adulthood for this. On the other hand, this difficult placement at the onset may also be very positive with a nurturing and insightful parent who helps John work into adulthood with balance between home and profession. There are two sides to each placement and either or both may occur at various times. Again, the North Node in Sagittarius suggests John may want freedom from home but will not achieve it until he learns to deal with it. This North Node is square Jupiter so he may be unbalanced in his actions at times. Since Sagittarius is ruled by Jupiter in John's seventh house of partnerships and marriage, he must watch balance with a spouse and home, and not idealize a situation only to be disappointed later on.

From these first four karmic retrograde placements we can see a life-long theme of a need for a calm, secure foundation coupled with a need for control of assets to feel secure. John's quest for these will probably be paramount throughout his life. There is also a core need for acquisition of assets to balance or be aligned with his personal values.

Fifth House of Creativity, Romance, Speculation and Children

John has Capricorn on the cusp of this house at zero degrees. Therefore, anything to do with these areas may be of critical importance to John, including his own children. Capricorn is ruled by Saturn in the eleventh house of dreams, wishes, friends and groups. Placed in Cancer, it suggests home and family are important to John's dreams for the future. He is willing to gamble and speculate for his wishes. He will probably take a plodding, practical approach to anything creative or speculative, and will be patient in child rearing. Children will be a source of security, as will investments. He may not outwardly appear romantic but he will be a practical and dependable partner and parent. He is likely to meet romantic interests through his friends or a group he belongs to, and may draw creative people toward himself with the Vertex here. Creativity is healing for John.

Sixth House of Work, Service and Health

John has Aquarius on the cusp of this house and no planets sit here. The ruler of Aquarius is Uranus retrograde in the second house of money, possessions, and personal values. Therefore, it is very important to John, almost a core need, that his work be of value to him, not just a way to make money. If he does not feel value, his health may even be affected. In Aquarius he may find unusual ways of making money and, moreover, will be at the forefront of technology in his field. His inventiveness may come out in work. However, his Sun and where he will shine is in his tenth house of career and honor and this says he should be able to earn outstanding achievements. As a child he must be free to work on his own in order to understand why he must do his work. Give him the choice of which chore he wants to do and he will do it. Eventually he will understand all chores must be done, although he will do them in his own way. He will be the first to want a computer.

Seventh House of Partners, Marriage and Binding Contracts

John has zero degrees on the Descendant, suggesting that partnerships and marriage are of great importance; but with Pisces, there may be more than one. Pisces on the cusp suggests that at the outset he may see his partner through rose-colored glasses and may not be realistic with regard to either a marriage or business partner. Since the cusp is at zero degrees, lessons learned this lifetime are of a partnership nature. The ruler of Pisces is Neptune retrograde in the fourth house of foundation and home. Therefore, it appears as though John is looking for a spouse with the same foundational values that he has and one who will give his adult home a good foundation. His home is very influential on the partners he chooses. He may consciously choose someone with the traits of a parent or he may consciously decide he wants someone totally different than a parent. His entire chart suggests a parental figure has a strong influence on who he becomes as an adult. Remember, Neptune is retrograde so this innate need for peace and calm is carried into the marriage and any conflicts in the marriage may result in separation. His spouse also must allow him a sense of freedom.

Jupiter in Pisces also sits in this house. This suggests he is looking for the perfect wife and perfect partnership. As a child he is an idealist and attracted to the mystical, fantasies and fairy tales. As an adult he may also look for this in a mate. With the Pisces influence and the Jupiter expansiveness, coupled with the fact that the ruler of Pisces is in the fourth house in Sagittarius (the sign that is also an idealist and wants freedom), when John's mate fails to live up to the fairy tale world in his mind, he will be disappointed and probably seek freedom. Although personally practical, he may not be so practical with regard to a spouse. This is a life lesson for John. He must get over any childhood problems, discard the rose-colored glasses and look for someone who will share his foundational values. This is not an easy lesson to learn. But, John has a strong chart and he will be able to transcend this lesson if he tries.

With Jupiter here, John sees the value in relationships and will go a long way to make them right. There may be a mystic quality to his partnerships and a joint seeking of universal good. Jupiter is square the Sun, suggesting there may be a conflict between marriage and career just as there is the opposition from the fourth house home and career. This just means that John must find an acceptable balance between what he is so good at from previous incarnations (his job) and what he is here to do now with regard to home, foundation and family matters. These lessons begin as a child, and although they do not have to be difficult or negative, they must be done. With Pluto and Uranus in Libra, hopefully John will find his balance sooner rather than later.

Eighth House of Shared Resources, Power, Investigation, Intimacy, Sex, Inheritance, Hidden Matters and the End of the Matter

John has Pisces on the cusp of this house, with its ruler in the fourth house in Sagittarius. This brings the home and foundation into yet another area of the chart. How his foundation was is how he will handle such matters as shared resources as an adult. Any problems or any really great sharing with regard to intimacy will also stem from his foundation. As an adult he can grow into a sharing relationship.

Chiron in Aries indicates the teacher or a lesson to be learned, and here involves intimacy; John or his spouse, or both, will learn the value of true intimacy. There also will be a lot of energy and fire with regard to eighth house issues. Chiron is square Mars in the house of dreams and friends, suggesting that with regard to finances, John's and his spouse's dreams may conflict and perhaps his spending on generational issues or on friends may affect his marriage. With Chiron opposition Neptune, the push-pull of joint resources and/or control thereof is also reinforced by this placement. Chiron in Aries also suggests someone who may be good at therapy or with investigation, perhaps as a teacher. This does not show up in a lot of other areas but is an option; since it is on the cusp of the ninth house, perhaps a workshop at college level comes into play.

Ninth House of Higher Philosophy, Religion, Law, Science, Higher Education, Travel and Foreign Matters

John has Aries on the cusp of this house, and the ruler, Mars, is in the eleventh house of dreams, wishes, friends and groups. As a young adult, a trip abroad with friends would be wonderful for John. As a child, anything foreign will broaden his horizons and expand his universe. He will approach higher education, personal philosophies of life and any travel with a lot of energy and drive. He has Venus in Taurus in this house, which suggests that even as a child, part of John's higher consciousness and philosophies may go toward sensual pleasure and nice things; but he also has high ideals and a desire for freedom. He should like to learn and will like things that are exciting. As an adult, these traits just increase and excitement may mean travel or nice things. If John is looking for the perfect partner, he may try again and again, and this placement reinforces the Jupiter in Pisces placement in the seventh house. If he finds a partner with his same beliefs and goals, he should be happy.

Comfort and physical gratification are also important, but he must watch for excess. Venus is inconjunct the fourth house retrograde North Node, so seeing how others live and looking at different cultures may help him deal with his own foundational values. With Venus sextile Saturn in the eleventh house, friends and groups help shape his personal philosophies. Venus is trine the Ascendant so higher education and travel are personally beneficial. He will probably have a very strong, personal philosophy of life, which may include some self-indulgence but also care for others.

Tenth House of Profession, Career, Honors and Authority

John has Taurus on the cusp of his tenth house, ruled by Venus in John's ninth house of higher consciousness, philosophy, higher education and foreign matters. This placement suggests that John would find any career dealing with foreign matters or travel fulfilling, as well as any career he achieves through higher education or perhaps something along the lines of philosophy or religion. Venus is in its ruler Taurus so anything that brings physical pleasure or beauty by way of career would also be rewarding. The Taurus cusp suggests John will be a steady worker and will not necessarily like change. He must have nice surroundings or probably will not be happy. If he does not receive higher education, he will learn on his own in order to advance.

John's Sun is in the tenth house so it stands to reason that John will shine career-wise. Also, the Sun is in the same house as his South Node, where he came from karmically, and this means that in previous lifetimes he shined in his career. Therefore, career endeavors are quite comfortable for John because his core feelings of ego and worth—the Sun—are in the career house. He should be a natural for a good career. According to Koparkar, the South Node here suggests he will contribute to society via business and economic growth. The Gemini Sun suggests John will have more then one choice of career and do more than one thing at a time. If not, he must have variety and activity in his career in order to be fulfilled. Gemini is an air sign ruled by Mercury in the eleventh house of groups, friends and wishes for the future. Taken one step further, Mercury is in Cancer so this placement suggests that part of John's honor or what is important to him this lifetime is that family be tantamount to career. So although he will shine in his career, family is also very important. John's identity is tied to what he is or to his profession and he will be a good authority figure. With the Sun in Gemini, he will be verbal and seek recognition for his mental abilities.

The Gemini Sun indicates a child who has to be very busy, going from one thing to another. This does not mean he is flaky but that his mind is so active he cannot stay too long in one place. It helps if at an early age the parent can begin directing him to finish a project by showing him another way to do it or, even better, by suggesting he try to find a better way himself. This will help in the early years of school. As stated earlier, the Sun is square Jupiter in the seventh house and John's career may at times be at odds with his marriage.

The Sun opposition Neptune retrograde indicates that at times his career may be at odds with his home life. Also, this opposition and the Scorpio Moon at a critical degree suggest that home life as a child may in some way be difficult to overcome; or, it could indicate insight and intuition concerning himself and how he can achieve. The fourth house is the derivative partnership house to the tenth house, so John should read partnership paperwork and contracts very carefully as there could be some confusion or even deception. Since John's Sun is in Gemini and he has a very quick mind, he can certainly make sure what he enters into is sound.

John has Cancer, the sign of the nurturer, on the cusp of the eleventh house, so if John is a step-parent, he should be very nurturing. Cancer is ruled by the Moon in the fourth house, suggesting John may also be a nurturer to his friends, even as a little boy. He may try to take care of any friend in need. In a group setting, he will be the one others come to for help. Saturn is in this house in Cancer. With Saturn in Cancer, as a child, although John has deep emotions, he probably will not be able to express them. He may look to his friends or groups for stability when he is a little older. As an adult, he may be stoic in expressing his emotions. With Saturn in the eleventh house, John will always identify with the group and although associations may cause obstacles at times for him, he probably will always be happy in a group setting.

John may feel limited by groups or friends at times and also probably feels some sense of obligation to his friends. His true friendships develop over a long period of time. Saturn rules Capricorn, which is on the cusp of John's fifth house. With this placement, John may have a sense of being friends with his own children or a need to be a friend to them. Any step-children will be a karmic link. Saturn is sextile Venus in the ninth house of personal philosophies so John will probably really share his generation's values. Saturn square Pluto retrograde was discussed earlier. Saturn in the eleventh house suggests he may feel he owes a debt to a particular group (an innate feeling) and in career suggests his attempt to repay this debt may interfere with his home life. He needs balance between the two.

Mercury is also in Cancer in the eleventh house sextile Venus and square Pluto retrograde. The first inkling of this placement probably occurred when John was quite little and everyone was in awe if his remarkable memory and vivid imagination. Creativity is a plus for John, and he needs to learn via all senses. As an adult John's mind will be open to ideas and he is not afraid to push the envelope, finding new ways of doing old things. He is imaginative and dreams are often quite revealing.

Again, the placements in Cancer emphasize the strong influence of the family on the child and how important it will be to the adult. John is prone to emotional thinking. Mercury is square Pluto retrograde in John's second house of money. With Mercury in the eleventh house, John will think about, communicate and often work with the finances of his career, and with this square to Pluto, he may feel he is not adequately compensated or that he must give too much for the good of the whole company. Power struggles or control over finances is again apparent. However, the squares are where John will learn to work hard to achieve his goals. We all learn through obstacles.

Mars is also in Cancer in this house. As a child, John was probably drawn to tantrums to express his feelings. Even as an adult his emotions may boil over. On the other hand, Mars in Cancer can suggest one who holds back feelings, which is the negative point of this placement. Both the adult and the child are seeking emotional security, and family is very important. With Mars in Cancer in the eleventh house, friends may often be thought of as family. If he has problems at home, this is his escape and will keep him sane. If things are going smoothly at home, this placement is beneficial and fun for John. The caveat with this placement is to watch for feelings that the world is overpowering for John and to recognize his own personal power. With Mars trine the Sun in his tenth house, John will have a lot of energy and drive toward success in his profession. He almost cannot fail.

Twelfth House of Subconscious Mind, Hidden Matters, Institutions and Mysticism

John has Leo on the cusp of the twelfth house which is ruled by the Sun in the tenth. There are no planets here, but by rulership John is subconsciously drawn toward career and honors. His South Node is in the tenth house so career and honors are his comfort zone. Leo is charming, the actor and showman, so John will be subconsciously drawn to being the important one, the center of attention in his career. Pride, integrity and honesty are natural traits for John, and an important career will give him a strong sense of worth.

We see two strong themes for John: power and control issues, along with career versus home and family issues, and a family foundation shaken to its core. This is what forms John the adult and takes him where he should go. Although the eighth house Chiron does not stand out a lot at first glance, it becomes important in light of his family members' charts and common eighth house lessons.

Chapter 7

Molly

MOLLY IS THE SECOND STEP-CHILD (see Figure 5). She has two cardinal planets in a cardinal house with a cardinal Ascendant, and is strong, energetic and active. Molly has three cardinal planets, a cardinal Ascendant and a cardinal Midheaven; three fixed planets; and four mutable planets. Therefore, her planets are quite balanced. She has four fire signs, two earth signs, three air signs and one water sign planet. The lack of water suggests possible difficulty in expressing emotions, perhaps seeking to be too self-sufficient and that emotional considerations in this lifetime are not as important to her as other pursuits. The planets are completely balanced between the left- and right-hand side of the chart so she is neither too much in charge nor too reliant on others; this is a perfect balance. There are seven planets below the horizon so she may be more comfortable in the background than in the foreground. However, with a stellium in the first house and a first house Aries cusp, she may overcome a desire to be in the background.

(While reading the delineations throughout the remainder of the book you will notice that themes are repeated again and again in the same chart and then often in the charts of family members. I may seem to repeat myself; this is because of the various placements that suggest the same theme. It is this reappearance of traits that lead to conclusions drawn in delineation, and is of particular importance in synastry between two charts.)

Aries Ascendant

The Ascendant is how Molly appears to others, to her family and her personality. Thus, with Aries rising, Molly appears to be the leader, the one who forges ahead with great energy, the in-

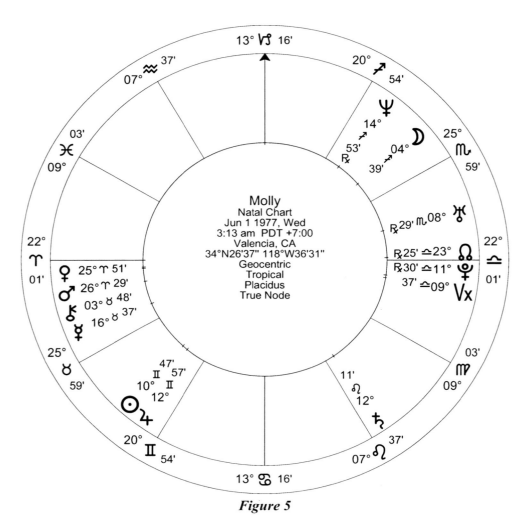

Figure 5

stigator, the one others follow. She may also be impatient or seem to lack consideration for others. Sports and physical games are important to the Aries energy, and Aries is independent. As the child grows into an adult, these Aries traits just become stronger. The first house is personal identity, how you take action and how the world sees you (much like the Ascendant which is the cusp of the first house).

The South Node is conjunct the Ascendant and retrograde. Thus, Molly is coming from a place of personal consideration and a lot of energy directed toward self-fulfillment; the retrograde makes these traits very strong. The South Node retrograde is opposition the North Node retrograde in the seventh house so partnerships and cooperation are the lessons to strive for. This

South Node retrograde is also conjunct Venus and Mars, making it a very strong placement with which to work. With the South Node conjunct Venus, Molly has tremendous energy, perhaps geared toward the arts and pleasure. This is her comfort zone, something she has done many times in the past. If a step-parent relates to her creativity, it will go a long way in the bonding process. According to Koparkar, the South Node in the first house suggests people who are an intellectual or creative impetus for society.

Molly has Venus in Aries in this house, complementing the previously mentioned creativity. However, she wants quick results for her energy. With Venus semisquare the Sun and Jupiter by a wide orb in the second house, Molly will have to reconcile her personal values with what she does and how she spends her money. She may tend to be extravagant and not save as much as she should. Venus is opposition the North Node retrograde, so artistic endeavors have been done before and this is what Molly feels comfortable with. What is a struggle and what she needs to work on this time around is partnership and balance (North Node in Libra in the seventh house). As an adult, Venus in Aries suggests the artist, musician, dancer and creator. She probably begins relationships quickly but is very independent. Molly's challenge is to balance her needs with the needs of others.

She also has Mars in Aries in the first house, giving Molly a double dose of energy. She may begin projects and get bored long before they are finished. The challenge is to find projects she can complete and feel good about before bouncing to something else. She may also have a temper. Mars in this house can suggest a combative child, but dance, sports and physical activity can help direct her in a positive manner. Her energy is a challenge for any parent or step-parent who cannot keep up. She will become an independent adult with a strong identity, retaining the abundant energy. Although Molly may anger quickly, she cools down just as fast. Mars is also semisquare the Sun in her second house, suggesting that personal values and finances may be an obstacle to personal action at times.

Chiron is also in the first house in Taurus, suggesting lessons of over-indulgence or seeking too much comfort. Since Taurus is ruled by Venus, also in this house, these lessons are very personal. With the South Node and Chiron both in the first house, lessons of selflessness, sharing and giving are important. Chiron opposition Uranus also suggests personal lessons dealing with partnerships, and they may be unexpected or very unusual. Chiron is quincunx the Moon in the eighth house, suggesting difficulty in projects concerning other people's money or perhaps intimacy issues which would go hand in hand with this lifetime's work in the partnership area. In fact, this is probably Molly's life lesson. It is interesting that this is also one of her brother's lessons; both were born into the same household. On the other hand, she may also be the teacher and help a partner in these areas. Remember, Chiron is either the teacher or the lesson to learn. Or, perhaps she and a partner would teach each other at different times in their relationship.

Mercury is in the first house in Taurus, indicating that Molly thinks things through, steadily and thoroughly. This placement also suggests a more sedentary or calm child so it can somewhat balance all the Aries. Also, this placement suggests a love of the arts and perhaps music or singing, as well as active Aries dance or sports programs. But this placement can also mean that Molly tends to get into a rut at times. All in all this is a good, strong first house. Mercury in Taurus brings in business skills and money acumen along with the artistic side. This placement suggests a quick and active mind, but she may be self-indulgent under stress.

Wherever there is a stellium of plants in one house, this is where strong emphasis on life will be. Therefore, personal action is very strong in Molly's chart.

Second House of Money, Possessions and Personal Values

Molly has Taurus on the cusp and Taurus is ruled by Venus in the first house. This immediately suggests Molly has strong personal values and will probably feel the need to earn her own money and acquire her own assets. How she makes money must not conflict with her personal values.

Molly has the Sun in Gemini in the second house. This suggests she will shine with regard to her personal value system, as well as the accumulation of wealth and assets. The Sun is opposition the Moon in the eighth house of other people's money so there may be tension over joint finances (a common theme with her brother as well). As a child, the Sun in Gemini suggests that Molly will always have to be doing more than one thing at a time and as an adult will probably do that with regard to making money. She is quick-witted, a lot of fun and a handful as a child. With the Sun in the second house, Molly's possessions are very important. Moreover, the Sun is part of a yod. In Molly's case both the Sun and Jupiter in the second house are sextile Saturn in the fifth house of creativity and quincunx the Midheaven. Therefore, with the yod and Saturn in the house of creativity, she feels a karmic link and at home doing something creative, possibly in her future career. Saturn suggests hard work or obstacles, but this should not stop Molly.

The fifth house is also speculation and children, which could be viable careers for Molly, but with Venus in the first house of personal effort and planets in Taurus, creativity is very strong. Creativity can be anything artistic or creative such as writing, music, dance, singing or art. So if you look at the South Node in the first house as where Molly is coming from and Saturn as a karmic planet in the house of creativity, combined with the Sun and Saturn pointing toward the career house, you begin to get a sense that even as a child, Molly is directing herself to where she is comfortable. She has been there before and it is what she is good at. The trick this time is to combine the yod with the seventh house of relationships. Think of the yod as a yellow marker highlighting a very viable path. One does not have to follow the path but it is there for the taking. Back to the Sun in the second house, Molly's self-esteem is tied to her sense of self-worth. She may at times spend impulsively and in Gemini will have more than one iron in the fire at a time to make money. She prides herself on versatility and intellect and is quite verbal.

Jupiter, planet of opportunity and expansion in Gemini, is in the second house and part of the yod. Molly should have a lifetime of opportunity if she works very hard (hard work is the Saturn part of the yod). Jupiter in Gemini suggests a child who has high ideals, is a quick learner and is skillful. In the second house it suggests that sensual pleasures and the accumulation of personal possessions and money are important. As an adult, Jupiter in Gemini continues with a large range of interests and a desire to mentally explore nearly all areas of life. Jupiter here as an adult suggests Molly values security and comfort, and feels she will always be able to get that from life. She is accepting and desires pleasure. Jupiter and the Sun in Gemini in the second house gives Molly both high ideals and the drive to get what she wants.

Third house of Conscious Mind, Siblings, Lower Education and Short-Distance Travel

There are no planets in this house, and Gemini on the cusp indicates an active, agile mind. Ruled by Mercury in the first house in Taurus, comfort is important to Molly's peace of mind. Her scattered, active Gemini mind is somewhat stabilized by Mercury in Taurus and this gives her effective mental ability, both active and stable. She is active around siblings and may try to out-smart them. Brothers and sisters will see two sides of Molly and not know where she is coming from. She should do well in school.

Fourth House of Home and Foundation

There are no planets in the fourth house and the cusp is Cancer, which suggests a homebody or that Molly may tend to crawl into her shell under adversity. Home and family are important. Cancer's ruling planet, the Moon, is in the eighth house. Placed in Sagittarius, it suggests that although home is important to her, she may also wish to escape at times. Also, her idealism may come from the home situation. But, very importantly, the eighth house is that of hidden matters and intimacy, joint finances and investigations, and this suggests some things may be hidden at home or intimacy may be a foundational concern. Although not so strong in this chart, after looking at brother's chart with Neptune, it does seem that control of joint finances and intimacy issues may be of concern to Molly as well. On the other hand, the Moon in Sagittarius is a good placement for adventure, philosophy and idealism, looking outside oneself for inspiration and looking to higher education or travel for fulfillment. These things will also come from the home and foundation.

Fifth House of Creativity, Speculation, Romance and Children

Molly has Leo on the cusp of the fifth house and its ruler, the Sun, in the second. This suggests that in fifth house areas she brings a lot of personal values into play. Whatever she does creatively or speculatively must conform to what she personally feels is important. She may make money using her creativity, and children will be of great value to her and she will treasure them.

Saturn is a karmic planet. It determines where hard work should be placed and where Molly can accomplish a lot in this lifetime through hard work. It also indicates where Molly may meet obstacles. Saturn in the fifth house in Leo suggests something to do with creative arts such as acting, dance, theater, music and art that is shown to the world. With Saturn here, Molly has been creative in the past; it is what she is good at and where she can excel with hard work. In matters of speculation she will want something creative and exciting for her investments. With regard to children, her children will be a definite karmic link and very active with the Leo influence. They may also be difficult with Saturn here—but worth it. Whatever Molly chooses, she will be very practical and energetic about it, and will work steadily toward her goals. As a child Saturn here suggests Molly will want to be very sure of herself before she shows her stuff. She may feel inhibited with her creativity until she is sure she has it right. Molly's creativity may be structured and well planned. Since Leo is ruled by the Sun which sits in her second house of money and personal values, she is likely to make money through her own creativity and speculation but she must do what has personal value to her. Since Saturn is trine the Moon in the eighth house, Molly will bring her emotions into her creativity and since this is the house of joint resources and other people's money, she may receive funding of some sort. Taken one step further, the Sagittarius Moon suggests she must have freedom in her creativity. Molly may feel a little tied down (more than most) if she has children (even though she would highly value them) so she will need to plan very carefully for them.

Saturn is square Mercury in her first house, suggesting hard work and thoughtful planning. Saturn is sextile Jupiter and the Sun in her second house, again bringing personal values into her creativity. Creative endeavors may provide her with a good income as well as personal satisfaction. If Molly were to go the speculative route rather than the creative one, she would do well to invest in areas that have to do with creativity. More important for the child, Saturn rules Capricorn which is on the Midheaven, suggesting honors and recognition may come from creative and artistic areas. Creativity is a good place to develop a strong ego. Molly's step-parent may wish to encourage Molly in creative endeavors and help her gain recognition, as this will go a long way in the bonding process. As an adult, honors may also come to Molly through the creative process.

With Saturn it is important to look at Saturn returns to see if Molly's growth is on track. Saturn suggests a place where she begins a long-term project that requires a lot of work or a place where work of the past comes back to her, either successfully or unsuccessfully. Therefore, around age twenty-eight, was she on track with what she was seeking creatively? Have years of past work paid off and is she coming into a career or some type of artistic endeavor that she is happy with or does she have children she is proud of? If so, then the next twenty-eight years will be a reinforcement, stabilization and fulfillment of a career and some creative endeavor or perhaps children that she is proud of. If she is not there yet, she should spend the following few years catching up so at the next Saturn return, she will be proud of her accomplishments.

Saturn is square Uranus retrograde in the seventh house. There may have been past chaos around partnership versus the arts, creativity or children that cries out to be worked through. Thus, personal creative efforts or motherhood should not be at the expense of the partnership.

Remember, Saturn and retrograde planets suggest heavy, past conditions. Uranus in Scorpio again brings in the intimacy or joint resource issues, as well as therapy, investigation or hidden matters. However, Saturn is trine retrograde Neptune in the eighth house, suggesting a good energy flow for working out relationship matters via eighth house issues, and helping to lessen the Saturn blocks.

Sixth House of Work, Service, Health and Pets

Molly has Virgo on the cusp of this house. Ruled by Mercury in her first house, it indicates personal effort and energy directed toward work and service. Also, since Mercury is in Taurus and Virgo is also an earth sign, Molly really has a double dose of steady, reliable, plodding movement toward her work goals, and she wants nice surroundings in her work. She has great attention for detail and may be concerned with health and a desire for cleanliness. She will be very good at detail oriented work.

Pluto is in the sixth house in Libra. Since Pluto is an outer planet and often represents generational issues, Molly may choose to work in something important to her generation. As a child, since Pluto represents control, Molly would want control over what she does, be it school work, home work and chores. She wants to make her own structure. This is one place that a step-parent can really create a bond: give her enough room to have some control and as she shows maturity, give her more and more space. This will create a very good understanding with Molly. With Pluto in Libra Molly will focus on fairness and relationships through work and service. Regarding generational issues, Pluto in Libra from 1971 through 1983, saw further political reform for minorities, and the excessiveness and overindulgence demonstrated in the 1980s. These areas may be of interest to Molly. Libra is ruled by Venus which sits in Molly's first house, suggesting that she will personally work hard and since Venus is in Aries, she will probably work tirelessly and with great enthusiasm in whatever she chooses to do.

Pluto is trine the Sun and Jupiter in Molly's house of personal values, further reinforcing that she may work toward the values she has acquired from her generation. It is also sextile Saturn in the fifth house of creativity so here is another placement suggesting creativity as a viable option for Molly's work. It is sextile Neptune in the house of shared resources or other people's money, suggesting work that is funded by others or, perhaps, with Saturn in the fifth house of speculation, some type of investment work. Since Pluto is retrograde, there are deep-seated control issues; this is also indicated by the conjunction with the Vertex. No matter how many people are around, Molly needs to work independently. Powers of regrouping for her job are strong, and she may have a deep desire to work with animals. Her lesson is to let go a little and watch out for manipulative actions in the work arena. Since Pluto and the Vertex are in Libra, she will demonstrate a lot of tact and charm with coworkers.

Seventh House of Partnership, Marriage and Contracts

Molly has Libra on the cusp of this house ruled by Venus in the first house, suggesting partnership and marriage are personally important and that she will work hard toward success in this area. Molly has the North Node retrograde here, indicating partnership issues are something she should work on in this lifetime. In Libra, a dual sign, she may tend toward more than one partner in this lifetime or perhaps be indecisive about a partner. The North Node is opposition Venus, Mars and the South Node retrograde in the first house so partnerships may be difficult and require a lot of give on Molly's part. With the North Node retrograde in the seventh house, there is an innate attraction to any partner. Uranus retrograde is also in this house in Scorpio. As a child Uranus retrograde in the seventh house suggests Molly will be attracted to children who are unusual and exciting as well as those who are outside her norm. Parents should expect the unexpected when she brings friends home and just enjoy them as she does. As an adult, this will become an attraction to unexpected people, chaos in relationships and perhaps quick changes in relationships. This placement makes the North Node a little more difficult because of the types she is attracted to. She may be torn between a desire for freedom and breaking the rules or maintaining the relationship, or her partner may feel that way. Anyone she marries must give her a sense of freedom and keep things new and unexpected. She needs friendship with her marriage partner since Uranus rules the eleventh house, as well as an exciting sensual, sexual world because Uranus is in Scorpio. There will be something unique as to how they share their lives. Uranus is square Saturn in the house of creativity, speculation and children so Molly may have obstacles with a partner in these areas. In the past she may have had to take sides between a paratner and a child and may have difficulty again.

Eighth House of Joint Finances, Power, Taxes, Inheritance, Intimacy and Investigation

Molly has Scorpio on the cusp of this house. Scorpio is the natural detective of the zodiac and since this is the house of in-depth investigation, her natural curiosity and ability to ferret out the truth is quite strong. Scorpio is co-ruled by Mars and Pluto in her first and sixth houses so she would make a good investigator or therapist. She has the Moon in this house opposition (wide orb) the Sun and Jupiter so there tends to be a degree of difficulty between Molly's personal finances and shared resources. The Moon in Sagittarius suggests she wants to be free of restriction in shared finances or perhaps free to express intimacy her own way (or freedom from intimacy). As a child, she needs freedom for adventure and to do with as she pleases with her allowance. Sharing may not be her strong suit.

As an adult, Molly may desire to travel, and emotional security may come from a knowledge of the world as well as from intimacy with a partner. She is naturally intuitive and will just know when she meets her mate. There also may be fluctuation in joint resources and extravagance with the Moon in Sagittarius. Early nurturing, especially from her mother, may play a key role in who she bonds with now, and her mother can have a great impact whether she is nurturing and secure or fearful and manipulative. Since Molly also has a full-time step-mother, she receives the imprint of both mothers. Part of Molly's learning process this time is to learn to handle and cope with deep-rooted emotions, forgive and go on with her life. With the Moon in Sagittarius, she may idealize rather than face reality. And with the Moon opposition her Sun and Jupiter in her second house, her personal values may be consciously developed. The eighth-house Moon suggests there may be hidden matters surrounding the mother figure or issues of vulnerability. Her mother may have been nurturing of her independent and curious spirit. There are always two sides to a coin and the individual may choose either side to relate to and grow from.

Neptune in Sagittarius is also retrograde in this house. This planet suggests imagination and possibly idealizing someone or something, even to the point of traveling far to find it or the perfect person. Avenues of escape are also a caveat with this placement since they tend to make one feel something may be better than it is. Molly is definitely an idealist. Neptune in Sagittarius indicates Molly may see freedom and high moral values as important or she may idealize her mate. She wants both the perfect person and the freedom to do as she pleases. Neptune can also mean deception or self-deception. It is important to look at everyone realistically and not through rose-colored glasses. She may be inclined to compulsion or obsession, and probably displays strong intuition. Molly is probably looking for a mate to share everything; however, this placement opposition the Sun and Jupiter in the second house also wants personal control of shared assets or joint resources. With Neptune retrograde here, Molly may not realize she is sending out this dual message. The lessons here are equality and personal values versus shared values. Neptune is sextile Pluto, so she may meet someone through work. It is trine Saturn in the fifth house of creativity, so Molly may find true harmony through joint creativity and/or children.

Ninth House of Higher Education, Travel, Foreign Matters and Higher Consciousness

Molly has no planets in this house, and Sagittarius is on the cusp. Sagittarius is the idealist and visionary, the freedom-loving traveler. These are the traits Molly brings to ninth house matters. Thus, her ideals are strong and important to her. Sagittarius is ruled by Jupiter, which sits in her house of personal values, reinforcing her elevated value and belief system. Jupiter is expansion and opportunity so she should have opportunity to travel. Molly feels she is not doing enough unless she is doing more than one thing at a time.

Tenth House of Career, Profession and Honor

Molly has no planets in this house, and Capricorn is on the cusp. The cusp of this house, the Midheaven, is part of the yod focused on her second and fifth houses, pointing toward this house. So, even if she has no planets in this house, it is very strong because of the yod. Although most of her planets sit below the horizon, which suggests she will work more in the background than the forefront, because of this Yod her chart is actually very strong for career and she may indeed work in the foreground and be known. She has the choice as to which she wishes to do: work in the background or take advantage of the yod and bring the energies of her Sun, Jupiter and Saturn into this tenth house of public recognition, honor and career. Again, since her planets sit where they do, the arts and finances are strong career options. With that in mind, Capricorn is ruled by Saturn, which sits in Molly's fifth house of creativity, further reinforcing a creative career for her. Also, Saturn in her house of speculation and investments should be lucrative. Although at first glance her career does not seem to be a strong, it is actually a very strong point. This also goes along with the fact that this time around, career comes naturally and partnerships are where she needs to work. This is not to say to let the career go, but while she is having a magnificent career, she shouldn't neglect to work on relationships and put her energy there as well. Career is her comfort zone and relationships are her work zone. Because of Aquarius on the cusp of her eleventh house she could also have a technology career.

Eleventh House of Dreams, Wishes, Friends and Groups

Molly has Aquarius on the cusp of this house and so is drawn to friends and groups that have advanced ideas, perhaps new technologies or new ways of doing things. Molly will be drawn to technology and should be good at it as well. Aquarius is ruled by Uranus in her seventh house of partnerships and contracts so she will may meet her spouse or business partners through groups endeavors or friends, all of whom will probably be unusual, do the unexpected and the like. With regard to the money house of her career, there are probably contracts or partnerships or groups associated with finances; funding will come from unusual means.

Twelfth House of Subconscious Mind, Hidden Matters and Institutions

With Pisces on the cusp, Molly's imagination if very active and she probably also has vivid dreams. Pisces tends to idealize or feel the problems of the world upon their shoulders so Molly should be cautious about making everyone's problems her own. This can be very draining. She may be drawn subconsciously to people she feels need saving or those considered the underdog. Since Molly tends to be idealistic, she may actually end up being a victim in a relationship. The key here is to look for balance in relationships. Pisces is ruled by Neptune in the eighth house in Sagittarius, another idealistic influence. She should watch getting bogged down in either her mate's or other family member's problems. Don't let prescriptions or alcohol be a problem and this problem may not be hers but becomes a problem when trying to help others. The higher self represented by the Pisces nature can work for the ultimate good if Molly doesn't let others get her down. The best part of this placement is such an innate, vivid imagination and creativity. It really goes along with and reinforces Molly's chart.

All in all, Molly has a really strong, creative chart with a lot of potential in business and technology. She has a lot of good things to work with that can add to the strength of relationships and those areas that she is looking to work with this time around.

Like her brother, Molly has a lot of karmic placements in her chart. This is really a good thing when step-parenting because you have readily identifiable places to look to where one can bond, help Molly grow and realize her potential. Karmic placements may at times be difficult for the individual, but they are great for insight. Molly's areas to reconcile, much like her brother, are a push-pull between self and relationships, control versus intimacy and control over joint finances. These two siblings alone give much insight into the family dynamic.

Chapter 8

Mary

MARY IS THE STEP-MOTHER of John and Molly. Her natal chart is Figure 6. Mary has two planets below the horizon and six planets above it. Thus, she has the potential to be a public person and to working more in the public than in private. Her planets are evenly balanced on either side of the chart, suggesting she is not controlled by others but is flexible and will listen to them. She has five cardinal planets, three fixed planets and two mutable planets. Five cardinal planets suggests a lot of activity and perhaps a taxed nervous system. There are three fire planets, two earth planets, two air planets and three water planets so elements are well balanced, indicating a balanced person with a lot of potential to shine in the public eye.

Sagittarius Ascendant

This Ascendant suggests that Mary appears idealistic, benevolent, broad-minded and with a strong sense of freedom, and possibly aloof or detached at times. This is her personality and how she appears to the outside world; it is the persona she carries. It is also her persona in the family situation or how the family perceives her. However, her family will know her better and her high sense of idealism will be very important to the family. Sagittarius is ruled by Jupiter in the third house of communication and mental ability, so expanding her mind is probably very important to her and she should communicate well with others. The Ascendant is part of a grand trine with the Sun and North Node. This is quite interesting in light of the charts of her step-son, step-daughter and husband. These charts suggest eighth-house issues such as intimacy, power and control over joint finances, investigation, therapy or research, all of which appear to be life

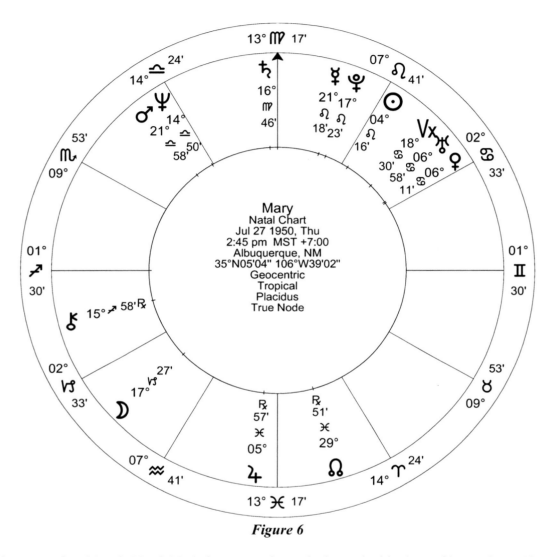

Figure 6

lessons. Also, Mary's North Node is retrograde so she has a double dose of karma here. Since this is part of a grand trine, it appears as though Mary may be of great assistance to the entire family in issues of the eighth house. In other words, her chart dovetails into the domestic life of the pre-existing family unit.

Chiron in the first house is retrograde and square karmic Saturn in the tenth house of profession, career and honors. This is an interesting square because the South Node (also karmic) is in the tenth house. Therefore, career and honor is what Mary is good at, has done before and is very comfortable with; and personal lessons of home and freedom are what she is working toward.

With a square to Saturn, there may be obstacles in the career path and this may actually make is easier to choose something other than a career outside the home. Saturn suggests she needs to work on something careerwise but since traditionally the tenth house is the mother perhaps that could be a big part of this placement. Chiron suggests personal healing throughout her lifetime.

Chiron is trine Mercury in the ninth house, so philosophy, idealism, higher education, travel and foreign matters are personally important to Mary.

Chiron is also in the first house in Sagittarius, and since Chiron is the teacher or the lesson to learn, it suggests there may be personal lessons with regard to freedom or idealism or she may be here to help others with lessons of freedom and idealism. Chiron is retrograde, suggesting Mary may take it onto herself to help others or be the teacher and try to express the high ideals of Sagittarius to others. Chiron here suggests a lot of personal responsibility.

Second House of Money, Possessions and Personal Value System

Capricorn is on the cusp of the second house, and ruled by Saturn in the tenth house. Since this is the house of personal values, Mary's career must be personally fulfilling and rewarding and meet her personal standards as to what is of value. Hard work is also indicated. Capricorn suggests accounting, law, business and the like as good sources of income and rewards.

The Moon is also here in Capricorn, indicating fluctuation; but since it is in an earth sign, there is not as much fluctuation in finances as there could be in another sign. The Moon also suggests emotions over assets, and a need for physical comfort and material security. Mary is emotionally serious and stable, and nurturing leads her to accept responsibility at an early age so hard work just comes naturally. Also, Mary may feel inhibited in her emotional response to others or inhibited with intimacy issues. The Moon in Capricorn is a very good placement for business acumen. The Moon's natural sign, Cancer, is prominent in the eighth house of joint finances, so there may be emotional issues concerning joint finances. At the very least, joint assets are very important to Mary, and anything she does for income or to acquire possessions must also meet with her standards regarding home and family. The Moon is trine Saturn so she should be able to personally acquire assets that meet her needs; but it will require hard work and long term planning. The Moon is square Mars, suggesting tension around assets and dreams for the future, and square Neptune, suggesting some sort of veil over assets, perhaps a lack of full understanding.

Third House of Conscious Mind, Communication, Lower Education, Siblings

Mary has Aquarius on the cusp suggesting she is far-thinking and an independent thinker, and that new technologies appeal to her. Aquarius is ruled by Uranus in her eighth house so eighth house matters such as joint assets, intimacy, power, hidden matters are all subjects of interest. Mary will be mentally attuned to the issues of her step-children with the emphasis on eighth house issues in their charts. Jupiter is in this house in Pisces and trine Venus in the eighth house, strengthening the Aquarius cusp with its ruler also in the eighth house. Since Venus is in Cancer conjunct the ruler of the third house cusp, thoughts also run to home and foundation. This is what is consciously important to Mary. Jupiter here suggests that she has an ever-expanding mind and that she is always learning. Teaching is also a good option with this placement. Mary tends to trust her logical reactions over emotional ones. There is a lot of communication with siblings, and Jupiter in Pisces suggests an empathetic nature. She also probably has very intuitive dreams, and a strong faith, conventional or not.

Jupiter is retrograde here and it may take quite a while before Mary can express herself as she would like. Although she will develop an expansive relationship with siblings, she will probably do that as an adult. There is a definite debt owed to siblings which she will pay over her lifetime.

Fourth House of Home and Foundation

Mary has Pisces on the cusp of this house. Pisces is ruled by Neptune in her eleventh house of dreams, hopes and wishes, friends and groups. With Pisces there, the foundation that is important to Mary would be compassion and sensitivity to others. Also, friends are probably very welcome in her home and her dreams and wishes for the future center around family. Since Mary has the North Node here, home and foundation are what is important in this lifetime, and with the North Node retrograde, Mary gets a double dose of its importance. With Pisces in this house, Mary's home and foundation are probably where she has the most insight and where she dreams. There also may be problems with prescription drugs, alcohol or the like, as well as overly emotional persons or someone who sees the world through rose colored glasses, or does not face reality well. Some foundational influence (male or female) may be a lot to cope with but he or she really affects who Mary becomes.

Where Pisces appears in a chart does not mean there is a drug or alcohol problem, but there is the potential. The potential for insight and dreams is just as strong, as these are two sides of a coin. Remember, drugs do not necessarily suggest a drug problem per se but perhaps there may be a needed prescription or too many prescriptions are prescribed at times. There also may be confusion or lack clarity of foundational values at times. Whatever the fourth house holds, it is a very important part of Mary's life since it contains her North Node. Also, remember this North Node is part of the grand trine with the Ascendant and Sun in the eighth house of shared resources, suggesting again that shared assets and intimacy, and all eighth house issues, as well as home and foundation are very important.

It is interesting to note that step-son John has the Moon at 29° Scorpio (critical degree) in the fourth house. Mary's North Node is retrograde at 29° Pisces in her fourth house. These placements are trine each other so you can see there is a great deal of empathy between them even before going into the synastry placements. Both will have critical things happen on the home front that greatly affect them. The Moon trine North Node is a core understanding of each other.

Fifth House of Creativity, Speculation, Romance and Children

Mary has Aries on this house cusp; it is ruled by Mars in her eleventh house. This brings her step-children into the house of her own children or, in other words, she may literally become their mother. Since I know Mary and her spouse had custody of her step-children, this placement is very appropriate. This cusp also brings friends and groups into creative or speculative areas. In fact, creativity is one very strong way for Mary to relate to her step-children. Anything creative or artistic she can do with them or help them do will create a sense of fulfillment in their relationship. These are areas Mary and her step-children can relate to with each other to form a strong bond. Also, Mars is in Libra in the eleventh house so balance is important to their relationship. Mars is fiery and energetic and may be combative so it is important to focus this tremendous energy into positive areas rather than combat or tension. Mary should be able to find a balance with Mars in Libra. But with Mars square Mary's Moon in her house of money and personal values, she may have conflict over how money is spent or in relating her values to her step children.

Sixth House of Work, Service, Health and Pets

Mary has Taurus on the sixth house cusp; it is ruled by Venus in Cancer in her eighth. Cancer suggests work, service and health issues may be related to home. Also, since the eighth house, where the ruler of Taurus lies, is that of intimacy, shared resources, hidden matters and power issues, her work may be in these areas. When you look at the charts of her step-children and Mary's other placements, you get a very strong sense of work in these eighth house areas. With Taurus on the cusp, Mary would feel fulfilled with work relating to any type of business and also with something creative. Since Taurus is ruled by Venus, creativity and beauty are important in the workplace. With the ruler in the eighth house, one possible field is investments or perhaps tax work.

But if Mary were to go the business route, rather than the creative route, she would need lovely surroundings in order to be happy. Taurus on the cusp of this house suggests Mary may work in a methodical, plodding manner, slowly and steadily getting to where she wants to go but with determination. And with Taurus ruled by Venus in her house of shared assets, she may work with a partner or share assets with her spouse and either work with him or work in the home as part of her shared responsibilities. Since Venus is in Cancer, it is very likely that the home will be her workplace or she may work out of the home on projects. Taurus rules the neck and throat so with regard go health, she should watch for problems in these areas.

Seventh House of Contracts, Partnerships and Marriage

Mary has Gemini, a dual sign, on the cusp of this house, suggesting she may have more than one partner or perhaps a marriage and business partner. In any event, if she has one spouse in her lifetime, he will have a very active mind, must be doing things all the time, and will communicate quite well. Communication is very important to their partnership. Gemini is ruled by Mercury in her ninth house so her partner must share her philosophies and probably will be well educated. Foreign travel would also be fulfilling for Mary and her partner, and business dealings with a foreign company or foreign persons is also a possibility.

Eighth House of Shared Resources, Intimacy, Hidden Matters, Investigations and Therapy

Mary has Cancer on the cusp of this house, ruled by the Moon in the second house, so shared assets are brought into personal assets. Her personal values are shared by a partner. She has three planets in this house: Venus, Uranus and the Sun, which is where Mary will shine. The Vertex in this house indicates other people and Mary's involvement with them, as there is a karmic quality to the Vertex in that others help us complete ourselves. Although Mary has free choice to follow her Vertex placement, it is very strong and one that many just fall into rather than consciously select. Since the Vertex is in Cancer in the eighth house, it appears that part of who Mary is deals with intimacy issues, shared assets, hidden matters, investigations, therapy, etc. In Cancer, the home and foundation are involved. *This sounds very much like a homemaker who shares assets and helps others to understand eighth house issues: power struggles over joint finances, passion and sex, strength in facing and working on the dark side within yourself and others, in depth or covert investigations and the like.*

Since I know a little about Mary's life, I know she is truly living her chart in her role as a step-mother as well as a mother. The eighth house issues faced with the members of her family as shown in previous charts fall right in line with her eighth house placements. If she did not marry into this particular family, she would have married into a family just like it. This is where Mary appears to be needed for herself and her family: spouse, children and step-children.

Although there is no stellium in this house, there is a stellium if you consider the Vertex. This is where most energy will be expended. Venus is here in Cancer, suggesting Mary wants a lot of passion with her mate and one of them may have lessons in sharing or they may have a very sharing relationship with regard to assets. However, with the Vertex opposition the Moon, it may be more of the former at first until this lesson is learned as the years evolve. Mary or her partner may be selfish or self-absorbed or they may be very sharing and motivate each other, or it may be a little of each at different times.

Since Mary's spouse is a Taurus and ruled by Venus, if he is self-absorbed at first, he should learn to share and motivate. Venus in Cancer suggests Mary really is fulfilled by home, family and food, and that her security is in the family and nurturing. She is probably cautious with family assets, and desires closeness. Venus is trine Jupiter in Mary's third house, suggesting easy family communication. Also, since Jupiter is in Pisces, Mary instinctively knows her family's motivations, or they may be confusing to her; most likely, both. Mary must trust her instincts.

Uranus is in Cancer in the eighth house, which suggests an unusual or unique approach to family, as well as a desire for freedom with regard to family. In this house it is an unusual approach to intimacy and dealing with deep emotions, as well as an unusual approach to shared assets, therapy or investigation. Mary probably wishes for freedom while at the same time has a desire to be with her partner. Uranus is also trine Jupiter in the third house so unusual communication skills may also be present. Finally, Mary has the Sun in this house in Leo and part of the grand trine with the North Node and Ascendant. With the North Node in the fourth house of home and foundation and the Sun in the house of joint resources, intimacy etc., she will shine at home and with her partner. Another viable alternative for her is in-depth investigation or research she could do at home. Strong traits are control and insight. The Leo Sun suggests she will feel fulfilled when she shines through creative efforts. This is a very good combination with her step-children since they both show a lot of creativity in their charts. It is a place to relate and form a good bond. Leo Sun signs have a charisma all their own. Also, she may take risks with joint finances or risk in order to attain more intimacy or to find and conquer the dark side of human nature. Since the Sun is in Leo in the house of shared assets, she is creative and generous with shared assets. This somewhat offsets the opposition to the second house of personal finances versus joint finances, and control issues. It may help temper any problems in this area. By far this is the most important house in her chart for planetary placement and seems to fall in line with other placements in her chart. With the Sun in the eighth house, a career in finance, therapy, research or investigation would be fulfilling, but with so much Cancer in the eighth house so would home and family.

Ninth House of Higher Education, Philosophy, Religion, Travel and Foreign Matters

Mary has Leo on the cusp of this house, and it is ruled by the Sun in the eighth. This brings eighth-house matters into her higher conscious philosophies and also into higher education or travel. A combination of research and foreign travel would be fulfilling for Mary, as would philosophy or psychology. Pluto and Mercury are both in this house in Leo.

Pluto in the ninth house suggests a strong sense of faith or belief and perhaps investigation or control of belief systems. Mary will probably reform whatever beliefs she chooses into her own method of thinking. Since Pluto is trine Chiron in the first house, ideals and personal philosophies are important to Mary's sense of self-worth. She may feel the need to impart these philosophies to others. Pluto in Leo suggests a lot of drive and a good outlet would be sports. She will feel fulfilled in the limelight but would seek to control that which is in public view. Leo, ruled by the Sun, is in the eighth house so, again, control over joint finances is a very important issue for Mary. Also, Pluto adds to the area of in-depth investigation. Philosophically, Mary will probably be inclined to investigate very thoroughly before choosing personal philosophies. Pluto always suggests power and control issues and conjunct Mercury suggests mental power and control are very important to Mary.

Mercury in the ninth house suggests thoughts of travel and thoughts of any issues dealing with faith and philosophy. This is a good placement for a teacher. Mercury in Leo suggests drama or a dramatic way of communicating. Mary is creative and outgoing. Mercury is sextile Mars in the eleventh, which is the house of step-children. Therefore, communication with them is very important and creativity is a good way for Mary to present her higher ideals, either through the arts or travel, while bonding and having fun. Thoughts are of shared assets and partnership since the ruler of Leo is in the eighth house. Also, since this is a good placement for a teacher, Mary is probably able to constructively and creatively help her step-children come into adulthood. Remember, the Sun, ruler of her ninth house Mercury, is in the eighth house and this house is part of the overall theme in the family's charts.

Tenth House of Career, Honors and Fame

Virgo is on the Midheaven or cusp of the tenth house. This brings a sense of practicality, hard work and business acumen into Mary's profession and career. Virgo is ruled by Mercury in the ninth house, so any career she would choose would have to meet with her sense of ideals and higher conscious philosophies in order to be fulfilling. It may also include foreign companies, travel or education. To all those around her, she would appear practical, dependable, steady, a methodical thinker and maybe a little critical.

Saturn is here and also in Virgo. This suggests a desire for control or a feeling of great responsibility. On the other hand, Mary may feel obstacles or that others are controlling her destiny. In Virgo, business or a profession such as accounting or law would be fulfilling. However, with Saturn here, Mary may have a sense that career is blocked from her. Remember, Saturn has a karmic quality. Because the South Node is here, also in Virgo, Mary has had success in career and this is where her comfort level is. However, she now may feel that success or career is blocked from this comfort level or will have to work very hard to attain it. Since the South Node is here, she would feel in control but also that she must do everything correctly and possibly have anxiety over mistakes or just over getting the job done perfectly. Self-criticism would be very difficult for her.

Mary is a hard worker and very productive. Saturn in Virgo suggests that hard work, plodding and effort will connect Mary with a profession that will be fulfilling if she lays a proper foundation. If she does not, she will not achieve the professional honor she may wish. This hard work should come naturally with the South Node here and, again, it would be her comfort zone. But this placement is totally different from her strong family-oriented sharing and nurturing placements and her North Node. Her options would be to try to do both and perhaps do well or neglect one facet of her life, or to choose one facet of her life to really work on. With the placements, choices probably came very naturally to Mary. She is a part of the many pieces that make the entire complex family puzzle. Saturn would actually help that South Node-North Node retrograde push-pull from the fourth and tenth houses be an easier choice, leaning toward the fourth house, because of the difficulty and obstacles suggested by Saturn.

Eleventh House of Dreams, Wishes, Groups, Friends and Step-children

Mary has Libra on the cusp of this house. Venus rules Libra so issues of shared resources and all eighth house matters are tied to her step children. As you can see from Mary's entire chart, it is strongly geared toward children, step-children, issues of power, control, joint resources and shared values, with a very creative undertone. Mar is really fulfilling her chart's potential in this regard. The Libra cusp on the eleventh house suggests balance, love, charm and all the positive that describes Libra and is a truly wonderful cusp for the house of step-children. Using Libra approaches will lead to a good, balanced family. Of course, any step-child/step-parent relationship may take years of work but this is a good eleventh house cusp to start with. Mary has Neptune in this house also in Libra.

Neptune in Libra suggests a very fertile imagination. It also suggests friendships and humanitarian endeavors. Mary must watch taking on the problems of friends or groups as her own and draining herself of energy. The same can be said of problems of step-children. She should have insight into her friends. With regard to step-children, she may have insight but also may at times be confused by them. She will strive for balance in their relationship. She should have insight into new technologies and new ideas, and this should be an area of interest to both Mary and her step children. Neptune in Libra may be interest in psychology and an interest in equality of all persons. Drugs or alcohol may be indicated but is not necessarily a problem. Mary and the step-children have artistic talent as well from the Neptune placement and this is a positive side of Neptune. Neptune is square the Moon in Mary's house of personal values so there may be some conflict with her step children regarding values or finances.

Neptune is sextile Chiron in her first house, suggesting either that she is the teacher or the lessons learned from the step children are of great value and benefit, and lessons will flow both ways in an easy manner. With Chiron in Sagittarius, the lessons are those of ideals and personal freedom. Mars in the eleventh house suggests a pioneering and courageous spirit. It is in Libra so this goes along with balance and partnership. This is a progressive placement. However, with regard to her step-children, they will probably have these traits as well but may get bored easily and may be combative at times. They may actually cause fights in order to feel a sense of freedom. Since Mars is in Libra, they should be reasonable and able to see all sides of issues. They are people oriented but may be indecisive. Mary may also feel indecisive in how to act regarding them. Again, Mars is square the Moon so this suggests conflict between Mary's personal values and imparting them to her step-children. It is better to reason than dictate with Mars in Libra.

Twelfth House of Hidden Matters, Subconscious, Institutions

Mary has Scorpio on the cusp and it is co-ruled by Mars and Pluto. Pluto is in the house of higher consciousness and philosophies so deep down Mary is really motivated by what she holds in high esteem. Mars is in her eleventh house of groups, wishes, friends and step-children. Thus, the values of her generation are also very important to what motivates her; and her step-children will also motivate her. Scorpio is the natural detective of the zodiac so if you combine this subconscious attribute with Mary's eighth house planets, including the Sun, investigation or research of some type, as well as psychology or the occult, religion or something esoteric may be a very fulfilling career, or at least something she can do that will be important to her sense of accomplishment. Also, the co-ruler is in the house of step-children so success in their upbringing is important to Mary's self-fulfillment.

Mary, the step-mother, is aligned with her step-children's placements. The synastry of their charts in the next chapter is enlightening. Family themes are repeated again and again—one reason why this family has chosen to be together.

Chapter 9

Synastry Between Step-Parent and Step-Child

THE SYNASTRY BETWEEN THE CHARTS of a step-child and the step-parent is particularly important in helping them to develop a positive connection and grow into a well-bonded family unit. In this chapter, I will look at specific placements in the child's chart and then how the synastry with the step-parent's chart can enhance the bonding process. I will also point out areas of concern but my concentration in this book is to look at the potential for growth with the help of planetary placements.

Molly and Mary

Figure 7 has Molly's natal chart as the inner wheel and Mary's natal planets surrounding Molly's natal chart.

To begin, look at Molly's natal chart, the inner wheel. With the Ascendant in Aries, this is an energetic, self-confident, excitable girl who eagerly goes into whatever task she is trying to accomplish; but she may quickly change to something else. She may anger quickly but soon something will grab her attention and the anger will subside. Molly's first house cusp is Aries, and as that is the natural cusp for the first house, the Aries personal traits are quite pronounced. Also, Aries is ruled by Mars (which sits in Molly's sixth house) so Molly will bring work, service, pets and health issues into her personality—who she is and what she does as perceived by her family members. She should be perceived as a hard, steady and energetic worker with a strong constitution. However, if you look at her tenth house cusp, it is the Capricorn traits that she may personally identify with as far as what she brings to the table. Molly is confident in her depend-

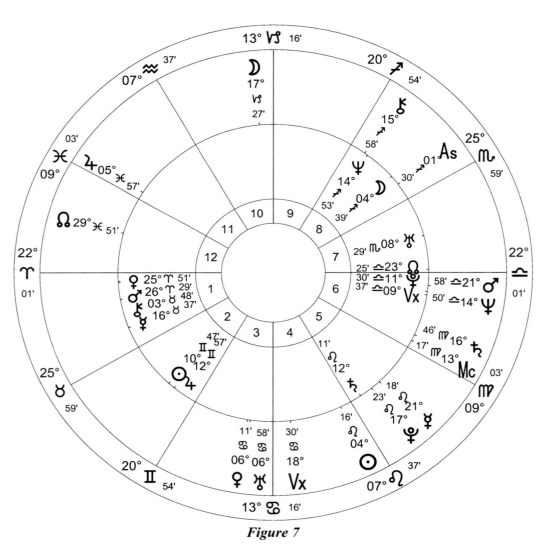

Inner Wheel
Molly
Natal Chart
Jun 1 1977, Wed
3:13 am PDT +7:00
Valencia, CA
34°N26'37" 118°W36'31"
Geocentric
Tropical
Placidus
True Node

Outer Wheel
Mary
Natal Chart
Jul 27 1950, Thu
2:45 pm MST +7:00
Albuquerque, NM
35°N05'04" 106°W39'02"
Geocentric
Tropical
Placidus
True Node

Figure 7

114

ability, structure and work ethic. She feels these are her strong points and she will be most comfortable preparing and executing projects. Again, this is what she feels is what she brings to the table. This is where her ego is tied. Her Sun is in Gemini and her mental ability is a place where she will shine. Since the Sun is in the second house, she will shine in her ability to control finances, acquire assets but most importantly, she will sine through her ethical or personal values. On the other hand, the Sun rules Leo which is the creative force and Molly's Sun is sextile her fifth-house Saturn, suggesting that another way to shine is through creativity, although it may be hard work. Working toward something creative is personally rewarding. Also, creativity (with Saturn in the fifth) is a karmic force. Thus, helping Molly in the creative process would be a good place to bond with her, both in her value system and just having fun. Just from these few placements, you can see where a step-parent can relate to Molly, help bond with her and gain her trust.

The Descendant, or seventh house cusp, is also very important in relationships. Molly has Libra on this cusp so she needs balance and harmony. A home with conflict will be very difficult for her. The Nadir, or cusp of the fourth house, is also very important when looking at step-children. This is their foundation; this is security for them. Molly has Cancer on the cusp, and this is Cancer's natural placement in a solar chart. Cancer is ruled by the Moon in the eighth house and its ruler is in the house of hidden matters, joint resources and intimacy—the areas emphasized in her brother's chart. These are the positions to look at first in synastry with a step-child and step-parent.

Now look at Mary's planets as they relate in synastry with Molly's chart. Mary's Moon is square Molly's Ascendant and South Node. This is a karmic placement and there is some natural tension to work out. This may seem obvious since you can guess that a step-mom and daughter will have some tension; but in this case it may be felt more than usual. The Moon brings in a lot of emotions and up and down feelings. On the other hand, Mary's Midheaven is trine Molly's Mercury so Mary should be good at helping Molly reach her mental goals and is a good sounding board regarding career and honors. Here is where the tension of the Moon square Ascendant and South Node can be worked with and worked out. Thus, although there may be tension, there is a real mental tie with these two people.

Mary's Moon is conjunct Molly's Midheaven. The tenth house is often associated with the mother (it can be father or mother). With the Moon here, Mary is taking on a mothering role. This also indicates a deeper spiritual connection between the souls and considering that Mary's Moon is square Molly's Ascendant and the karmic South Node, the strong tie and need to work things out is evident. However, this tie is significant and there is a good, core connection here that should be felt by both parties.

Mary's Mars conjunct Molly's Descendant is also a strong connection. There is a lot of drive for balance and equity with Mars in Libra; however, this Mars is opposite Venus in the first house so again there may be some emotional tension. Both parties are looking for equality, harmony and justice. They also both want lovely surroundings along with the harmony.

There may be some combativeness because Mary's Mars and Molly's Mars are in opposition. This negative energy would be well directed into sports or physical activities they could do together. As you can see just by these few placements, there is a real mother-daughter push-pull.

Now look at Molly's fourth house. Mary's Vertex and Sun both sit here. The Vertex suggests a lot of new people being brought into the home (in Cancer it is probably family members) by Mary and the Sun is a real show of strength. Therefore, Molly will get a feeling of strength from Mary in her foundational house. The Sun here is where Mary will shine and give a lot of herself to Molly, and this is strong force to help Molly in creative endeavors since Mary's Sun is in Leo. Since Molly is very creative, this is a place where the two can bond and become family. Sharing in creative endeavors or even just Mary driving Molly to art, drama, dance or music class will go a long way in the bonding process.

Mary's Pluto is conjunct Molly's Saturn in the fifth house of creativity so Mary may help Molly to reform or reorganize her direction. Mary should watch trying to control though. Mary's Mercury is also here, in Leo, so creativity and even types of speculation are very strong relationship builders. Mentally, Mary should be tuned into Molly's creativity.

Pluto is usually an area where there may be power struggles or control issues. In this case, it may be Mary trying a little too much to control the child—a past reaction with Pluto conjunct Saturn. Mary's Pluto is square Molly's Mercury and Molly's Mercury is in the stubborn sign of Taurus so there may be a lot of head butting but that is also part of the bonding process. This same Pluto is trine the Ascendant and more importantly Neptune in the eighth house. Remember, eighth-house issues are very important in all of the family charts and with the trine to Pluto, Mary is bringing reorganization regarding eighth issues in a positive light to Molly. A difficult placement at times? Yes. A good placement overall? Yes!

Mary has a stellium of planets in Molly's sixth house of work, service and health. She will be a strong influence on her work ethic but may feel value conflict with the Midheaven square Molly's Sun in the second house. Also, Mary may make Molly work and pay for things when Molly feels she should not do so. Again, this is pretty much a mother-daughter thing, not just step-mother and step-daughter. The Midheaven also is square Jupiter and Molly may feel her freedom is being thwarted by Mary. Mary's Saturn in this house is also square the Sun and Jupiter so there is a lot of hard work to be done here with core karmic ramifications. It is important to try to balance out this area of difficult energy with the creativeness and strength of Mary at home. There is a Neptune-Vertex conjunction here which will mellow out the difficulties a little, and bring a dream or optimism into work. With all this Libra, both are seeking a balance. Neptune trine the Sun and Jupiter will also help alleviate the difficulty of the Midheaven and Saturn squares. However, Mary may not wish to see everything or see things with rose-colored glasses at times in order to gain harmony. In this case, it is not a bad thing. With Molly's Pluto in the sixth house, she will want to control and reform, and again, the Mars contact may indicate combativeness.

One of the most telling placements of this relationship is the eighth house. Remember, Molly and her brother have eighth house issues and Mary's Ascendant and Chiron sit in Molly's eighth house. The Ascendant is conjunct Molly's Moon (emotions). Mary brings her personality and being into the issues of hidden matters, investigations, joint resources and power, and intimacy issues. She is a catalyst for the work it seems the family must do by eighth house placements and aspects thereto. Molly may feel the need to nurture with her Moon here but since it is in Sagittarius, it may be hard for her to express and she may seem detached. Let's not forget that the Moon rules Cancer, the cusp of the fourth house, so this placement of the Ascendant-Moon conjunction fits right into a home where both reside. Mary's Chiron is also conjunct Molly's Neptune. Chiron is the teacher/healer/lesson learned and Neptune is the confused one who often takes on the problems of others; the Moon is in Sagittarius this placement suggests someone in search of the truth. Thus, with Chiron here, both may learn from each other relating to all eighth house issues. This is one of the strongest placements for bonding in the chart.

Mary's Jupiter (in Molly's eleventh house) is square both the Moon and Sun, so while Mary may help Molly grow and expand her wishes, the groups she is involved with and to look broadly at generational issues, she may still feel difficulty with the eighth house issues, including control over money and assets. Although Mary is very good for Molly in expanding her horizons and dealing with issues of the eighth house (intimacy, hidden matters, joint resources, creating a secure home and the like), there will be conflict with issues of earning and spending money and struggle over what Molly feels she should have or what she is given. All of this is very normal in any household and can be worked out.

Mary's North Node (in the twelfth house) is trine Molly's Moon in the eighth house so again I feel Mary's strong point is relating and bonding through eighth house issues.

The conjunctions involving Pluto-Saturn and Vertex-Pluto-Mars, indicate power or control issues, as do the Ascendant-Moon and Chiron-Neptune conjunctions, which are very strong. Therefore, you see immediately issues of power, control, intimacy, teaching, feeling and dreaming. But, as much as these things are issues, they are also the ties that bind. These charts are very connected so it is no wonder that Mary was a custodial parent for a part of Molly's childhood.

The Effects of Progression

See Figure 8, which is Molly's natal chart surrounded by her secondary progressed planets. Molly came to live with her father and Mary in June 1986. The secondary progressions are an indication of inner maturity rather than outside influence.

Molly's Mercury had progressed into her second house of personal values, money and assets. It is at a critical degree, 29 Taurus so this is an important time for Molly in her value system. Obviously, previous family values of family are shattered and part of Mary's role is to help Molly build back and perhaps create some new values. This is a difficult time.

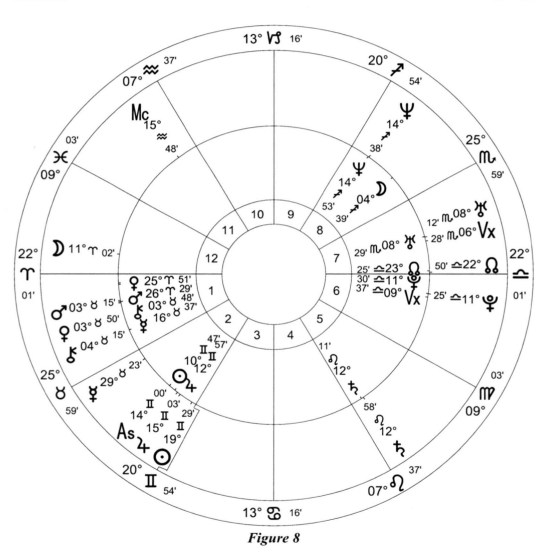

Inner Wheel
Molly
Natal Chart
Jun 1 1977, Wed
3:13 am PDT +7:00
Valencia, CA
34°N26'37" 118°W36'31"
Geocentric
Tropical
Placidus
True Node

Outer Wheel
Molly
Sec.Prog. SA in Long
Jun 30 1986, Mon
8:56:09 am CDT +5:00
Minnetonka, MN
44°N54'48" 093°W30'11"
Geocentric
Tropical
Placidus
True Node

Figure 8

118

The other major progression that is important to maturity is that the Vertex has moved into the seventh house conjunct Uranus. This suggests that Molly's perception of partnerships is shaken. Molly's Midheaven is in her eleventh house now and what was once her personal ego has shifted and possibly changed as to what she wants for the future. Also, her Moon (her emotions) has moved into the twelfth house of subconscious. Thus, you can see that at the time Molly came to live with her father and Mary, she was going through a period of change that affected her emotionally and on a deep, subconscious level. Her values and ideas of marriage and partnership were shattered and what was her sense of importance and ego was shifted into hopes for the future. It is also a time where she may identify with groups and friends for support rather than those at home. Just knowing the effect of these progressions gives Mary a head start in how to relate to Molly. The charts are heavily linked and there are places of great bonding potential, learning and loving, but with the effects of progression, Mary must make an effort to help Molly regain what was lost. In this case, progressions are very effective in helping the step-parent relate to a step-child. This is one place where I feel progressions are used very effectively.

John and Mary

Figure 9 is John's natal chart (inner wheel) surrounded by Mary's natal planets (outer wheel). With John's 0 Virgo Ascendant, he appears practical, methodical and hard working and can be critical or self-critical. He likes stability so anything else such as divorce will be a problem. Although not necessarily a pessimist, he does not get excited and methodically decides what to do. The practicality and stability are offset by his Gemini Sun which gives him a quick mind, versatility and energy; but at first glance the Virgo Ascendant is what is presented to the world. John's tenth house cusp is Taurus so again the earth sign practicality comes through; he also has the Taurus traits of liking fine things and luxury. He will work toward this end. He also has a desire for peace and harmony. Although he is not necessarily one who keeps secrets, he will work methodically toward what he wants without spelling out each step to others. Just from these two important placements we can see that stability along with peace and harmony are very important; his parents' divorce does not fit with this pattern.

Although all children suffer terribly from divorce, some placements really add to the stress. John's Descendant is 0 Pisces so he will be highly intuitive around partners but may tend to take on all their problems. This tendency to take on problems of others may be difficult when he sees a marriage dissolve. The Nadir is Scorpio which suggests he may feel home life is difficult. He may not be secretive but he perceives secrets in the home. And his Moon is 29 Scorpio, a critical degree, on the cusp of his fourth house of home and foundation. The Moon is associated with change, so its placement on the cusp at a critical degree indicates his home will change and it will be a deeply emotional experience during his childhood. This change of home and the emotional trauma is a pattern he will carry with him into adulthood. Childhood conditions of change and perhaps discord may gear him toward cautiousness as an adult. On the other hand, he is very intense at home, has a lot of energy and will be the magnetic charmer in the family.

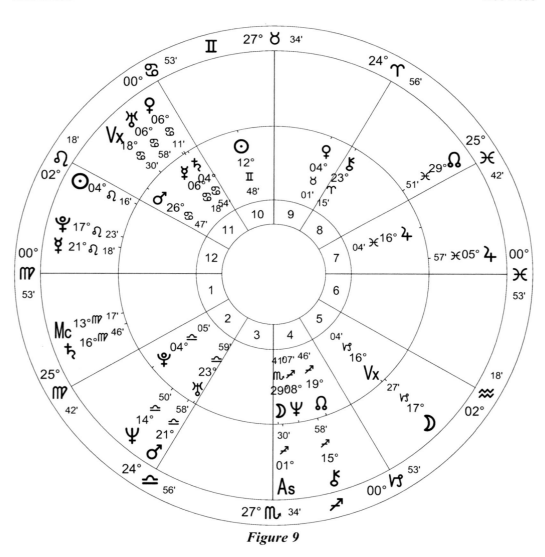

Inner Wheel
John
Natal Chart
Jun 3 1974, Mon
11:46 am PDT +7:00
Whittier, CA
33°N58'45" 118°W01'55"
Geocentric
Tropical
Placidus
Mean Node

Outer Wheel
Mary
Natal Chart
Jul 27 1950, Thu
2:45 pm MST +7:00
Albuquerque, NM
35°N05'04" 106°W39'02"
Geocentric
Tropical
Placidus
True Node

Figure 9

John's Sun and where he shines is in Gemini in his tenth house of career and honors. This suggests he will probably do more than one thing at a time in order to feel fulfilled. He also will feel strongly about his mental capabilities and this is where he will shine. His ego is tied to what he does, honors, recognition and mental matters. His South Node is also in his tenth house so his feelings of self-worth are core inner needs and feelings. With his Sun in Gemini, a dual sign, and his Moon at a critical degree in the home showing a pattern of change, he may tend toward more than one marriage as an adult.

Now that we have quickly analyzed John's chart, let's look at Mary's planets in synastry to it (the planets around the inside wheel) and how she can be a positive step-parent. At first glance, it appears he may be a bit more difficult than his sister just by aspect and planet placement. That is not to say this relationship will not bond in a positive way; it just may be a little more difficult.

Mary's Midheaven and Saturn sit in John's first house. Thus, Mary's ego and self-esteem are related to Saturn, which would be considered an obstacle to John so there may be some head-butting in this relationship. On the other hand, Saturn, a karmic planet, sits in John's first house so this is a relationship that is deep and there is a core connection. With all these placements in Virgo, there is a practicality and dependability to the relationship, but there also may be some criticism that should be avoided. If you look at the aspects of Mary's Midheaven to John's planets, there is a square to his tenth-house Sun, again suggesting a bit of head-butting. There may be a contest of egos and wills. Mary's Saturn is also square the South Node so this is a karmic condition; these two people definitely chose to work things out during this lifetime no matter how difficult. Remember how strong the nodal contacts are between these two charts. The good part of this placement is that it suggests a nice place to work.

Mary's Midheaven is trine John's Vertex in his fifth house of creativity, speculation and children. This is great. She will be a positive influence in these areas and work with John in creative endeavors is a good place to bond and a place to work out difficulties in a positive manner. She will also be a good step-grandmother for his children and probably babysit in later years. Because her Midheaven is opposition his Jupiter in the seventh house, he will gain positively from her input when he chooses a mate or partner, even if their own relationship seems difficult at times. Mary's Saturn square John's North Node in his fourth house suggests that this is where they both should be, even with obstacles suggested by the square aspect. Mary's ego and self-assertion in the home is something John must acknowledge and grow from into adulthood. Although they both may find living together difficult at times, it indicates positive growth, especially if creativity is used for positive bonding.

Mary's South Node, karma, is sextile John's Moon in the fourth to the exact degree. The Moon in the fourth house or home at a critical degree sextile this planet of karma is a very strong tie. It seems impossible that these two people would not be together in some fashion with their charts. John may feel that Mary is too strict with his spending money or that she tries to get him to adjust to her values but with the sextile to the Moon, the home should come together and things should work out. Her Moon is opposition (wide orb) his Mars in his eleventh house so she will make a home that he will be able to have friends visit or groups he is interested in be a part of. She may also help and give insight into his wishes for the future.

Mary's Neptune sits in John's second house and is trine John's South Node and Sun in his tenth. Mary's personal values and/or lessons regarding finances and assets will inspire John in his own achievements, his career and honors he may receive. Mary's value system is good for John's positive growth. Mary's Neptune is square John's Vertex so Mary should have a lot of insight into John's friends, wishes and generational issues or she may be easily deceived—two sides of the same coin. Now the tough part: Mary's Mars is square John's Mars in the eleventh house regarding what John wants for the future. They may butt heads. Mars suggests energy and quick action but also combativeness. One thing they could do together to tame this is sports or physical activities. It would be very good for bonding and releasing frustration with each other.

Also, since John's Mars is in Cancer, the tension may be around the home and with Mary's Mars in Libra, she wants peace and calm there. Now the really unpredictable placement: Mary's Mars is conjunct John's Uranus which suggests no one will be able to predict what will happen between these two. This placement can be really exciting when working together toward something, or explosive when opposing each other. The key for them is to know themselves and work toward something without exploding. With this placement that is a tall order. Since the placement is in Libra, they both would like harmony and beauty. If they look to something artistic or creative and beautiful, there is no end to what can be created; this is a good avenue to positive bonding.

Mary's Ascendant is conjunct John's critical twenty-nine degree Moon in the fourth house so it is apparent that she will be in his home. It is no wonder she and her husband are the custodial parents. The Moon-Ascendant aspect can be very supportive and is often found in friends. Mary's Ascendant is also conjunct John's Neptune so there is a lot of intuition on the part of John; he can probably read Mary pretty well but also may be confused and lack clarity.

Mary also has Chiron in John's fourth house conjunct his North Node. Chiron is the teacher or healer and conjunct the karmic North Node suggests that Mary will help John in his childhood. Chiron opposes John's natal Sun so again there is the push-pull and head-butting, but Chiron in the fourth house should be soothing for John. Also, Chiron suggests the lesson learned so John is probably going to do his share of teaching as well.

Mary's Moon is conjunct John's Vertex in his fifth house of creativity. This is a good placement for bonding when creating together. The Vertex is where other people come into play and Mary should be very helpful to John and have a lot of insight. Since the Moon rules Cancer (John's eleventh house) there should be a lot of friends around the creative process, as well as generational issues viewed in a creative way but also in a practical one since the Moon and Vertex are in Capricorn. Mary's Moon is square John's second house Uranus so things may also be quite unusual and unpredictable. The Moon is also square John's Chiron which is in his eighth house.

Eighth house lessons seem to be a theme running in the family's charts and the Moon square Chiron here just falls into place with eighth house lessons of shared resources, hidden matters, therapy, investigation and intimacy being brought into play. Emotions and home are a big part of this placement. With this and the second house placements, John will not like being advised on what to do with his money. He will want control, especially with Pluto in the second house.

Mary's Jupiter sits in John's seventh house. John's Jupiter is also in his seventh house but the Jupiters are out of orb for a conjunction. This suggests Mary will help John expand his horizons in partnership matters. Both are in Pisces so again there is a lot of intuition or on the other hand confusion and lack of clarity. Mary's Jupiter is trine John's Mercury in Cancer in his eleventh house. It is also trine his eleventh house Saturn (karma). She may try to be overly expansive with regard to his thoughts and may actually be an obstacle by trying too hard. There is a psychic connection and if they go with their feelings they can work through the Saturnian obstacles and have sympathetic thoughts for the future as well as for the home represented by his Cancer planets.

Mary's North Node sits in John's eighth house so Mary relates to John via these matters. Thus, the motif that runs throughout this family is once again emphasized and this is where Mary needs to work with John. Since the North Node is in Pisces at a critical degree, this is an important placement. Mary will have a lot of insight and intuition into John and also may be confused. She may try to see things through rose-colored glasses to alleviate any tension. Mary may also try to take on too many of John's burdens or at the least will feel deeply with regard to John's feelings. It appears as though Mary is a critical person for John when working with on eighth house issues. The North Node is trine John's twenty-nine degree Moon in the fourth house so Mary's role in the home is quite critical to John's growing up. Do you see a sort of destiny in these two people? Mary's North Node is also trine John's Mars in the eleventh house so Mary will help positively influence this area; but Mars is in Cancer which again suggests home and foundation. The North Node is also sextile John's Midheaven so Mary's influence is positive toward career and honors. Mary's North Node is an incredibly strong influence in John's chart. This is one of the most important placements in their synastry and almost suggests a common destiny.

Mary's Venus, Uranus and Vertex sit in John's eleventh house, suggesting a positive influence on his wishes for the future and at times possibly a startling suggestion from her. Venus-Saturn suggests a fondness for each other despite age. In Cancer, this is good for the home environment, and the relationship should develop into a mutual benefit for both. However, Venus is also square John's Pluto in his second house and again the idea of resources and power-control comes into play. This is one of John's lessons and since Mary's North Node is in the eighth house and Venus is square Pluto, there appears to be a tug of war over resources with John trying to come out on top. Venus is conjunct Mercury as well and this is a natural, easy relationship with qualities of help, love, respect and joviality. This is good and can offset some of the power struggles. Mary's Uranus is conjunct both Saturn and Mercury. With Uranus-Mercury both may feel they understand what the other is thinking only to be totally surprised. But there is a real sensitivity here, and in Cancer it is quite strong. Saturn/Uranus suggests unusual circumstances or chaos, as well as obstacles or periods of difficulty. Uranus is chaos and Saturn is stability, so this push-pull can cause mishaps which may actually bring the parties closer together. John will be quite surprised by his step-mother at times. Uranus also is square John's Pluto and again there are the control and power issues, especially over finances or resources. John will want Mary's input into how he handles money and she will surprise him every step of the way with her suggestions. With regard to control, this is the place where they will really get to each other and may vehemently argue or at the least be at odds. There may be some tantrums.

Mary's Vertex sits in John's eleventh house and suggests she will bring persons into John's life who are beneficial to his future wishes and dreams. She will also be influential in groups or associations he may be interested in. The Vertex is trine John's Jupiter in his seventh house so Mary should be a good influence regarding Joe's future partnerships.

Mary's Sun, Pluto and Mercury sit in John's twelfth house. With the Sun in the twelfth house, Mary will know what motivates John as she can read him like a book. Her action and energy are a positive influence on his psyche. With the Sun here, Mary can help John develop his interests. This Sun is trine John's Moon and Neptune by a wide orb in the fourth house so this is a positive influence for John and what helps to ground him. The Sun is square John's Venus in his ninth house so there may be conflict with philosophies of life.

Mary's Pluto here suggests that she may help John examine life on a deep level and this goes along with the eighth house placement of her North Node. On the other hand, he may act out because he does not want to examine his life. He may feel she really knows his weaknesses and try to live up to them. This is a tough placement no matter who the people are. John will subconsciously feel that Mary has the control or power and we know that power is one of his issues. This Pluto is trine John's North Node in his fourth house so he must feel at home with Mary even though there may be power struggles. Mary's Mercury in the twelfth house suggests she will probably know what John is thinking. This may be kind of tough for the child if he feels that step-mom knows what he is thinking and what motivates him. Mercury is fairly well aspected and suggests that Mary will give John good advice and, although may not admit it, he will probably respect it.

The Effects of Progression

By looking at John's progressions at the time he came to live with his father and step-mother, we can see where he is developmentally, or his maturity level, and how this may also affect the relationship between step-son and step-mom. See Figure 10.

John's progressed Ascendant entered his second house of finances and personal values and was conjunct his Pluto and Mary's South Node. Thus, personally, the power struggle was strong and a major factor when he moved into his father's and step-mother's home. This was a very per-

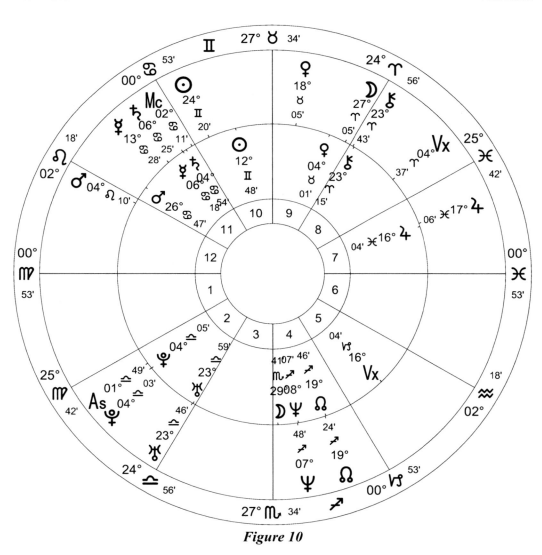

Inner Wheel
John
Natal Chart
Jun 3 1974, Mon
11:46 am PDT +7:00
Whittier, CA
33°N58'45" 118°W01'55"
Geocentric
Tropical
Placidus
Mean Node

Outer Wheel
John
Sec.Prog. SA in Long
Jun 30 1986, Mon
8:56:09 am CDT +5:00
Minnetonka, MN
44°N54'48" 093°W30'11"
Geocentric
Tropical
Placidus
True Node

Figure 10

125

sonal struggle for John. Control issues were both personal and important to him. Personal values were also very important to John at this time and may have to reform or reorganize his values. His progressed nodal positions were at exactly the same degree as at birth, a karmic placement and one which would encourage positive growth. His Vertex had moved into the eighth house, and eighth-house issues are very strong in John's natal chart as well as the charts of his family. Again, issues of control over joint resources, hidden matters, investigation and intimacy were at the forefront at this time. However, along with these issues, the Vertex suggests more people would be brought into his life to influence him at that time. These are energetic, compulsive, aggressive, exuberant Aries type people and Aries is a fire sign, just like his step-mother's Leo Sun.

John's progressed Moon in th ninth house in Aries indicated emotions regarding life philosophies and higher ideals that were in a state of flux as one would imagine with the change of residence. His Midheaven and Mercury had moved into his eleventh house in Cancer so there was a lot of thinking about the future, hopes and wishes, and with Cancer involved, so were the home and foundation. There was probably a lot of thought about friends, those left behind and trying to make new ones.

Other than the Nodes being at their exact degree as the natal Nodes, his progressed Mars really tells the tale. It is in the twelfth house, suggesting a lot of subconscious tension and is conjunct his step-mother's Sun. This Mars-Sun conjunction in John's twelfth house in Leo suggests a lot of strong will on the part of both parties and there may be a lot of energy and give and take, but there may also be a lot of tension and combativeness. This is the initial adjustment period and is filled with tension. It will have a very strong affect on John's psyche. If Mary and John use this energy in a positive way, it can also be very exciting and physical activities such as skating, playing ball and the like will be a positive way to relate to each other. Since the Sun and Mars are in Leo, this is an innately creative relationship so creativity is a good way for Mary to bond with John. So while this is tense, it can be exciting and help bond on a deep level.

Chapter 10

Use of Decanates and Dwads

PROGRESSIONS ARE SYMBOLIC, connecting one time with another. The most common is secondary progressions which equates one day with one year. Thus, if a child is ten years old, the positions of the planets, Ascendant, Nodes or other points ten days after the birth date are symbolic of age ten. I use secondary progressions as indications of levels of maturity rather than an outside influence.

Decanates divide each sign of the zodiac into thirds of the same element. Let's use Aries for an example. The first ten degrees of Aries is the Aries decanate of Aires, the second ten degrees of Aries if the Leo decanate of Aries and the last ten degrees of Aries is the Sagittarius decanate of Aries. Each decanate may change the flavor of the sign somewhat but the underlying elemental definition of the sign remains the same. For example, look at Taurus. Zero to ten degrees is the Taurus decanate of Taurus so the traits of dependability, steadiness, plodding toward goals and over indulgence and love of luxury are strong. At eleven through twenty degrees of Taurus, you are in the Virgo decanate and you may see a lessening of the over-indulgence or quest for luxury and perhaps a critical or self critical trait will appear while the earth sign elemental traits of dependability and a steady, methodical or plodding nature remain in tact, and so forth. Decanates give a tone or flavor to a sign but do not have the specificity of the dwads as described below. Thus, I normally stick to the dwads in synastry, but you can use one, the other or both.

A simple definition of a dwad is that each sign of the zodiac is 30 degrees and each sign is divided into 2½ degree parts beginning with zero degrees. Thus, if you look at Aries, the first 2½ degrees of Aries are in the Aries dwad. The dwads proceed as the zodiac does so the second 2½

Figure 11, Decanates and Dwads

Decanates

0°	♈	♉	♊	♋	♌	♍	♎	♏	♐	♑	♒	♓
10°	♌	♍	♎	♏	♐	♑	♒	♓	♈	♉	♊	♋
20°	♐	♑	♒	♓	♈	♉	♊	♋	♌	♍	♎	♏

Dwads

0°	♈	♉	♊	♋	♌	♍	♎	♏	♐	♑	♒	♓
2½°	♉	♊	♋	♌	♍	♎	♏	♐	♑	♒	♓	♈
5°	♊	♋	♌	♍	♎	♏	♐	♑	♒	♓	♈	♉
7½°	♋	♌	♍	♎	♏	♐	♑	♒	♓	♈	♉	♊
10°	♌	♍	♎	♏	♐	♑	♒	♓	♈	♉	♊	♋
12½°	♍	♎	♏	♐	♑	♒	♓	♈	♉	♊	♋	♌
15°	♎	♏	♐	♑	♒	♓	♈	♉	♊	♋	♌	♍
17½°	♏	♐	♑	♒	♓	♈	♉	♊	♋	♌	♍	♎
20°	♐	♑	♒	♓	♈	♉	♊	♋	♌	♍	♎	♏
22½°	♑	♒	♓	♈	♉	♊	♋	♌	♍	♎	♏	♐
25°	♒	♓	♈	♉	♊	♋	♌	♍	♎	♏	♐	♑
27½°	♓	♈	♉	♊	♋	♌	♍	♎	♏	♐	♑	♒

degrees of Aries are in the Taurus dwad, the third 2½ degrees in the Gemini dwad, and so forth. In Taurus, the next sign of the zodiac, the first 2½ degrees are in the Taurus dwad, the second 2½ degrees in the Gemini dwad, and so forth. Thus, a person with the Moon at 4 Taurus would have a love of nice things, emotional stability and an emotional need for security; but with an underlying influence of Gemini, the emotions would be offset somewhat by logic and mental energy. Suppose you have the Sun at 14 Leo, which is in the Capricorn dwad. This is a heavy influence on a Leo Sun. The Leo Sun wants to readily go ahead, show off, be the actor in the limelight, while the Capricorn influence will temper this and help the Leo Sun move along in a steady fashion, analyzing things and perhaps not taking so many chances. See Figure 11 showing the decanates and dwads for each sign.

The use of dwads can be enlightening when looking at a child's secondary progressions. Since the slower planets may not change degree or perhaps only change a few degrees during childhood, if you look at the dwads you are one step ahead when analyzing the child's maturity level. Many astrologers use dwads to see differences in twins. You can take hours and hours, pages and pages, to analyze a chart using dwads. I use them more with progressions to see the maturity level of a person in light of the astrological placements at birth. I also use them in synastry with parents or step-parents because they shed a lot of light on the bonding situation and parenting.

For example, consider a child with a Leo Sun in the Capricorn dwad, now progressed to the Pisces dwad. This is someone who as a small child was energetic but also practical. Now he may be more dreamy than active, which would seem out of character. In synastry, how one reacts to the sign of the dwad may differ greatly from dwad to dwad. If you are a Leo, you can relate to a child with the Sun in the Leo dwad even if the child's Sun sign is one a Leo wouldn't normally relate to. If you look at two planets that are in different signs and/or different houses, but both have progressed to the same sign in their dwad pattern, you may get a very strong underlying behavior theme. For example, suppose both Uranus, representing chaos, and Mars, representing action or aggression, have progressed to a Cancer dwad. You may have a child who is unpredictable or erratic and may be angry or aggressive in an attempt to find nurture and comfort. Perhaps the child who acts up does so for attention. If you recognize this pattern, rather than reinforcing the child's anger with negative attention, you can divert his energy into something positive and reinforce him with nurturing attention even before the fact. Take him roller-blading, hiking through caves or something unusual to reinforce the Uranus influence. Combine something you usually do not do together with something physical to reinforce the Mars. *These hidden dwad messages in the secondary progressions can really help bonding with a child.*

I look at the dwads of the secondary progressions of the Ascendant, Midheaven, the luminaries, and the Nodes as having the most importance. If any of these or an outer planet have progressed to an aspect with another person's planets in synastry, then the dwads are of utmost importance in understanding the child's maturity and the way to relate to the child. I do not find any dwad to be of more importance than any other, but they are of importance in understanding. The sign the planet is in is still weighted far more heavily than the dwad. The dwad simply gives an underlying understanding of a placement. John's and Molly's charts are a good illustration of this (see Figures 8 and 10). First of all, a planet that remains in the same dwad is also of great significance. Look at John's Uranus. It is at 23 and 24 Libra in the Gemini dwad. With this we can see a shake-up in his mental processes by events that affect his value system since Uranus is in the second house of finances and personal values. This has not changed since birth and you may be assured that sometime in childhood there will be a shake ups affecting his mental processes that affect values. Since Uranus is in Libra, he is seeking balance. Mary's Mars is conjunct this placement but in the Taurus dwad so her drive may be toward comfort and security and this will help John with his mental changes regarding values. Mars-Uranus is tough, but you can see that if Mary focuses energy on comfort and security, this will help John and the bonding process. Although Mars-Uranus does suggest a lot of tension and chaos and is not an easy placement, Mary's input toward nurturing and security will help John. The Taurus dwad can help this tough placement and is a point the astrologer should emphasize for these clients.

John's Ascendant has gone from 0 Virgo (practical, steady approach) to 1 Libra (need for balance and harmony). The Libra Ascendant is in the Libra dwad so this need for balance, harmony and beauty is very important. His Midheaven has progressed to 2 Cancer so it remains in the Cancer dwad; thus home and foundation are very important at this time. His personal ego seems tied to family and foundation, suggesting his new environment will greatly affect who he becomes. It is in the eleventh house of dreams and wishes, it goes without question that his dreams do not include a divorce or moving in with a step-parent. Mary's Venus is conjunct the progressed Midheaven in Cancer but with a Virgo dwad bringing stability and practicality into the home. This is good for John.

John's Midheaven has gone from Taurus to the Cancer dwad of Cancer in the eleventh house. Thus, his 27 Taurus Midheaven in the Aquarius dwad has progressed from the child whose ego is tied to his ability to think outside the box but still appear practical to the child whose wishes are consumed with Cancer things such as home, family and security. This Midheaven placement really shows a dissolution of the parents' marriage and concerns with home or a new home and that the child has a lot of wishes about his future. His ego has been somewhat deflated and is now tied with his new home and his place therein.

The Nodes remain at their degree at John's birth: 19 Sagittarius and 19 Gemini in the fourth and tenth houses. They are in the Cancer and Sagittarius dwads respectively. Thus, with both placements, there is a desire for freedom and mental capacity, freedom in the home and freedom to pursue ego-involved activities. Mental abilities may be very imaginative and John may seek freedom from worry through intellect. Mary has Chiron at 15 degrees, conjunct by a wide orb to John's North Node and opposition his South Node. Chiron suggests that at the time John came to live with Mary, there was a great need for healing and that they would both learn lessons from this experience. This Chiron-Node placement was discussed in the delineation of the synastry of their charts and by progression has not changed.

The Sun has progressed from 2 Gemini to 24 Gemini, from the Gemini dwad to the Aquarius dwad, but remains in the tenth house. This is actually positive because the Sun remains in the house of honors and helps John keep his ego strong. Aquarius gives John that sense of the far-ahead thinker, and brings in new technology, perhaps science. John should have the newest electronic toys and a computer system comparable to that of his school. This will help bring his strengths into the home and he will fee comfortable. *This Aquarius influence with the Sun placement is a great help in helping John to adjust and bond through joint play of computer games and scientific endeavors, encouraging his ability to think outside the box.*

The Moon has progressed from a critical 29 Scorpio in the Libra dwad to 27 Aries in the Aquarius dwad. The first thing to remember is that the natal Moon at a critical degree suggests a tremendous shake-up and change in home, and in the Libra dwad suggests equilibrium and balance will be completely thrown off. John must have beauty and harmony in the home so a shake up, even to a new and lovely home, will be traumatic. By progression, the Aquarius dwad suggests again a need for the latest gadgets and technology will be a good place to bond with John. Since the Moon is now in the ninth house, John may discover a newly found love of things foreign or desire to see foreign countries. He may also change his ideas about higher education, especially if it deals with technology.

When a child is subjected to divorce or change in residence, look at Saturn and its secondary progression since Saturn suggests obstacles, difficulty and hard work. John's natal Saturn is at 4 Cancer, suggesting difficulty and obstacles with regard to the home; placed in the Leo dwad, he copes with this by being the show-off and using charm. He is energetic and an actor, and no one may grasp his true feelings. Saturn has progressed to 6 Cancer and is now in the Virgo dwad. This suggests John may have a sense of fear of mistakes around the home and/or self-criticism or criticism of others. There may also be health issues created by this trauma. This is the time to build up his ego and help him realize that this change is not his fault and he could do nothing about it. Friends could be helpful (with the eleventh house placement), but that will be difficult since he had to move. This Saturn has now reached the exact degree of Mary's Uranus so he will definitely feel the shake-up around her. However, Uranus tends to throw the chips in the air and let them fall where they may. Thus, when things calm down, this can be a very promising relationship, and a friendship of unusual quality is suggested by natal and progressed placements and their synastry. It is interesting that the natal Saturn by progression sits with Mary's Uranus in Cancer, the home and foundation. This is hard but can be good.

Since Mars suggests tension, drive, ambition, combativeness and focused energy, it is good to look at its progression when a child is the product of a divorce and changes residence. John's Mars has moved from 26 Cancer in the Taurus dwad to 4 Leo in the Virgo dwad. John's natal Mars suggests tension in the home but also a desire for beauty and calm so the Taurus dwad tempers the Mars energy. This is a good placement of Mars in the home. The new Virgo dwad now suggests that John still displays a lot of Mars energy but it is now tempered with the Virgo influence that like Taurus is steady and plodding, but may now involve self-criticism or criticism of others (remember Saturn has also progressed to a Virgo dwad so these traits are emphasized). John should not be too hard on himself and this includes any acting out (Mars energy) to live up to his own self-criticism. Mars has moved into the twelfth house so this mental tension is affecting John's subconscious; again, he may act out and not even know why.

Although I believe all children who are products of a divorce should have some counseling, with the progressed Mars in the twelfth house and in a Virgo dwad, it would really help John cope and adjust. He may not fully realize just how much he may place blame on himself or somehow feel guilty. Certainly someone who is not trained in counseling is unlikely to recognize this. This placement also suggests he may perfect the use of charm to get his way. Mars in the twelfth house can be very good and often suggests personal action geared toward achieving one's place in the universe. Thus, while mental tension may be suggested, it is also a time of growing and seeking what is right for John. It suggests a quest for a personal, inner meaning, and with the Moon in the ninth house, it suggests perhaps looking for something that will help John feel he has what is needed to be strong.

There are also some interesting placements in Molly's secondary progressions. Her Ascendant at 22 Aries has progressed to 14 Gemini in the second house. Thus she has gone from a self-assertive, energetic, kind of a "me" person to someone who is thinking a lot about personal values.

The progressed Ascendant in Gemini shows a duality in her approach, and its placement in the Scorpio dwad adds a lot of emotion. This suggests a personal questioning of values, a confusion or going back and forth over values and a period of vacillation in thoughts and emotions. It is a time of confusion over what is of real value. It is also a time of growth and mental search. The progressed Ascendant is also conjunct her Sun so this is a very personal time for her. She is mentally seeking where she will shine. She is mentally intense.

The progressed Midheaven has gone from 13 Capricorn to 15 Aquarius. Thus, it has gone from practical steadiness and an almost dogmatic approach to a pioneering, technological and far-thinking approach. It is interesting that Aquarius plays an important role in both her and her brother's charts at this time. Molly's Midheaven is in the Leo dwad in the eleventh house. Therefore, her hopes and wishes are tied to technology and the arts. It seems to broaden Mary's approach to her future. She is expanding her universe. *As with her brother, a new computer and technological games would be a good place for Mary to bond with Molly.* Friends are also of concern and Molly will probably make friends with ideas toward technology, computers, and those that are far-thinking. This new/unusual approach is a very strong theme for both Molly and her brother and one wonders if in the case of these siblings, a divorce actually put a new spin on cognitive thinking and looking toward the future in order to cope.

Both the natal and progressed Suns sit in the second house of values. Molly's personal values are thus greatly affected by the divorce. She probably feels she is being divorced. Her natal Sun in Gemini suggests a quick mind and all the things Gemini connotes. In the Libra dwad, the suggestion of peace, balance and harmony is essential to her being. It is part of her value system. When this is progressed to the Capricorn dwad, we see a much more serious approach, steadily plodding to gain goals. It takes peacefulness and turns it to tense seriousness. That feeling of "all is in balance" is gone. There is a need to control mentally as well as to steadily work toward control of her surroundings, so that her values are once again in sync. The Capricorn dwad is a tough placement for Gemini.

Molly's Moon has progressed from 4 Sagittarius in the ninth house to 11 Aries in the twelfth house. The Moon in the twelfth house suggests a lot of emotions that carry to a subconscious level so this is a time where her emotions will be deeply buried and possibly suppressed. The Moon in Aries suggests rapid shifts in mood, running either hot or cold, and a time of subconscious upheaval. The Moon here suggests looking for a tie to humanity or the universe for security rather than a person or home which makes sense given the circumstances. It is in the Leo dwad so Molly may act out, not knowing why, in an attempt to get attention. This is a difficult time.

The South Node remains within one degree in the first house but has gone from the Capricorn dwad to the Sagittarius dwad. Thus, the South Node in the first house or the place of karma takes on a Sagittarius tone. Molly is looking for escape and freedom from problems and her ideas are shaken. This is a past life feeling she is re-living through no fault of her own. The break-up of her parents, a second marriage of her father and a new home will really color who she becomes.

Molly's Saturn remains at 12 Leo in the fifth house of creativity. Her need for a creative outlet is innate and her work ethic in the arts is very strong. It is in the Sagittarius dwad so Mary's Pisces Jupiter, trine by wide orb to Molly's Saturn, can relate to Molly so creativity is a place to bond and grow. More importantly, Saturn in a Sagittarius dwad brings in issues of freedom of artistic expression and expressing higher ideals through art. The arts are a place to work through and gain insight into other areas of life for both children.

Natal Mars is at 26 Aries and has progressed to 3 Taurus, both in the first house. She has gone from a very active, assertive, energetic, combative Aries-type to a person with a need for security, a lovely home, the importance of possessions and over-indulgence, but also with an active mind since Mars is in the Gemini dwad of Taurus. She will probably be viewed as moody rather than outgoing at this time, seeking comfort and security rather than asserting herself. However, Mars is still Mars and she should have a lot of personal energy.

Molly's Mercury has gone from 16 Taurus to 29 Taurus, a critical degree. It has also shifted from the first house to the second house. Natal Mercury is in the Scorpio dwad, suggesting eighth house matters that are so strong in both her and John's charts. The 29 Taurus placement is in the Aries dwad, suggesting energy expended searching for this harmony, comfort and balance. This suggests an active mental search for that which is of value at this time. This is a critical time mentally for Molly, and her mental perception of values is at a crisis point. She has gone from a natal eighth house type quest to a quest for baeuty and peace. This is quite a change at the time of divorce.

You can ascertain just from these few progressed placements how important secondary progressions are in delineating a child's chart, especially with regard to synastry with a parent or step-parent.

Chapter 11

Others in the Mix and Using the Moon

IT IS INTERESTING TO LOOK at the charts of other family members and how they relate to the step-parent/step-child relationship. For example, a new sibling who is the product of one parent and one step-parent can really mix things up. If we look at Molly's chart and its synastry with her sister and step-mother, it is quite informative as to family dynamics (see Figure 12).

Although I will not delineate all the charts of other family members in full, look at the synastry and how other family members interact with the step-child and the step-parent. Molly's chart in synastry with her sister (the product of her father and step-mother) and her step-mother show where motifs are repeated and where family dynamics come into play. Molly and her sister Ann have some close conjunctions and seem to have chosen to be together. Ann's 29 Aries Mercury, a critical degree, sits in Molly's first house conjunct her Venus and Mars. Here is a strong personal, intellectual and energetic tie. Ann's Ascendant, North Node and Sun also sit in Molly's first house with a North Node-Mercury conjunction again suggesting strong mental ties. Ann's Ascendant is conjunct (slightly wide) Molly's Chiron, suggesting lessons and healing between the two. There is a Pluto-Uranus conjunction in the seventh house in Scorpio which is also a strong tie. However, with the step-mother, there are the eighth-house issues and the theme that runs throughout the family. There is a Neptune conjunction at 14 Sagittarius (Molly's chart) with Uranus at 16 Sagittarius (Ann's chart) and both conjunct Chiron at 15 Sagittarius in step-mother's chart, all sitting in Molly's eighth house. There is intuition, dreaminess, psychic ability, compassion and escapism (Neptune) combined with chaos, the unexpected, humanitarian ideals and a desire for freedom (Uranus) combined with the healer, teacher and lesson learned, all in Sagittarius, which brings in enthusiasm, idealism, quest for freedom, philosophy,

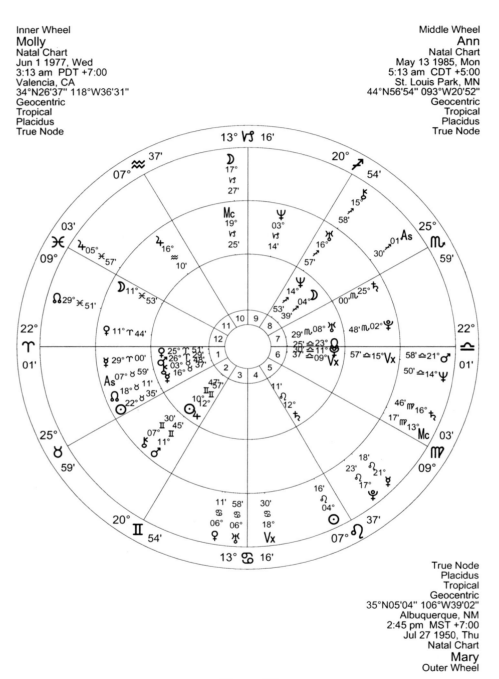

Inner Wheel
Molly
Natal Chart
Jun 1 1977, Wed
3:13 am PDT +7:00
Valencia, CA
34°N26'37" 118°W36'31"
Geocentric
Tropical
Placidus
True Node

Middle Wheel
Ann
Natal Chart
May 13 1985, Mon
5:13 am CDT +5:00
St. Louis Park, MN
44°N56'54" 093°W20'52"
Geocentric
Tropical
Placidus
True Node

True Node
Placidus
Tropical
Geocentric
35°N05'04" 106°W39'02"
Albuquerque, NM
2:45 pm MST +7:00
Jul 27 1950, Thu
Natal Chart
Mary
Outer Wheel

Figure 12

136

truth and justice. All of this sits in the house where the family theme of eighth house issues is strong. If you remember from the initial delineation of Molly's and John's charts, eighth house issues are where the family must work and where attention is needed. This one placement really tells the tale of the step-mother's role in regard to the interaction of these two siblings. These placements are in the Aries and Taurus dwads of energy and action combined with peace, harmony and a nice home.

John's chart in synastry with his sister Ann's and step-mother's charts (see Figure 13) also is revealing. Ann's Uranus is conjunct John's North Node in the fourth house so she causes quite a shake-up and the step-mother's Chiron is conjunct this placement, showing how she fits into the home and foundation of these two people as the healer and teacher. All of this is in Sagittarius, which is a theme running throughout these charts. Ann's Midheaven is conjunct John's Vertex in the fifth house of creativity, and the step-mother's Moon sits there, suggesting again that creativity is a good way of bonding for this family. There is a practicality to approach with the placements in the sign of Capricorn.

Ann's Moon is conjunct by a wide orb with John's Jupiter in the seventh house and they should form a strong bond, almost a partnership. Ann's critical-degree Mercury is conjunct (also by a slightly wide orb) John's Venus in the ninth house and they should share philosophies as well.

The same themes are present in the synastry of Molly, her father and step-mother (see Figure 14). For all three persons, the synastry starts in the fifth house with father's Pluto conjunct by a slightly wide orb Molly's Saturn and the step-mother's Pluto conjunct both, the exact degree of the father, David. Herein lies the creativity bonding placement with hard work and power struggles. The sixth house also has strong placements and work, service and health issues come into play. Molly's Pluto in Libra is conjunct David's Neptune by a slightly wide orb and David's Neptune is conjunct Mary's Mars by a slightly wide orb. This brings power and control issues into play with insight and intuition, or the opposite of looking at things through rose-colored glasses, energy and combativeness. There are a lot of power and control issues along with extremes in drive going on here. Since it is all in Libra, harmony is sought and this is not as combustive as it would be in a lesser harmonious and peace loving sign. All are seeking balance. David and Molly have South Nodes sitting in Virgo in Molly's sixth house so this is a very strong and karmic type of placement. Both father and step-mother also have Saturn here. Molly's father will be a tremendous influence on her work ethic and she may even feel a need to work as hard in order to keep up as an adult. The key here is for Molly to learn to work hard but not let work be everything; her career will probably be detailed oriented. Maintaining good health is also something Molly will probably learn from her father and step-mother.

The themes repeat in the synastry of John, his father and step-mother (see Figure 15). David's South Node sits in John's first house so there is a personal connection even if the South Node is not conjunct a planet. It is square John's Sun and North and South Nodes so there is personal work to be done. David's Vertex is conjunct John's Vertex in the house of creativity and specu-

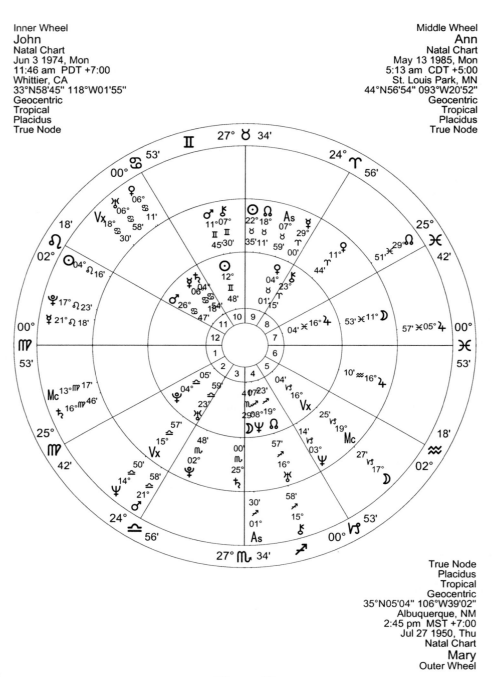

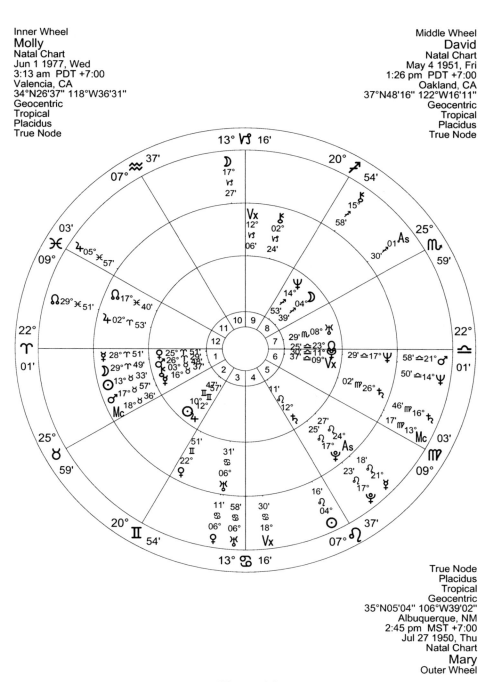

Inner Wheel
Molly
Natal Chart
Jun 1 1977, Wed
3:13 am PDT +7:00
Valencia, CA
34°N26'37" 118°W36'31"
Geocentric
Tropical
Placidus
True Node

Middle Wheel
David
Natal Chart
May 4 1951, Fri
1:26 pm PDT +7:00
Oakland, CA
37°N48'16" 122°W16'11"
Geocentric
Tropical
Placidus
True Node

True Node
Placidus
Tropical
Geocentric
35°N05'04" 106°W39'02"
Albuquerque, NM
2:45 pm MST +7:00
Jul 27 1950, Thu
Natal Chart
Mary
Outer Wheel

Figure 14

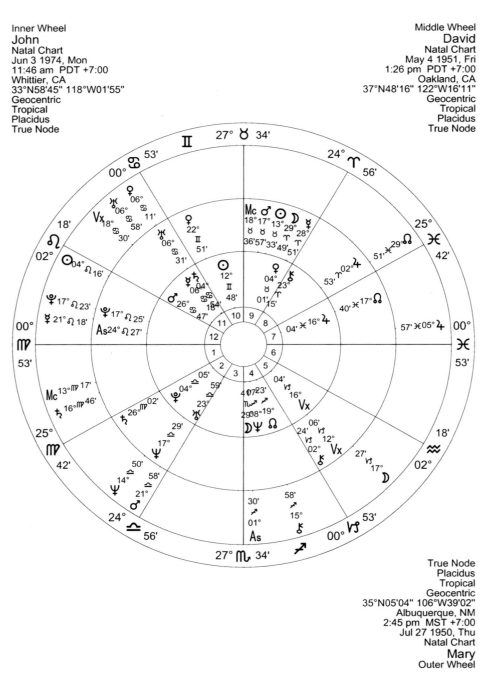

Figure 15

lation so there is a creative tie and both should enjoy people brought into the creative process. Also, David and John should have some insight into joint speculative ventures. There are, however, three very telling placements. The first is David's North Node conjunct John's Jupiter in John's seventh house, both in Pisces. There is a partnership feeling here with a lot of expansion, and with Pisces, perhaps also creativity. David may tend to look at John in an unrealistic light at times but this is a true partnership. The next telling placement is the Moon-Venus conjunction (slightly wide ob) in the ninth house of philosophy, religion and higher values. This is a good and harmonious placement. The third placement that is very strong is David's Uranus conjunct David's Saturn in the eleventh house. Saturn is the planet with karmic ramifications and conjunct Uranus suggests shake-ups; with both in Cancer, shake-ups occur in the home. It will affect John's wishes for the future and he will probably look toward friends and groups during times of crisis. Uranus is also conjunct John's Mercury so there will be a tremendous shake-up in thought processes as well, again concerning home and foundation. Although John has three T-squares, one of them is with his Ascendant, Moon and Midheaven, and David's Moon is trine John's Moon, suggesting he may be of help throughout David's life with regard to career and personal life. Remember, John's Moon is at a critical degree in his foundational house. This critical degree Moon suggests a broken home when in the fourth house and with David's Moon in a trine with John's Moon, you can see why he chose to live with his father (his nurturer).

With such a difficult placement as a T-square, David is quite good for John. He will help John with any ego problems related to his parents' divorce. Also, David's Pluto, the reorganizer, sits in John's twelfth house of subconscious and is trine John's North Node in his fourth house so this is also a benefit for John. Since David's Pluto is in Leo, it adds fire to John's already fiery North Node, lending to a strong subconscious link between the two and also helping with the home situation. Now add Mary into the mix. First, Mary's Saturn is conjunct David's South Node within one degree (very karmic) and this placement sits in John's first house so together they are very influential for John. Mary's South Node is conjunct David's Saturn in John's second house of values and this is another karmic placement that is very influential on John's personal value system. Also, Mary's Nodes are at a critical degree. There is a Neptune-Neptune conjunction of Mary and David in John's second house and a Mars-Neptune conjunction of Mary and David in John's second house. Mary's Mars is also conjunct John's Uranus so again there is an influence of perhaps confusion and a shake-up but also energy and a search for balance since the placements are in Libra. Mary's Moon is conjunct both John's Vertex and David's Vertex in John's fifth house, indicating the family theme of creativity and changes brought by Mary. Mary's Venus is conjunct the eleventh house conjunctions of David's Uranus with John's Saturn and Mercury and she actually brings peace into the home when there is chaos. *These are very strong astrological placements for all three people to help them work together.*

It is interesting to look at the synastry of the charts between Molly's and John's mother, Patricia, and their step-mother, Mary (see Figure 16). They are close in age so a lot of the outer planetary placements are close in degree. However, there are some really telling placements.

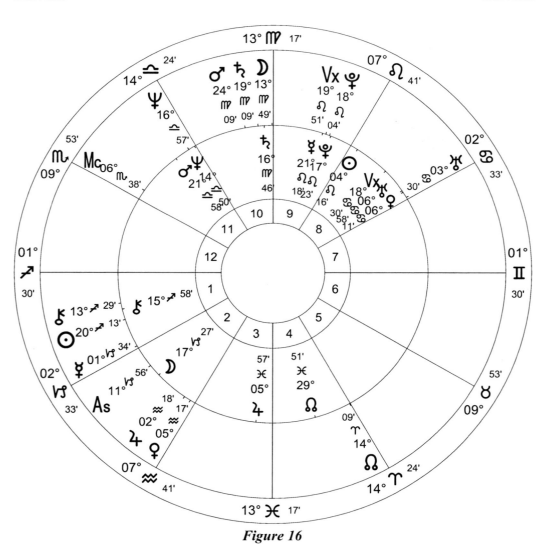

Inner Wheel
Mary
Natal Chart
Jul 27 1950, Thu
2:45 pm MST +7:00
Albuquerque, NM
35°N05'04'' 106°W39'02''
Geocentric
Tropical
Placidus
True Node

Outer Wheel
Patricia
Natal Chart
Dec 12 1949, Mon
8:49 am EST +5:00
Queens, NY
40°N43' 073°W52'
Geocentric
Tropical
Placidus
True Node

Figure 16

142

Patricia's Sun sits in Mary's first house, suggesting they will probably get along, and with their Chirons conjunct, both will teach and learn lessons, and perhaps need healing. Patricia's Uranus is conjunct Mary's Venus in the eighth house in Cancer. There may be conflict between shared resources and the home. At the least, shake-ups will occur occasionally. One of the most interesting placements is Patricia's Moon conjunct Mary's Midheaven, suggesting changes in what will fulfill Mary and where her ego finds peace. Since it is the Moon it suggests home and foundational changes or that Patricia will contribute on a foundational level to Mary and what could be more of a contribution than two children sharing their homes. This Moon is also conjunct Mary's Saturn, suggesting some hard changes but changes that must be worked toward. Patricia's Sun also is square this Saturn by a wide orb. The Moon and Saturn in Virgo indicate stability for the Moon and rigidity for Saturn. There is also a Mars-South Node conjunction and the South Node is at a critical degree so both must be cautious regarding combativeness and explosive situations. With the Moon in Virgo, Patricia must be cautious of being critical of Mary.

The eleventh house is that of step-children and Mary's Neptune is here and Patricia's South Node and Mary's Neptune are conjunct. Perhaps another indication of Mary's step-children? The South Node-Neptune placement suggests idealism or perhaps confusion and lack of clarity, and this is something that must be worked out. Although these two charts show some difficulty, they are strong and, used positively, the relationship between the two should be good. They must get through the Neptune-South Node placement though. Interestingly, this conjunction affects Mary's eleventh house or the house of the step-parent and Mary is the step-parent to Patricia's children. Patricia's Midheaven is also in Mary's eleventh house and conjunct the cusp of Mary's twelfth house, which should be good.

Molly's (see figure 17) and Joe's (see figure 18) charts in synastry with mother and step-mother are also revealing. Both Patricia and Mary have Pluto sitting in Molly's fifth house of creativity and should help both relate to Molly through this house; but both may have power struggles with Molly. The Midheaven-Moon conjunction between Patricia and Mary sits in Molly's sixth house, a good placement to help Molly with her work ethic, changes in what she may want and health issues. Both have Saturn here as well and tension may affect Molly's work or health. The Neptune-South Node conjunction that affected Mary's eleventh house also sits here, and if there is tension between Patricia and Mary, Molly may find it difficult to concentrate on work or school. The relationship between Mary and Patricia could also affect Molly's health. Fortunately, the Neptune-South Node placement is in Libra and both parties are looking for harmony, peace and beauty so this placement should work itself out. Since this placement is also conjunct Molly's Pluto, she will reorganize herself as part of the lesson.

In John's chart, Mary's Midheaven conjunct Patricia's Moon sits in his first house so they affect him personally. The Neptune-South Node conjunction sits in his second house of personal values and he may be confused at times, and at others really understands the situation. With Mary's Mars here as well, there is a lot of tension regarding values and finances. There is a Chiron-Chiron-North Node connection in the fourth house, suggesting that both Mary and Pa-

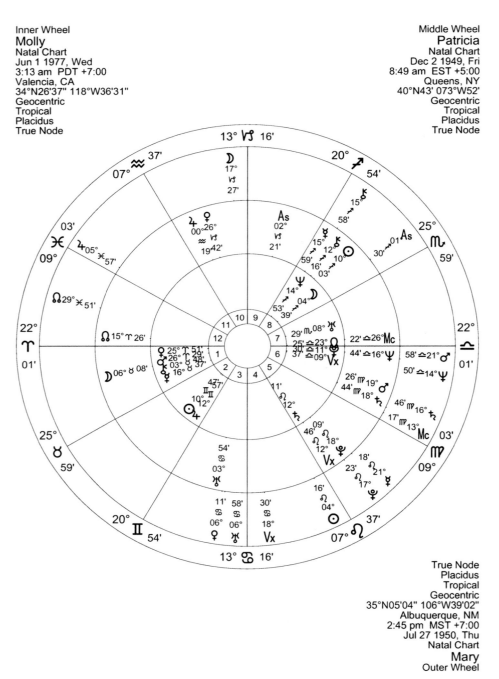

Inner Wheel
Molly
Natal Chart
Jun 1 1977, Wed
3:13 am PDT +7:00
Valencia, CA
34°N26'37" 118°W36'31"
Geocentric
Tropical
Placidus
True Node

Middle Wheel
Patricia
Natal Chart
Dec 2 1949, Fri
8:49 am EST +5:00
Queens, NY
40°N43' 073°W52'
Geocentric
Tropical
Placidus
True Node

True Node
Placidus
Tropical
Geocentric
35°N05'04" 106°W39'02"
Albuquerque, NM
2:45 pm MST +7:00
Jul 27 1950, Thu
Natal Chart
Mary
Outer Wheel

Figure 17

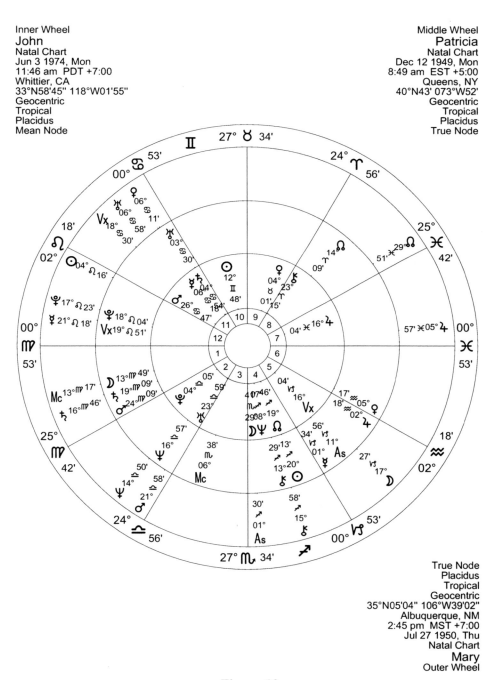

Figure 18

145

tricia are teachers, healers and may learn lessons about the home from John. The Venus-Uranus conjunction sits in John's eleventh house and is conjunct his Saturn so dreams and wishes are deeply affected; how Mary and Patricia play out this conjunction will also affect John's wishes for the future and perhaps the groups he is attracted to. Pluto in both of the women's charts sits in John's twelfth and both have a tremendous affect on his subconscious. Any power struggles between them will deeply affect him. In combination they are quite reforming in his subconscious.

Use of the Moon

Every member of the family brings something to the table in light of the relationship of a step-parent and his or her step-child. There are a lot of factors to consider in step-parenting, and in order to help the family bond into a comfortable unit, you can use timing devices such as return charts to target opportune times to grow as a family. The lunar return can be useful here to begin the bonding process. For example, creativity or eighth house issues are a good way for the example family to bond and work together. Let's say that either John or Mary has a lunar return chart with the Moon in the fifth house of creativity; this is the time to push forward in this area, to begin a project. Then, as the Moon transits the lunar return chart, they can work on each facet of life that the particular house it is transiting represents.

Solar returns are good for long-term work, but lunar returns afford more opportunities with impatient children. Returns are just an aside to aid in the start of the bonding process and the topic of another book down the road but they are something to think about when dealing with children.

Chapter 12

The British Royal Family

THERE ARE SOME IMPORTANT karmic placements and aspects that highlight the step-parent/step-child relationships between Prince William, Prince Harry and Camilla Parker-Bowles, wife of Prince Charles.

Prince William

Prince William has a stellium of planets in his ninth house: Mars, Saturn, Pluto retrograde and Jupiter retrograde conjunct the Midheaven. Philosophy and foreign matters are very important to him, as perhaps are higher consciousness and religious or humanitarian causes. This is good for a future king. With Pluto and Jupiter both retrograde, part of his karma appears tied to ninth house matters, along with his ninth house Saturn. Mars in Libra in this house suggests mental tension and indecisiveness. It also suggests concern for foreign matters and perhaps fighting for justice. William should watch his safety and security when abroad. Things may erupt when he is in another country.

The stellium carries over into his tenth house with the Jupiter conjunct the Midheaven, so career and honors are important as well. His education and development of higher consciousness are all geared toward what he will be: king of England. Jupiter is at zero degrees which suggests the start of something new. Jupiter coupled with Pluto suggests he will reform the monarchy or at least the public perception of it. He will expand the monarchy according to his personal beliefs and may hit obstacles with Saturn in the ninth house. The Mars in Libra indecisiveness may be tied to concern over foreign wars.

He has a T-square with Mars in the ninth house, the Moon in the seventh house and the South Node retrograde in the first house. When I look at a T-square I always look at what is missing or what would create a grand cross, and for Prince William it is Aries in the third house of communication. This is important later on when looking at Camilla Parker-Bowles' (step-mother's) chart along with his. There is a grand cross out of Prince William's T-square when looking at synastry with Camilla's planets. Also, Prince William may have difficulty in personally communicating his ideals or trouble with a partner. He is almost fighting himself to live up to his ideals. With the South Node in the first house he has been in this position before and reigning a country may be personally comfortable to him but doing it on a high, idealistic plane with a selfless attitude may be new and different. His mother's influence goes a long way here.

Prince William has a yod, as do many of William's peers because Pluto and Neptune move slowly; thus the yod will probably be directed toward generational themes. Pluto in Libra suggests balance, beauty and reformation. He will use his power to create what he thinks is right and beautiful as well as just. With Neptune in Sagittarius in his twelfth house Prince William subconsciously knows what he should do and will search for the freedom to do so, or possibly search for freedom from his responsibilities, or both, throughout his lifetime. With Neptune in his twelfth house, he should take care what type of freedom he chooses.

The yod is comprised of retrograde Pluto (ninth house) sextile retrograde Neptune (twelfth house) and pointing to Chiron in his fifth house and cusp of his fourth house. Since Pluto and Neptune are both retrograde, this is a karmic yod. Thus William's own personal philosophies, as well as his subconscious, point to his foundation with Chiron in his fifth house of creativity, romance and children and also on the cusp of his fourth house. His Chiron may be serving the fourth house as much as the fifth house. This brings changes to his foundation (the monarchy) and a need for healing or lessons. Remember, his mother died when he was young and this may be a part of his need for healing, with Chiron's influence so close to the cusp between the fourth and fifth houses. He may also feel very protective of his children when he is older because of the loss of his mother at a young age. He will both teach and learn from his children. Just with this superficial look at his chart, we see a lot of heavy aspects that go a long way in making Prince William what he will be as king of England.

When looking at aspects in synastry, I concentrate on conjunctions and oppositions, then trines and squares. I look at the Nodal placements and Saturn, as well as retrograde planets in terms of karma. I try to keep synastry simple and have found this works very well.

Just glancing at Prince William's seventh house, he has his Sun, Moon and North Node in Cancer (Sun-Moon conjunction). This is where he should shine, however his North and South Node suggest a push-pull between self and partnerships. He must find a balance. Coming from a place of I, me and my, he must find equality with a partner. With his Sun and Moon both in the seventh house, his royal (or maybe not royal) marriage should be loving and strong. Also, these placements are very important in synastry with both his mother and his step-mother. See Figure 19.

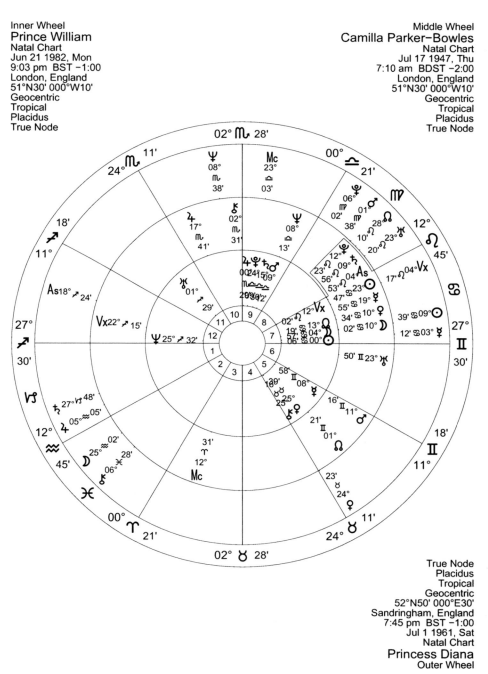

Inner Wheel
Prince William
Natal Chart
Jun 21 1982, Mon
9:03 pm BST −1:00
London, England
51°N30' 000°W10'
Geocentric
Tropical
Placidus
True Node

Middle Wheel
Camilla Parker-Bowles
Natal Chart
Jul 17 1947, Thu
7:10 am BDST −2:00
London, England
51°N30' 000°W10'
Geocentric
Tropical
Placidus
True Node

True Node
Placidus
Tropical
Geocentric
52°N50' 000°E30'
Sandringham, England
7:45 pm BST −1:00
Jul 1 1961, Sat
Natal Chart
Princess Diana
Outer Wheel

Figure 19

Although Prince William has no natal planets in his tenth house, his Sun and Moon trine the cusp of this house and Jupiter, making his ability to garner honor and recognition very strong. He will be loved for his feelings, as well as his strength.

Again, his Nodal placements suggest he must learn to focus on less on himself and more on his partner. In William's case, with his Sun and Moon trine the Midheaven, his partnership must also include his partnership with Great Britain.

William's Chiron, Venus and Mercury all sit in his fifth house of romance, creativity and children. Thus, a love for children and thoughts about them are very important to him. He will probably bond with his own children through creative means such as art, music and sports. Chiron suggests wounds he needs to heal and that they will be healed by and through his children. He will be both teacher and student with them.

William's North Node, or what he is working toward this lifetime, has some heavy aspects as well. It is square karmic Saturn, a difficult aspect and a double dose between the seventh and ninth houses. Different partnerships may shape his personal philosophies and higher conscious attitudes or perhaps a difficult partnership will have a great influence on him. His seventh house North Node is parallel his Moon in the seventh house, suggesting emotions around partnerships but also intuition, insight and especially strength since his North Node is also parallel his Sun. The North Node is also square his ninth house Mars, again bringing in issues of partnership and philosophy or religious beliefs and foreign matters.

Neptune is contraparallel his North Node and Moon so his subconscious reactions are shaped by partnership influences and difficulties, probably in light of a feminine figure. Thus his personal placements highlight or reinforce his synastry with Camilla. His South Node-North Node conflict is coming from a place of personal attitude and learning to work in a partnership manner with neither party being more important than the other. Since he is working with a seventh, eleventh and third house trine with his Nodes, this suggests someone working toward peace and societal harmony. His goal would be protection of society, perhaps a warrior or at least a warrior for a cause. Since the North Node, Sun and Moon are all in Cancer, this is based on his foundation and home. His true partnership is to his home, and since he is royalty, his true partnership is to Great Britain.

Jupiter in the ninth house is trine his Moon and Sun, and helps offset the square to Mars, as does Pluto trine his Sun. The Pluto-Sun trine will make him a strong reformer.

William's Sun is opposition his Ascendant, reinforcing his South Node-North Node opposition. He is working toward equality. His Sun is trine his Midheaven, bringing in career and honor to his partnership status and again, since the Sun, Moon and North Node are in Cancer, this tie is to his foundation.

William's tenth-house cusp is Scorpio, ruled by Pluto and Mars, both in the ninth house, so he will rule England based on his higher consciousness and philosophies of life, and his higher education will also play an important role. He will have high ideals for his country. Mars and Pluto in Libra are ruled by Venus so the dispositor is in the fifth house, making children are important to him as well.

Karmic Saturn in the ninth house is trine Mercury in the fifth house, suggesting karmic placements with children, but Saturn helps stabilize the Mercury in Gemini and he won't jump from one thing to another in a flighty manner, yet will be able to efficiently multi-task.

The Sun (where he shines) is trine Pluto, the Midheaven and Jupiter so he will definitely reorganize the royal household or at least the public perception of it with the Cancer foundation and Jupiter at zero degrees. It will be reorganized according to personal philosophies and higher values.

One placement I find a bit troubling is his twelfth-house Neptune in Sagittarius. He has an innate need to pursue spiritual matters, mysticism, morality and the like, and because Neptune is opposition his Sun and contraparallel his North Node in the seventh house, where he shines may be at odds with who he is deep down and balancing this may be difficult. He may have a deep need to escape when under pressure. On the other hand, with Neptune in his twelfth house, his imagination and intuition may be a great asset. He has an innate need to connect to his higher self that goes along with his ninth-house stellium. Although Neptune here is a savior/victim placement because he is working with the North Node and third, seventh and eleventh house placements, he should tend toward the savior role.

Now that we have briefly looked at what makes William a good candidate for king of England, this book is still geared toward creative step-parenting so we will look at Camilla Parker-Bowles in synastry with Prince William.

Prince William/Camilla Parker-Bowles

Prince William's North Node is conjunct Camilla's Venus and Moon in the seventh house, and Princess Diana's Sun and Mercury are conjunct his Sun and Moon in his seventh house. You can see that his mother's Sun will help him learn strength and how to shine and communicate through partnerships, following her example. Princess Diana was shy when she met Charles and during their marriage learned how to really shine and handle the media. She became an excellent communicator. This is what Prince William learned from her. Unfortunately, it ended up being a loveless marriage.

If you look at Camilla's planets, it seems as though he may learn about harmony (Venus) and emotions (Moon) in partnerships by her example. Despite any difficulties they may have, Camilla may help William learn how a loving marriage should be. Thus, both mother and step-mother add a lot to his chart in the seventh house areas. He is as much tied to Camilla (karmically) as his mother, which happens over and over again with step-family relationships. Lessons may be difficult but the karmic ties always exist. Camilla actually has her Moon, Venus, Mercury, Sun, Ascendant, Saturn and Pluto sitting in William's seventh house where Diana has her Mercury, Sun and Vertex. William and Camilla have a Moon-Moon conjunction by a wide orb and probably recognize each other on a deep emotional level. Camilla's Pluto and Saturn are conjunct William's Vertex. In fact, Camilla's Pluto is at the same degree as his Vertex. With Camilla's Pluto sitting in William's seventh house, he may perceive a power struggle with her in regard to his father (her husband). However, Camilla can go a long way in the bonding process by setting an example for William of how marriage should be. She will gain respect for this over the years and should try to cultivate this in order to bond with William.

As an aside, Princess Diana and Camilla have a Sun-Venus conjunction within one degree in William's seventh house, suggesting both are influential in his idea of partnerships. I have found that both mother and step-mother also have strong karmic ties.

Diana's Vertex is exactly conjunct Camilla's Ascendant. Is there any wonder that the people and media Diana brought around herself personally criticized Camilla? Since the placement is in Leo, everything said would be quite public and very dramatic.

With regard to William, where Princess Diana brought a lot of people into Williams's life and was good for him learning to deal with the limelight, Camilla brings herself and he must learn to cope with her on a personal basis. Diana's Mercury is conjunct William's Moon; she knows his emotions and he can read her as well. Diana's thoughts would always be of his emotional well-being and he would certainly feel this! There is a very emotional and intellectual connection between William and Diana, and more of a power struggle with emotions involved between Camilla and William.

Again, both women bring something to the table and the step-mother brings quite a bit.

Camilla's North Node is directly opposite William's retrograde Uranus in the eleventh house. This is a heavy aspect. Perhaps some of her creativity (North Node in his fifth house) will help him with regard to his wishes for the future or with groups or generational issues; however, an opposition, especially with Uranus retrograde, suggests this will not be easy. The nodal axis is a place they will have to work in order to bond. They can learn to work together when her North Node is transited by a benevolent planet. The Gemini (conscious mind) Sagittarius (superconscious or philosophical mind) are opposite but can compliment each other well if they learn to work together. With Sagittarius, William will have a very strong personal philosophy when it comes to both Camilla and foreign matters. With Uranus there are a lot of disruptions and chaos and they just don't know where things end up. It appears Camilla may be a disruptive influence.

Camilla's Midheaven sits in William's third house opposition his Mars and creates a grand cross with his T-square with Mars in the ninth house, the Moon in his seventh house and his South Node in the first house. There is thus a karmic link in the form of a T-square with his South Node in the first house, with William's attitude toward partnerships and his higher philosophies all coming to fruition in his third house conscious mind. It appears that Camilla at the very least may create a lot of personal anxiety for William. These are hard placements to work through and one must look elsewhere and at all areas of connection for places to bond and work together. This is why synastry between step-parent and step-child is so important. You must take such stressful placements and find ways to work with them. As I have stated, these people chose to come together and work things out this time around. A good example of working together would be for Camilla to take a somewhat public role (with her Midheaven in his third house of communication) and push a humanitarian project that is important to William. He may snarl while she is doing it but must appreciate any good that comes out of her work. This is the kind of activity that could take a truly tough karmic placement with the South Node and try to overcome it. Not an easy task.

As an aside, to add to the stress of Camilla's Midheaven creating a grand cross from William's T-square, Camilla also has a T-square and her Midheaven is part of it. Her T-square is from her 12 Aries Midheaven, her third house Neptune at 8 Libra to her eleventh house Moon and Venus in Cancer. So actually her Moon and Venus conjunct William's seventh house North Node, her Midheaven creating a grand cross in his third house and her Neptune conjunct his Mars in his ninth house are all part of her T-square. The difficulty of these placements flows both ways.

Also, Camilla's eleventh house is her house as a step-mother. It contains her North Node, suggesting she will be a step-mother this time around. Mars and Uranus in Gemini suggest a lot of mental tension and chaos for her as well. See Figure 20.

Camilla's South Node is conjunct William's Uranus in his eleventh house. Perhaps they have worked together before for generational issues and perhaps they have worked at cross-purposes. The South Node-Uranus placement can be tough to deal with and let's not forget his Uranus is retrograde. Karma, Karma, Karma! Uranus-South Node in the eleventh house may have extreme ramifications for William's hopes and wishes for the future. Uranus retrograde in the eleventh house is a pretty good placement on a personal level for William and will give him unusual and nonconforming approaches to generational issues. Per Lynn Koiner this placement suggests a "reformer complex." They see themselves as very normal, though. Camilla's South Node here is difficult. Again, if she were to help one of his humane efforts, it would go a long way in the relationship.

Camilla's Vertex is in William's twelfth house conjunct his Neptune retrograde, so people Camilla brings into his life may be disturbing or may offer insight. Neptune retrograde can be psychic and in the twelfth house probably insight comes to William in dreams, or it may cause paranoia. He may not trust people Camilla brings around. As you can see there are many karmic retrograde placements and aspects for Camilla and William to work toward bonding. There are more placements than I have covered but, as I stated, I usually concentrate on Conjunction or opposition, then square or trines. When I am looking for places for people to come together and bond, I look mainly at the conjunctions and then trines. If I look at where things may be more

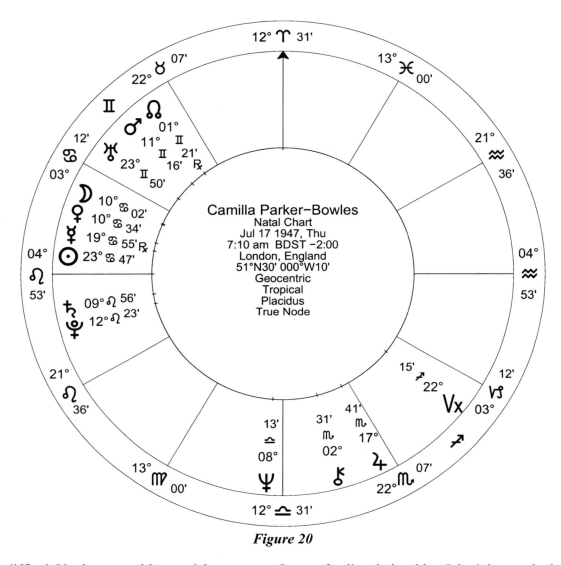

Figure 20

difficult I look at oppositions and then squares. In step-family relationships, I don't have to look too far for connections.

When looking at trines as places where bonding may occur in a more easy or more fluid manner, Camilla does have some planets trine William's planets. Some examples are:

Her Mars in his fifth house is trine William's ninth house karmic Saturn. Her creativity and mental drive (Mars in Gemini) may help push the plodding Saturn in Libra and she can use her Mars energy to move forward. Since William's Saturn is in the ninth house of foreign matters and higher consciousness, Camilla may actually help him with something idealistic and this also ties into the placements where she may help him with humane projects near and dear to William. Mars-Saturn is definitely tough, but in trine they may find a way to work together.

Any planet in one person's chart may have both difficult and easy aspects in synastry with planets in another person's chart. Look at the easy aspects as places to bond while trying to work through the more difficult aspects in the most positive manner. It is all a matter of choice as to how people interact with their charts.

Camilla's Uranus is trine William's Jupiter by a wide orb and Pluto by a tight orb. Uranus is difficult under the best of circumstances and in William's sixth house may affect his work, how he works or even his health. Since Uranus is in Gemini, it will probably affect his mental concentration or perhaps add to nervousness. However, with Pluto and Jupiter in William's ninth house and part of his stellium, Camilla may have some unusual or unorthodox thoughts that again help in ninth house matters, as well as a world-wide humanitarian project that William wishes to pursue. It is their choice to work with the trines and bond.

Camilla's Neptune is another place where both trine and conjunction may help her relationship with Prince William. Her Neptune is conjunct his Mars in the ninth house and her Neptune is trine his Mercury in the fifth house. Perhaps she may have some insight into creative ways he can further ninth house matters. They would have to overcome the Neptune square North Node in William's seventh house which probably includes feelings that he does not want her to understand him very well. But this trine and conjunction is a place to look toward bonding while working through the more difficult aspects of Camilla's Neptune.

Camilla's Chiron in William's tenth house is conjunct William's Jupiter in his ninth house and trine his Sun in his seventh house. This may facilitate any healing that needs to take place between the two of them, but again, it is their choice.

Some of Camilla's planets that sit in William's seventh house square some of his ninth house planets so all the trines that help with bonding in ninth house activities face obstacles from the squares. It all boils down to partnership and William's feelings in light of the seventh house placements of both Camilla and Princess Diana, the world and what he will do in light of his own higher consciousness. Thus, he should work with his step-mother when benevolent planets transit the trines, and back off when more difficult planets transit the squares.

Also, William has a lot of eleventh and twelfth house karma with Uranus and Neptune retrograde, and this is a place for him to work. Camilla's South Node and Vertex are here, with the South Node in synastry adding to William's already heavy karma. Her South Node is conjunct his Uranus in the eleventh house, suggesting drastic actions or persons who do not want to be restricted by each other. Since this is in Sagittarius, there is a double dose of the desire for freedom from the other party and a bit of chaos to boot.

William's South Node and North Node placements suggest a push-pull of partnership versus personal. He instinctively turns to the personal and it may be at the expense of the partnership. He learned to personally shine through partnerships from his mother but it appears emotional giving may be helped by Camilla's placements. He may learn by watching Camilla as she appears to stay somewhat behind the scenes. By helping or showing William how to achieve more of a balance in marriage, Camilla may also bond with him. Now that he is older, it is a time to really focus on how he wants a relationship to be. His comfort zone is I, me and my and so he must work on equality. This is perhaps Camilla's strongest positive point for William.

Pluto is associated with psychological reformation but when retrograde suggests the individual may not trust very much. This is in William's ninth house and suggests that perhaps he does not trust the foreign press, foreign matters in general or possibly religion. He probably has a lot of intuition regarding other people's motivations and this may in turn shape his personal philosophy. He is probably shy. This is a very good placement to work with for world reform. Pluto in Libra suggests difficulty with partnerships and power struggles and along with his Nodal placements we begin to see a pattern emerge. This Pluto is in the Cancer dwad so there may be an innate need to control his home and foundation, or reform his foundational values. This is another emerging pattern—maybe reforming the monarchy or how it is viewed by others—much like his mother whose Midheaven is conjunct this placement by one degree. This placement really emphasizes his mother's influence on him.

Again, Camilla's Uranus is trine this retrograde Pluto and sits in William's sixth house so help with work, service and with foreign matters may be a place to bond; but it is more than likely there would be chaos and unpredictability. For example, it may be difficult for William to resolve his mother's and his step-mother's roles since Camilla had a relationship with Prince Charles throughout his marriage to Diana. Camilla should try to use the trine energies to help bond even though Uranus may be difficult and unpredictable. Again, working on generational issues important to William is another good place of bonding with this placement.

Camilla's Sun is square this Pluto, again bringing in partnerships and foreign activities, influencing William's higher values regarding partnerships. Perhaps in some way Camilla may influence William's own personal philosophies toward partnership. There may be a power struggle with Prince Charles caught in the middle.

William's Jupiter is retrograde at 0 Scorpio in the ninth house. Zero degrees is important, although not as strong as 29 degrees. Jupiter here suggests expansion, connection to religion and opportunity, Jupiter retrograde suggests that perhaps he was once very religious and had difficulties because of it. He may now be cautious or even disdain religion and may not listen to that inner part of himself that needs a connection to something greater. Material goals will come up short in the overall scheme of things. He must give back now, not take. Jupiter retrograde in the ninth house is very strong and the child must dig deep to establish feelings of faith or connection. It is in the Scorpio dwad so there seems to be a lot of distrust or secrecy. He may be fearful of showing his wisdom or faith to the world. Camilla's Sun is square this so there may be difficulty dealing with her influence as well. It appears with many of their placements that William may have difficulty dealing with world perception in terms of Camilla. He may try to expand his horizons around her, possibly because of jealousy and therefore block where she can shine. She can bond with William if she takes an unobtrusive role and lets her light come slowly through. Her Uranus is trine his Jupiter by a wide orb, and although trines suggest an easy flow of energy, Uranus is still Uranus, so difficulty is also suggested, and again we see unpredictability and chaos. They can learn to work together and bond, but the learning process will not always be smooth.

William's eleventh-house Uranus is retrograde at 1 Sagittarius. This is the placement of the rebel. Also in the Sagittarius dwad, this is a rebel who wants freedom. Uranus here is not too difficult but this is tough for a royal who is expected to conform. He will fight the establishment for what he wants for the future, and again, he may be the king who reforms the monarchy. The lesson is to learn the art of compromise. His partnership placements may help train him for this since they also suggest he must learn the art of compromise. Remember, his lesson is between self and partners. His step-mother can have great influence here and help him learn, if only by example. It is a good place for them to bond. Camilla may also try to influence him with regard to his friends, who inspire him.

William's twelfth-house Neptune is retrograde at 25 Sagittarius. Neptune direct is the planet of dreams, psychic ability and escapism; when retrograde these may be hard to deal with and in the twelfth house these traits are very deep. This placement is often mediumistic, and coping with reality may be difficult according to an article by Lynn Koiner. Neptune retrograde can be a receptacle for all of the world's problems and this would be a difficult placement for a future king. On the other hand, a vivid imagination, a wonderful creative mind and spirituality are also possible and may help balance the retrograde Pluto in the ninth house. This is the placement of the artist, the spiritualist or the addict; he must reach for the higher ground.

Camilla's North Node and Mars in Gemini are in William's fifth house of creativity. Her natal eleventh house planets (what she brings to the table as step-mother) sit in William's fifth and sixth houses. This is one of the most karmic and strong places of coming together, possibly her ace in the hole. She may inspire him think more creatively and create more than he would have without her influence, even if the inspiration comes from difficult feelings. In other words, creativity is a place for them bond, and because of his twelfth house placement this is a very good place of bonding. They have some tough connections by aspect, but here is a place for them to come together. Her Mars is conjunct his Mercury, which may suggest some mental tension; however, fifth-house matters may ultimately lead to bonding. With her North Node in his fifth house, this is a good place for her to work on their relationship. Since he has Mercury and Venus here, it is another placement suggesting creativity. Camilla's North Node (what she should be doing now) in Gemini suggests communication and mental activity while working with William in a creative way. Although her Mars is opposition his Uranus by a wide orb, her Mars is well placed to add energy to William's creative mind. I can easily see them tossing ideas back and forth while collaborating on a creative endeavor. Sports is a good place for them to bond also. The Mars energy does not have to create tension if both parties try to work together.

Camilla's Saturn in William's seventh house is quincunx his retrograde Neptune, bringing partnership issues to the forefront. Although I do not usually look at the quincunx in step-relationships, because of previous placements indicating partnership issues and Saturn being a planet of karma, this is another tough area that is important. It suggests problems between them with partnership issues that are a core part of William's subconscious motivations. On the other hand, learning emotions and balancing the personal push-pull of self versus partner suggested by William's nodal placement may be hard but important lessons to learn from Camilla's Saturn influence. It sounds difficult but it is what they have chosen.

Camilla's Neptune is conjunct William's Mars in his ninth house. This placement suggests that she may help him with insightful suggestions and may try to bond over ninth house matters if they overcome the squares from the seventh house. Her Midheaven in William's third house is opposite his Mars and Saturn in the ninth house so her strength in communication with him may be difficult at times and at others may give him balance. The Midheaven opposition Mars may be difficult and there may be tension and testing each other's strengths, especially since this Midheaven creates the grand cross discussed earlier in this chapter.

In summary, since William's South Node is in his first house he will work through the grand trine of the first, fifth and ninth houses. Thus, his karmic retrograde planets in the ninth house are important and his work appears even more karmic. With his fifth-house Venus and Mercury, he is the intellectual and creative type and this is what he will add to society. Camilla's placements in his fifth house may help him and help them bond but will also affect how he works though his first, fifth and ninth house creative Nodal trine. Her placements in his seventh house are also very important to his natal placements, emphasizing personal versus partnership issues.

With the Camilla's South Node-William's Uranus conjunction at the same degree in his eleventh house, what do you think she did for his hopes for the future? Do you think they can work together for the good of society with the 1 Sagittarius placement or be at odds because of other placements? I am not sure! They must remember that they both love Prince Charles and learn to give and take with each other, working together where they can and backing off when need be.

Prince Harry

Prince Harry's chart is shown in Figure 21. His South Node is in the tenth house so he is working with a tenth, fourth and eighth house trine. According to Mohan Koparkar, Harry is to contribute to the economic growth of society. He has already gone abroad to help build infrastructure and homes.

His retrograde South Node is at 29 Scorpio in the tenth house. He may not be king but certainly has a role to play in society; this is his comfort zone. Though he appears fun-loving, Prince

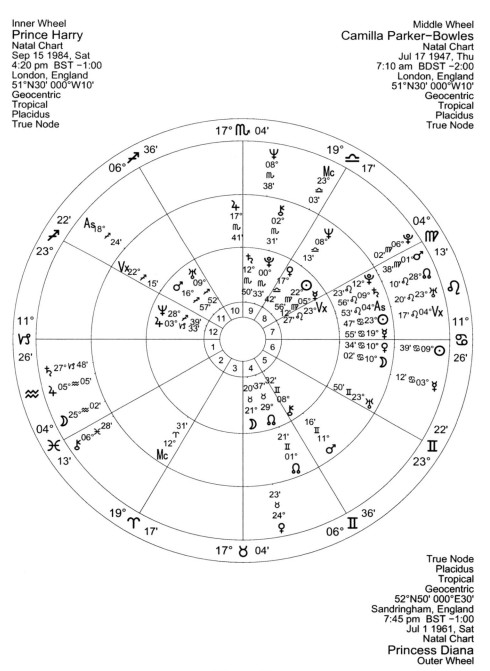

Inner Wheel
Prince Harry
Natal Chart
Sep 15 1984, Sat
4:20 pm BST −1:00
London, England
51°N30' 000°W10'
Geocentric
Tropical
Placidus
True Node

Middle Wheel
Camilla Parker−Bowles
Natal Chart
Jul 17 1947, Thu
7:10 am BDST −2:00
London, England
51°N30' 000°W10'
Geocentric
Tropical
Placidus
True Node

True Node
Placidus
Tropical
Geocentric
52°N50' 000°E30'
Sandringham, England
7:45 pm BST −1:00
Jul 1 1961, Sat
Natal Chart
Princess Diana
Outer Wheel

Figure 21

Harry won't have the same frivolous reputation as his Uncle Andrew had in his youth. Prince Harry's North Node is at 29 Taurus retrograde in the fourth house. His work is crucial for his foundation as well. While William seems more a dreamer, Harry may be more a worker. He is working for balance between career and foundation. Since his career is tied to his foundation, he probably will be able to synthesize these houses. In fact, being a royal is a perfect synthesis of these two houses.

Harry's South Node is in the Libra dwad so he is coming from a place where he achieved balance and harmony, or at least tried to do so, and this is his comfort zone now: career, public life and the achievement of peace and harmony. It is at a critical degree and this is of utmost importance to him. He may have been artistic in the past and will bring this type of nuance into his career. His North Node in his foundational house is also at a critical degree, and he was not very old when his mother died in the car crash, an incident that would shake any child's foundation to the core. The North Node in the fourth house suggests the importance of his foundation and in Taurus suggests that a nice home, security and comfort are important. It probably took him a long time to feel any sense of security after his mother's death. His North Node in the Aries dwad suggests that he may be a terror at home. At the least he brings a lot of energy and personal drive into the home, and this is a good placement for a royal.

Harry also has some interesting aspects. Like his brother he has a yod, but Harry's has the North Node where William's is with Chiron, suggesting that Harry has a more karmic placement and perhaps must work through something more karmic than his brother. His North Node is in the fourth house so he must work for the security of his home and foundation which in his case is his country. He has served in Afghanistan already. With the South Node in his tenth house at 29° Scorpio and going into Sagittarius, he may do a lot in foreign countries, possibly undercover because of the natal Scorpio Ascendant; he may truly be one of Great Britain's greatest assets.

Both brothers also have a T-square. Harry's T-square is Mercury at 5 Virgo in the eighth house, Uranus at 9 Sagittarius in the eleventh house and Chiron at 8 Gemini in the fifth house. His missing link is at 5 Pisces in his second house and conjunct the cusp between his first and second houses. His mother's Chiron at 6 Pisces fills in this missing link and shows a place where lessons are learned or healing takes place. Thus, his personal value system was greatly affected by his mother. His mother's Chiron creates a grand cross with Harry's placements. This suggests healing is needed or hard lessons are learned or taught. Since he lost his mother at such a young age, this may be the very tough lesson. Princess Diana should have a tremendous influence on his personal values. In fact, in a television interview, he stated he wishes to carry on his mother's legacy. His T-square is between his fifth, ninth and eleventh houses so, like his brother, he is working with foreign matters and personal philosophies, creativity and groups or wishes for the future.

Now back to Prince Harry's yod, which is karmic because it includes his North Node. His North Node is in the fourth house at the critical 29 Taurus, Neptune is in his twelfth at 28 Sagittarius and Pluto is in his ninth at 0 Scorpio, which is another important degree. Both his yod and his T-square involve the ninth house, suggesting this is a karmic house and important to his being. This would be good for foreign service. His critical degree is in his fourth house so his foundational values and what happens to him at home is crucial to his yod. Camilla and Harry should be able to work together for the good of the home/foundation with her North Node in a conjunction with his. This is a good place to bond. Pluto is at a beginning degree of Scorpio in his ninth house of foreign matters, philosophy, higher education and religion, and also in the Scorpio dwad Do you think he may do a little spying? In other words, his life probably will be geared toward foreign matters, behind the scenes actions or actions stemming from his subconscious motivations, pointing toward his royal foundation. The North Node is where he is working now, balancing his loyalty to family with personal recognition.

He also has Chiron retrograde in his fifth house conjunct Camilla's Mars, so fifth house matters are places of lessons or teaching or where healing will take place, and also where some karmic baggage is worked out. Her Mars is opposition his eleventh house Uranus in Sagittarius so there may be conflict with his unusual approach and ideals, his friends or groups and her tense mental state.

Harry's Part of Fortune, Mercury, Sun and Venus are all in his eighth house in Virgo with Venus in Libra, an indication of charm.

When using derivative houses, Harry's eighth house is the twelfth house (behind the scenes) to his ninth house of foreign matters. This indicates a lot of activity behind the scenes in foreign matters. With the Sun, Part of Fortune and Mercury in Virgo he will be very practical and this goes along with his Nodal placement of economic growth of society. The eighth house, among other things, represents other people's money and perhaps this is an emerging pattern for Prince Harry.

Pluto at zero degrees in the ninth house suggests power and control issues, again with foreign matters, and Saturn here suggests this is a karmic debt. Perhaps he also struggled a bit with higher education or feels thwarted or constricted by religion.

Uranus and Mars create chaos in his eleventh house of dreams, hopes and groups, and Uranus is part of the T-square that brings in the strong Mercury and eighth house issues. Between the eleventh house planets in Sagittarius and the eighth house planets, he will go to the ends of the earth for what he desires and specifically to economically benefit mankind.

Like his brother, Harry has Neptune in the twelfth house, indicating both insight and confusion. Neptune is square his eighth-house Sun which makes it difficult to follow his instincts in achieving goals. He may not trust his own insight. On the other hand, Jupiter trine Mercury can expand his subconscious and reach his conscious mind. If he can learn to trust his instincts, he will do well.

Interestingly, nine of Harry's planets are above the horizon so although he may work in the background of foreign matters he will be visible. Again, a little spying?

He does not have the number of retrograde planets that his brother has. William appears to have a lot more emotional baggage and debt to pay, but then he is to be king. Harry already seems to have started working well with his placements.

Prince Harry/Camilla Parker-Bowles

Camilla's and Harry's Nodes are conjunct within two degrees, a close connection. There are definitely some ties and obligations between them. The North Node conjunction is in the fourth house so she is definitely part of his foundation, and although his is in Taurus and hers is in Gemini, they recognize each other on a basic, innate and core level. They should learn to work together for the good of the crown at the very least. Camilla's Mars is conjunct Harry's Chiron in the fifth house so she would push him in creative matters and perhaps help him with his own children. She may be a little overbearing as a grandmother. With her Mars in Gemini, she should communicate well and forcefully with him. Just as with William, creativity is a good place to learn to bond and a place of healing for Harry. Camilla and Harry may bond more easily with the nodal contact or innately feel more conflict and not really know why. With a nodal tie though, they will remain connected throughout their lives. Diana's Venus is conjunct both Harry's Moon and North Node in the fourth house and he will gain feelings of security and love from her even though he must work with foundational issues with Camilla. Harry's Moon is in the Capricorn dwad which may cause him to appear emotionally stoic. He is not! Also, Princess Diana's Saturn is at 27 Capricorn (the sign of his Moon's dwad) so she will relate to him personally on an emotional level with this placement in his first house even though Saturn suggests some obstacles. This one placement is a good example of why dwads in synastry are so important. Saturn in the Capricorn dwad is karmic for Diana but when we see Harry's lunar dwad is also in Capricorn we can see another close emotional tie that is not apparent at first glance.

Camilla's Mercury, Sun, Ascendant, Saturn and Pluto sit in Harry's seventh house and although they are not conjunct any one planet, this is a large stellium in one house. She thus influences his reaction to partnerships.

As an aside, Diana's Vertex is conjunct Camilla's Ascendant by degree in Harry's and William's seventh houses. There is no doubt that they will be related through marriage to these boys. Diana's Part of Fortune is also conjunct Camilla's Ascendant and she probably benefitted from Camilla's negative publicity.

Camilla's Chiron is conjunct Harry's Pluto in his ninth house in Scorpio. Both are in the Scorpio dwad and this is part of his yod. She should help him in ninth, twelfth and fourth house matters. They may learn from each other; however, her lessons will be reforming to him or he may try to reform her. There may be some power struggles. She is giving and receiving lessons from the strength of his Pluto, a powerful combination. Camilla may help or influence Harry with his work in foreign matters. He may have trouble dealing with her and the foreign press or any publication for that matter. Her Jupiter in Harry's tenth house is also conjunct his Saturn in the ninth house by a wide orb, suggesting her influence will be expansive and perhaps difficult for him. Harry may feel inhibited or that she is some type of obstacle. She appears to try to expand while he tries to hold back and reform.

Just as they have the North Node conjunction in Harry's fourth house, they have a South Node conjunction in Harry's tenth house; hers is at 1 Sagittarius and his at 29 Scorpio. Her South Node should be positive for his South Node, and this placement goes hand in hand with her influence on the ninth house. Because of this placement, her influence may help him shine and gain recognition, or just her presence could cause discomfort. Because this is a South Node placement, they recognize each other, have been here before and this relationship whether difficult or easy is a comfort zone for both of them. Since both South Nodes sit in Harry's tenth house, they may have even been royalty in the past but also had difficulties; whatever happened was probably very public as it is now. Harry's South Node is in the Libra dwad and he is reaching for balance, peace and harmony; this is his quest in his career and where he will definitely shine. Libra likes peace and comfort and as stated previously, Harry built homes and infrastructure in other countries and has gone to Afghanistan.

Harry's North Node in the fourth house suggests that perhaps he was career oriented at the expense of his home and must concentrate on home this time. He did something critical in the past so now must think of foundation and others. This also suggests a close tie with his mother or father and that breaking away is difficult. As we know, parting with his mother must have been very difficult. Camilla's North Node here may help with growing up and away from his father as well. He may have to work hard for honor but while working hard must achieve balance between career and home and family. The real key here is a balance between security and doubt versus self-esteem.

Again, his South Node in the tenth house is at a critical degree so he is coming from a place where his work and honor reached a critical level and may do so again. For example, his humanitarian works or his military service may bring him honor and may be of critical importance. With Scorpio there may be danger and deception as well, and he may see the horrors of war.

Harry's Sun is in the eighth house in Virgo also suggests he may shine with regard to partnership assets, investigation, intimacy and other eighth house matters, and this is totally different from his nodal placements. Camilla's Sun is sextile Harry's Sun so there is an easy flow of energy and she may help here. Also, this is the derivative twelfth house to the ninth house and again he may work behind the scenes regarding foreign matters. This seems more likely to me. In any event Camilla's Sun sextile Harry's Sun and is a good place to bond.

Camilla's Sun is square Harry's Pluto by wide orb; although difficult, if they can work through the square and learn to work together she can help him with his yod placement. They must overcome great issues of power, control and reorganization of their roles and learn to feel equal to each other. In general outer planet energies trump inner planet energies in synastry but since this is the Sun-Pluto, the Sun is not easily trumped. There could be quite a butting of heads. I think her Sun square Harry's Pluto may have a lot to do with his superconscious philosophies on seventh house matters and her role in partnership with his father/mother, as well as much as other ninth house matters.

Camilla's Sun is trine his South Node by a slightly wide orb so again there seems to be a karmic contact and she may help him with tenth house matters and is a strong influence. Working together for the crown is a good place to bond. This placement helps balance the Sun square Pluto. If he tries any sort of power play they will definitely butt heads.

Camilla's Jupiter sits in Harry's tenth house and is opposition Harry's Moon in the fourth house; thus her presence in the royal family may cause a lot of emotions around his home and foundation. Her Sun in his seventh house is trine his tenth house South Node, suggesting her influence as his father's wife may influence him in his own career and how he gains public honors. Her Mercury is trine his Midheaven, suggesting she will be kind to him in the media. Her Venus is also trine his Midheaven by a wide orb and is beneficial to his work and may help him gain honor and recognition for his work.

Their Mars in opposition is very difficult in synastry and since his Mars is in the eleventh house it suggests a step-relationship in the past, possibly where he was the step-parent. This ties into the nodal placements. Harry seems to have a lot more to work out with Camilla than does his brother William.

Camilla's Neptune is square Harry's Jupiter and Ascendant and since Jupiter is in the twelfth house this suggests her insight into him may be unnerving; but he will not know why.

If you look at Camilla's and Diana's planets, both are strong in Harry's sixth house and should influence how hard he works and how healthy he lives—Diana by her strength (Sun) and communication of thought (Mercury); Camilla by her emotions (Moon) and with Camilla's Uranus there, perhaps shock or surprise. Camilla's Uranus in Gemini is in the Pisces dwad and she may bring insight, emotional chaos or both.

Diana's Pluto is conjunction Harry's Mercury in the eighth so there is a much more intimate relationship than Harry has with Camilla. Diana has a reforming affect on him personally and has a great influence on where he will shine. He has said he wishes to continue his mother's legacy. Diana's Neptune is conjunct Harry's Saturn in his ninth house so she has great influence in this house as well; but Camilla has the placement conjunction his Pluto in the ninth house which influences his yod. Both women may be influential and bring a lot to the table.

Diana's placements are more personal to Harry: Saturn, Jupiter, Moon and South Node in his first (personal) house. Her Venus is in a conjunction by a slightly wide orb his North Node in the fourth house so there more of an emotional investment between them. Diana is Mummy and Camilla can be more of a helper if they bond.

Camilla's Saturn is square Harry's Saturn. This is karmic and tough. Her Saturn is in the seventh house of partnerships and his in the ninth house of higher consciousness and religion. This could cause difficulties especially since she had a friendly relationship his father during Charles' marriage to Diana and Harry is probably quite philosophically confused or opposed to this. Camilla's Saturn is in the Scorpio dwad and Harry's Saturn is in Scorpio—another example of dwads flavoring a placement. The Scorpio influence may also bring in some jealousy. Saturn in Scorpio is tough and with her dwad she is up to fighting the Saturn obstacles. However, Camilla's Saturn is trine Harry's Uranus and part of his yod, so although they may have to work at it she may help him with his hopes for the future if they can work through the karma and bond.

Camilla's Neptune in Harry's eighth house is square his Jupiter in the twelfth house and also the Ascendant. They recognize each other on an unconscious level. She may intuitively know what motivates him and try to avoid the square energy and use Neptune intuition to bond.

Diana's Midheaven and Neptune sit in Harry's ninth house so her influence on his education and life philosophy is strong. Camilla has Chiron there and they may learn from each other, as well as come together in a healing sense.

Both William and Harry do not have that warm, fuzzy feeling with Camilla that they had with their mother and rightly so. However, if they try, Camilla may be helpful to them.

Dwads Revisited

Camilla and Prince William

You will see over and over how the dwad can flavor step-relationships in synastry. Thus, I will go over some of the astrological placements again and add secondary progressions to the mix.

The dwads and the dwads of the secondary progressions are just another part of the mix to be thrown into the blender for a complete astrological cocktail. There is a Moon conjunction with William and Camilla in William's seventh house. His is in the Leo dwad and hers in the Scorpio dwad. They recognize each other's core emotions with a Moon conjunction, but William learned how to handle the press from Diana (his Leo dwad coming out) and perhaps he learned of the jealousy or almost fanatical love from Camilla (her Scorpio dwad coming out), who was in the background for many years. He may have been aware of scheming on an emotional level while also recognizing true love in a partnership. This Moon in Cancer conjunction takes on a whole new dimension when looking at the dwads.

On Charles and Camilla's wedding day William's secondary progressed Moon was 27 Aries, which is in the Pisces dwad. Along with the Aries energy and enthusiasm showing outwardly, William probably had a lot of emotional turmoil and even at his age perhaps confusion. His natal lunar dwad in Aries is quite different from his secondary progressed lunar dwad in Pisces.

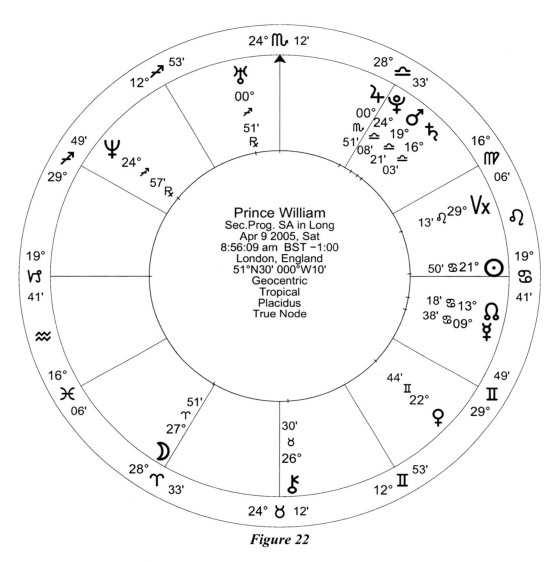

Figure 22

Let's look at a tough opposition. Camilla's 12 Aries Midheaven is opposition William's ninth house Mars in Libra and Saturn at 15 Libra. Her Midheaven is in the Leo dwad, his Mars is in the Capricorn dwad and his Saturn is in the Aries dwad. This adds an interesting twist on his T-square which her Midheaven turns into a grand cross. We now have Leo and Capricorn dwads which are quite different. They can be practical and at least publicly learn to work together. The Capricorn with Mars stabilizes the Mars energy a bit but since William's Mars is in Libra; William will still weigh things back and forth, perhaps frustrating her Aries Midheaven.

Saturn in the Aries dwad helps William relate to Camilla's Aries Midheaven and suggests they have worked together before and this is another karmic placement. Whatever was done before, they have to tough it out now.

On the day Prince Charles and Camilla were married, William's progressed Mars was at 19 Libra and Saturn at 16 Libra, putting Mars in the Taurus dwad and Saturn in the Aries dwad. William's fiery Mars had progressed to a sign somewhat tempered by a desire for balance and beauty and one that is extremely charming, while staunch Saturn was now influenced by fiery Aries. These placements can be summed up by Saturn, his karma, feeling aggressive rather than held back, his energetic Mars being tempered and his appearance that of charming and harmonious. Although he had fire energy ith both placements, the Libra influence on Mars seems to come through here.

As I mentioned before, look at conjunctions and trines, or oppositions and squares when looking at synastry. Since Camilla's Moon is important in synastry to William's chart because her Moon is square his Mars. His Mars is in the Capricorn dwad and her Moon is in Cancer in the Scorpio dwad. Although Mars is fire energy, he is looking for balance and stability throughout the world. Foreign press reports may be hard for William, and Camilla is again in the background with a lot of emotion, perhaps jealousy, confusion or delusion (Moon in Cancer in the Scorpio dwad). This is a difficult square. On the wedding day, with William's 19 Libra Mars in the Taurus dwad in his eighth house, he put those old ninth house feelings behind the scenes and brought out the Libra charm.

Camilla's Venus is also square William's Mars and Saturn, and in the same Scorpio dwad as her Moon. Since Venus tends to be more benevolent, perhaps this will lessen the difficulty of the Moon placement; but the energy is still a square and difficult.

Camilla's Moon is opposition William's South Node which is 13 Capricorn in the Gemini dwad. Of course this South Node deals with karma and in the first house it is very personal to William, and with the Moon, very emotional for Camilla. Capricorn suggests inflexibility but the Gemini Dwad adds some intellect to this placement and may help a bit; but, I feel he stubbornly digs his heals in on issues of Camilla because that is what he feels he should do. It is a pattern.

Camilla's Venus is conjunction William's 13 degree North Node and this is beneficial in their synastry. Her Venus brings caring and balance to what he needs to do for future karmic patterns. His North Node is in the Sagittarius dwad. Sagittarius is the natural ruler of the ninth house where he has a stellium and although Camilla's Venus is square William's Saturn in the ninth house, this conjunction should open a door for Camilla to relate to William in regard to foreign matters or higher consciousness.

A less difficult and more helpful aspect is Camilla's Jupiter trine William's North Node in Cancer in the Sagittarius dwad, a natural and easy flow of energy. Camilla's Jupiter is in William's tenth house, suggesting she again may be a catalyst for the karma he chooses to initiate with regard to tenth house activities. Any time there is a benevolent planet transiting this Jupiter is a time for Camilla to relate to William and his sense of duty and honor (tenth house matters). *Despite all of the difficulty with other placements this is an example of a place where the step-parent can bond with the step-child.*

Camilla's Uranus is in William's sixth house in Gemini. She creates nervous tension that could affect his health. However, it is trine his Pluto in the Ninth house at 24 Libra in the Cancer dwad. A trine should be an easy flow of energy. Uranus is never easy and this trine helps lessen the erratic Uranus energy. Pluto-Uranus is tough even in trine. There are power issues and chaos. Again, Camilla is affecting William's ninth house, foreign matters, foreign press and his higher consciousness, and the trine is unpredictable. This placement includes family issues because of the Cancer dwad creating a whole new dimension to the placement. His progressed Pluto is also 24 Libra but direct, not retrograde, on the day of the marriage so it is possible there is a little easing of the karmic energy. Camilla's Uranus is also opposition William's Neptune at 25 Sagittarius in the Libra dwad and his 27 Sagittarius Ascendant also in the Libra dwad. Bringing the dwads into play reinforces the underlying pattern of Sagittarius and the ninth house, as well as a need for balance represented by Libra, and subconscious emotions represented by Neptune, as well as confusion and idealism. Camilla's speech and thought patterns are unpredictable that day and in William's sixth house may cause nervousness. More importantly, the Uranus-Neptune opposition would create confusion or flashes of insight, upheaval or erratic emotions, all with a desire for an idyllic situation, and perhaps not the marriage. Since Neptune is in the Libra dwad it suggests William will try for balance but it may be difficult. More importantly, as discussed before, her Uranus is opposition his twelfth house so many of his feelings may be buried deep in his subconscious only to come out later. With Neptune in the twelfth house, he wants to see the world with rose-colored glasses and may be in denial.

One important point is that Camilla's vertex is conjunction William's Neptune in his twelfth house so she may bring people around, although probably in the background, that are beneficial for William, his dreams and his generational values. This is another good place for Camilla to work on her relationship with William. Her Vertex is in the Leo dwad and his dwad is Libra which is also a good match—fun-loving or exciting and energetic people may help him balance his emotions.

Her Saturn is conjunction his Vertex, suggesting she may have difficulty dealing with people he brings around. There is a karmic connection to work through. His Vertex is in the Sagittarius dwad so we again see the Sagittarius theme and ninth house matters, since Sagittarius rules the ninth house. The dwads reinforce the ninth house placement issues.

Camilla's Neptune is trine William's Mercury in the Virgo dwad. First of all, Neptune-Mercury suggests William may not be able to consciously figure her out but she may say or do things with terrific insight that helps him again in ninth house matters. She may never understand how he thinks but at times may have insight into his mind. The Virgo dwad helps keep an over-active Gemini mind clearly focused. His Mercury by progression on the day of his father's marriage to Camilla was 9 Cancer and he must have been thinking of his own mother with Diana's 9 Cancer Sun. It is in the Libra dwad so he was charming and tried to stay balanced that day. Because Camilla's Neptune sits in William's ninth house and is trine his Mercury, he has the ability to use the foreign press to advantage and perhaps keep Camilla confused, much as his mother probably did. Just knowing this may bring him a little wicked peace of mind. Camilla's Neptune is square William's North Node at 13 Cancer in the Sagittarius dwad—yet another ninth house issue affecting his role in the world and her insecurity, emotions and insight.

Camilla's Neptune in William's ninth house is square his Moon at 4 Cancer in the Leo dwad in his seventh house, suggesting emotions around how public their situation is to the world. By progression his Moon was at 27 Aries in the Aquarius dwad on his father's wedding day. Moon-Neptune suggests difficult emotions and in the Aquarius dwad suggests William may be trying to reach for higher ground; but this is difficult for William even though he is an adult.

Camilla's Neptune is square William's South Node at 13 Capricorn in the Gemini dwad in his first house. She is personally difficult and he has done a lot of thinking about the situation and probably expressed himself verbally; he feels a core difficulty with her emotions, as well as her intuition. Since his progressed South Node is also in Capricorn, he may be personally stubborn but will be stable no matter what the situation. He will plod along even though ninth house matters are again involved. The ninth house is not just philosophy, higher consciousness and foreign matters, but also publishing and thus the domestic and foreign press could bring him a lot of heartache where she is concerned. Her Neptune is in the Capricorn dwad also so the two Rams may but heads. Her Neptune desire would be for an idyllic relationship and his would be more cerebral and thinking about how things really are.

We must bear in mind that Camilla's aspects to William's Mars, Moon and South Node activate his T-square energies as well so her Neptune square his South Node is quite difficult and again plays a part in his seventh and ninth houses. Even when looking at the dwads which flavor the placements, the seventh, ninth and first houses with Camilla's Midheaven in Williams third house creating the grand cross are most difficult. She really must concentrate on her ace in the hole placement for a binding experience.

Camilla and Prince Harry

As with William's chart, the placements are what they are but the dwads can increase or diminish an easy or difficult flow of energy.

Camilla's Moon is trine Harry's Midheaven at 17 Scorpio in the Taurus dwad. With a 17 Scorpio Midheaven Harry is dynamic and has a lot of charisma. The emotions felt are probably a bit of mistrust but he would not publicly show this. He will remain charming with his Midheaven in the Taurus dwad. Publicly he may appear to have a somewhat easier time than William. But

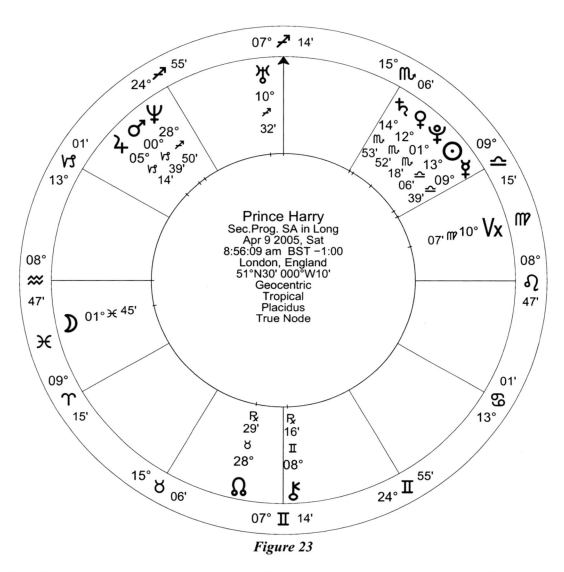

Figure 23

Camilla's Moon is also trine his Saturn at 12 Scorpio in the ninth house in the Pisces dwad which suggests a lot of emotion and confusion affecting Harry's higher philosophy, his private choices and the face he will always publicly present. He also has media-related issues with Camilla, and may feel restricted by her emotions. His Midheaven progressed to 7 Sagittarius on the date of the marriage of Prince Charles and Camilla is in the Aquarius dwad so publicly he wants freedom and privately he is moving beyond himself and more toward the world view. He will only show charm in public.

Camilla's Moon is opposition Harry's Jupiter at 3 Capricorn in the Aquarius dwad. Herein lies the rub! Aquarius may lessen Capricorn's rigid stance but also brings a need for a higher order to Harry that he won't show or possibly even recognize since it is in his twelfth house. Her emotions are an influence on his unconscious motivations and psyche. Jupiter is expansive and this may balloon or expand deep down, only to erupt at times and for no apparent reason. Jupiter in Capricorn takes on a new flavor when Aquarius is thrown in. His progressed Jupiter was 5 Capricorn on the wedding day in the Pisces dwad, suggesting he was very emotional that day. He may have felt confused.

Camilla's Sun is trine Harry's Midheaven and South Node by a wide orb. Again, Harry's Midheaven is 17 Scorpio in the Taurus dwad so Camilla's Sun in Harry's seventh house suggests that through partnership matters she may help Harry with his work toward public honor. He may be suspicious, but will show appreciation and be charming and kind. This is a good placement for Camilla to work with Harry and bond through seventh house matters.

Camilla's Moon helps tenth house matters, another good place to bond. Harry's South Node is in the Libra dwad and in the tenth house, suggesting he will be recognized for his balance and fairness. He will do well with investigation and any kind of eighth house matter such as economic help to others.

Remember that marriage changes the step-relationship with the child from someone on a par with the child to that of the parent's spouse and perceptibly no longer on a par. Thus any negative aspect to Pluto heightens issues of control and power are heightened. Camilla's Pluto is in Harry's seventh house, affecting his view of partnership and marriage. Saturn is in his ninth house of higher ideals so his view of any partnership may be greatly affected by her need to control. There is a real power struggle here. Her Pluto is also square his tenth house cusp, suggesting potential power struggles regarding public image and his career as a royal. Pluto in the Sagittarius dwad suggests she wants him to present her as ideal in public while she tries to be in control through partnership (marriage). She plays on his desire to remain charming, with his Midheaven in the Taurus dwad.

Camilla's Mercury is trine Harry's Midheaven and her marriage to Charles when Harry was almost twenty years old suggests she will talk about and treat him as an adult and may try to help further his public image even though it may be through her Pluto control. So this is a good placement to bond and may lessen some of the more difficult aspects. Camilla's Mercury is square Harry's Venus at 17 Libra on the cusp of his ninth house. His Venus is in the Aries dwad so he may feel like he feels, not wanting her thoughts or communication to matter.

Camilla's Venus is opposition Harry's Ascendant at 11 Capricorn in the Taurus dwad. It is trine Saturn as 12 Scorpio in the ninth house in the Pisces dwad and trine the Midheaven at 17 Scorpio in the Taurus dwad. On his father's wedding day, Harry's Ascendant was at 8 Aquarius in the Taurus dwad. Harry's Saturn was at 14 Scorpio in the Aries dwad and his Midheaven at 7 Sagittarius in the Aquarius dwad.

Camilla's Venus is in the sixth house of work and service, so a trine to Saturn helps with ninth house issues. Venus eases the obstacles and difficulties suggested by Saturn and promotes bonding with Harry in sixth house matters; this may help lessen some of the ninth house difficulties they share. Camilla may help Harry with emotional blocks since Saturn is in Scorpio in the Pisces dwad. He should probably learn to trust more and perhaps be less confused. It will help their relationship if Camilla uses this placement to bond. However, there is still the matter of the media and higher ideals that may not emotionally mesh with what he feels is ideal. Saturn in Scorpio is always difficult and often emotions or vindictiveness are one's own worst enemy. On the other hand, Harry is magnetic but may hide his true feelings at least in the public arena.

Camilla's Venus is trine Harry's Midheaven at 17 Scorpio in the Taurus dwad. *She should work toward helping Harry shine to gain recognition for his public efforts; this is great place to bond.* He has Scorpio magnetism and Taurus charm which is wonderful for a royal and is what he presents to the public. He appears more accessible than his brother and will probably will be more diplomatic about Camilla. Venus in Cancer gives Camilla some nurturing feelings toward what Harry will become. Unfortunately, this good placement is also opposition Harry's Ascendant at 11 Capricorn in the Taurus dwad. If you have to have an opposition, Venus is not such a bad planet with which to have it. Capricorn suggests practicality and Taurus suggests charm, so all will appear okay. Appearances help things to go more smoothly.

On the wedding day Harry's Ascendant had progressed to 8 Aquarius and was again in the Taurus dwad. Harry would appear charming but with Saturn at 14 Scorpio in the Aries dwad he would feel a lot of things, including the necessity to hide is true feelings. It may have been difficult for him, and he may have been more self-involved about his feelings.

Camilla's Mars is opposition Harry's Mars at 16 Sagittarius in the Gemini dwad and opposition Harry's Uranus at 9 Sagittarius in the Pisces dwad. It is trine Venus by a wide orb so the oppositions are what are prominent.

Mars opposition Mars indicates conflict, tension and a lot of opposing energy. However, Sagittarius is idealistic and Gemini thinks on both sides of an issue so it could be worse. But Sagittarius also suggests foreign matters and publicity so Harry, like his brother, may have trouble dealing with the press where Camilla is concerned, and with Mars may explode from time to time. Mars opposition Mars suggests power struggles and we have seen this with other placements as well.

Mars-Uranus is difficult, unpredictable and explosive in opposition. Sagittarius with the Pisces dwad suggests Harry's judgment may be clouded and unpredictable and he may also misjudge Camilla's Martian energy. Uranus is part of Harry's T-square so Camilla's Mars is setting off a difficult aspect in his fifth house with Chiron, the eighth house, the Part of Fortune and the eleventh house Mars energies. Since Chiron is included there is an obvious need for healing and lessons to be learned.

On his father's wedding day Harry's Mars had progressed to 0 Capricorn in the Capricorn dwad in the eleventh house and Uranus to 10 Sagittarius in the Aries dwad in the tenth house.

Harry is practical about what he wants and his dreams for the future and he has energy to achieve his goals. He was concerned on that day with disruption or chaos around his public image and thought a lot about himself and his role in the family. The Sagittarius theme is repeated again and again, and plays an important role here. Of course his role in the family comes into a great deal of consideration since the family dynamic has now radically changed.

Camilla's Jupiter is opposition Harry's Moon at 21 Taurus in the Capricorn dwad. Jupiter expansiveness may cause Harry to overreact emotionally but he has the help of an earth sign in an earth dwad to stabilize this. Since his Moon is in the fourth house, these emotions will center around home and foundation. Camilla will get a lot further if she does not push things at home. On the wedding day, Harry's progressed Moon was 1 Pisces in the Pisces dwad in the first house, suggesting overwhelming feelings of emotion, confusion, insecurity and at times insight and clarity this day. Things may have been personally difficult for Harry that day, not just because of Camilla but perhaps from remembering his mother. Camilla plays a role in the overall difficulty but is not necessarily a cause. Camilla's North Node was square this progression so there was a lot of future baggage created that day. As an aside, you can also look at Camilla's natal planets in synastry with Harry's progressions or her progressions in synastry with Harry's progressions, but it becomes unwieldy to work with. Natal to natal synastry and a look at the child's internal maturity with secondary progressions works quite well. Use the dwads with the secondary progressions to see the subtle and not so subtle changes in the early years.

Camilla's Jupiter is conjunction Harry's Saturn at 12 Scorpio in the Pisces dwad. This is a good placement for Camilla to work with Harry, and with Scorpio and Pisces her attempts at public image and helping Harry will go a long way in the bonding process. Again, the Midheaven Taurus dwad makes him a charmer and she can play to this publicly, which is a good spot for Camilla to expand (Jupiter) her relationship and grow with Harry. This may be her ace in the hole with him. With Saturn he may pull back or she may feel blocked by him, but Jupiter goes a long way toward lifting Saturn burdens, especially with Jupiter conjunct his Midheaven.

Saturn can be tough even with the trine and conjunction. This is where karmic lessons are learned and obviously there is tremendous karma suggested by their close nodal conjunctions and oppositions. Again, a lot of karma usually shows up in step-relationships. Poor Camilla has Saturn square Harry's Saturn at 12 Scorpio in the Pisces dwad. Talk about a lot of innate inhibition (Saturn) and confusion (Pisces) for Harry! Saturn square Saturn suggests tough lessons and Harry will hopefully have a good handle on them by his first Saturn return at age 28 or 29. There is a great deal of core energy they cannot explain and a great deal of work to be done. Whatever was done, they have done it over and over and hopefully will get it right this time. Saturn square Saturn often suggests each party feels justified in obstinance and each wants to create the structure of the relationship or, as with difficult aspects between them, power issues.

Camilla's Saturn trine Harry's Uranus affects his T-square and sets off energies of his fifth, eighth and eleventh houses. He is reminded of his mother's death with the eighth house, his hopes and wishes are somewhat shaped by the placement in his eleventh house and his health and possibly how he works could also be affected. Since Chiron is also part of this T-square, Harry could fear having children or that they would feel abandoned if he died. This is also suggested by the early death of his mother.

On his father's wedding day, Harry's progressed Uranus was 10 Sagittarius in the Aries dwad and Saturn was 14 Scorpio in the Aries dwad. Thus Harry was concerned with himself (Aries dwad) and felt shaken. He was inhibited in expressing his feelings. Uranus shakes things up so even an aspect with an easy energy flow may be chaotic.

Camilla's Uranus is square Harry's Moon in the fourth house with her Uranus in his sixth house. His health may be affected with her presence in light of fourth house and foundational matters.

Camilla's Uranus opposition Harry's Neptune is wide but can still be disruptive to his psyche, and since his Neptune is in the Pisces dwad, this suggests chaotic emotions and confusion. If you look at the effect of Camilla's Uranus on the fourth house and twelfth-house Neptune, this suggests Harry may intuitively or through dreams pick up a lot of chaos and images that do not necessarily fit together or make sense, and possibly thoughts between his mother and Camilla.

Neptune is part of Harry's yod along with Pluto and his North Node causing repeated themes affected by Camilla's planetary placements in synastry with his chart. This is why step-parents must look for those "ace in the hole" areas to work toward peace, harmony and bonding. It can be done.

Camilla's Uranus affects Harry's Pluto because of its opposition to Neptune which is part of Harry's yod with Pluto and the North Node. Again, ninth house issues come into play.

Pluto and Neptune are part of Harry's yod pointing to his North Node foundation that is conjunction Camilla's North Node, so there is entanglement here as well. Progressed Pluto remains the same. Progressed Neptune at 28 Sagittarius remained the same on Prince Charles and Camilla's wedding day.

Camilla's Pluto is square Harry's Saturn and the Midheaven. Camilla's Pluto is trine Harry's Uranus. Pluto is square the Midheaven at 17 Scorpio in the Taurus dwad. Camilla's Pluto sits in Harry's seventh house so her presence in a partnership role is a reorganizing force and there are power struggles. In the Taurus dwad Harry will dig his heals in. Her aspects to his yod also repeat this theme.

Again, Camilla's Pluto is square Harry's Saturn in the ninth house. Harry's Saturn is 12 Scorpio in the Pisces dwad so despite stoic Saturn there is a lot of emotion, perhaps jealousy or vindictiveness, confusion and a desire for something ideal. The ninth house among other things repre-

Inner Wheel
Camilla Parker-Bowles
Natal Chart
Jul 17 1947, Thu
7:10 am BDST −2:00
London, England
51°N30' 000°W10'
Geocentric
Tropical
Placidus
True Node

Outer Wheel
Prince Charles
Natal Chart
Nov 14 1948, Sun
9:14 pm UT +0:00
London, England
51°N30' 000°W10'
Geocentric
Tropical
Placidus
True Node

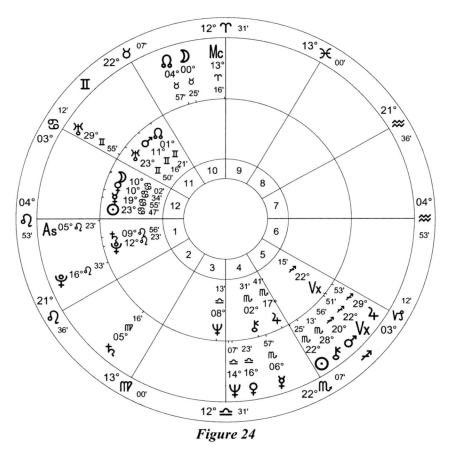

Figure 24

sents publications and the effects of this aspect may be hard to keep out of the tabloids. Fortunately, Harry's Virgo Sun helps him remain steady.

Again, Camilla's Pluto is trine Harry's Uranus at 9 Sagittarius in the Pisces dwad so the Sagittarius theme recurs and brings in ninth house matters to the eleventh house of wishes for the future. Pluto in trine lessens the power struggle and gives a bit of relief. There is still the Pisces confusion and need for the ideal with this placement, although the Pisces need for the ideal may lead to a little less tension. With Uranus there is no telling. Pluto in trine still wants power.

Camilla's Midheaven is square Harry's Ascendant at 11 Capricorn in the Taurus dwad so he may personally feel negative toward her public persona; but Capricorn is practical and Taurus is charming so he will put up a good front. Although this is a square, Camilla can work with him on public matters and with hard work it may be a place to bond, especially when there is a benevolent transit. Her Midheaven or public persona is square Harry personally so mutual work requires effort on both of their parts.

As an aside, the outer planet energies normally trump the inner planet energies, so Camilla's aspects to Harry's Pluto in general take a back seat to his strengths. However, her Pluto square his Saturn trumps Harry and it is through her Pluto strength that she can bond, using the square to her advantage while helping Harry in ninth house matters. Difficult as it may be, she can use her power and control with the square pattern to help Harry and thus bond. This is using negative energy wisely.

Camilla's Ascendant is square Harry's Pluto (part of his yod) so she may be at odds with his direction and power. Again, outer planet energy in synastry seems to trump inner or personal planet energy or personal placements such as the Ascendant so she personally may be at odds , but he has the power here. Then again, while Harry's Pluto and part of his yod trumps Camilla personally, Camilla's Pluto is square Harry's Saturn so in matters of partnership (where Camilla's Pluto sits in Harry's chart) she may trump Harry a bit. It is all in how they choose to use these energies.

Although the aspects are what they are, the sign and dwad can flavor the action of the planetary energies a bit. Certainly the energy of two earth signs would be more stubborn than earth and air, where more thought is given to a situation.

Prince Charles' Pluto and Ascendant are conjunct Camilla's so he may help with the trine but not with the square aspects to Harry (see Figure 24). But Camilla's Venus in Harry's sixth house is her ace in the hole and is trine Charles' Sun by a wide orb; her Mercury is trine his Sun so he may be of help there. Often the parent's aspects may help a little but primarily the step-parent must choose to bond.

If you cannot find conjunctions or trines that help in the bonding process, go to sextiles and parallels (they act like a conjunction) to find more places to help two people bond. It is not as strong but can be helpful. Sometimes it is just too difficult but I can always find someplace with common ground for a step-parent and a step-child to bond.

I hope everyone with step children will benefit from my experience and astrological knowledge and have a happy, healthy family life. Best wishes to you all.

Bibliography

Astrology

Astrology At A Glance, Barbara Harkins and Gayle Lakin-Geffner, Harlak Press, 1986.

A-Z Horoscope Maker, Llewellyn George, Llewellyn Publications, 1978.

Combination of Stellar Influences, Reinhold Ebertin, Ebertin-Verlag, 1972.

Rulership Book, Rex E. Bills, American Federation of Astrologers, 1991.

Yod, Miss Dee, American Federation of Astrologers, 1989.

The Twelve Faces of Saturn, Bil Tierney, Llewellyn Publications, 1997.

Decanates and Dwads, Stephanie Ennis, American Federation of Astrologers, 1983.

The Changing Sky, Steven Forrest, ACS Publications.

Karmic Astrology Vol. I, Martin Schulman, Samuel Weiser, Inc., 1975.

Karmic Astrology Vol. II, Martin Schulman, Samuel Weiser, Inc., 1977.

Lunar Nodes, Mohan Koparkar, Ph.D., Mohan Enterprises, 1977.

The Astrologers Node Book, Donna Van Toen, Samuel Weiser, Inc., 1981.

Childhood Development

Baby and Child Care, 8th ed., Benjamin Spock, Pocket Books, Simon and Schuster, 2004.

The Developing Person Through Childhood and Adolescence, Kathleen Stassen Berger, Worth Publisher, 1991.

Astrology Articles

"Retrograde Venus and Reincarnation," Maryanne Kremer, Today's Astrologer.

"Retrograde Planets," Lynn Koiner, http://www.astralis.it/lynn_koiner.htm.

"Saturn is the Gateway," Amanda Owen, http://www.amandaowen.com/saturn_is_the_gateway.htm

"Saturn, Karma and Astrology," Laura Paggiani, Ricardo Sottani, http://www.astralis.it/saturno2.htm

Childhood Development Articles

"Elementary School," http://www.counselorandteachertips.com/body.htm

"Stages of Child Development," Ladies Home Journal, http://www.lhj.com/stages-of-child-development.htm1

"Adolescent Development," http://www.aopmentalhealth.org/ad-dev.html

Breinigsville, PA USA
10 November 2009
227209BV00003B/1/P